About This Book

Why is this topic important?

It seems clear today that the source of competitive advantage that we have the most control over is our leadership talent. We know that effective leadership development makes a dramatic difference. There is mounting evidence that organizations that are the best at developing their leadership talent also perform best in the marketplace—and that's why this *Annual* was created.

What can you achieve with this book?

What you will get out of the *Annual* is first-hand information about where the field of leadership development is headed, from experts closest to the action—practitioners in charge of leadership development in leading organizations. You will also find in-depth case studies on major organizational leadership development programs and processes and thought-provoking chapters from leading thinkers (academics, consultants, and practitioners) on key issues such as leadership development strategies and systems, metrics, developing high-potential talent, engaging top executives, today's most effective learning methods, developing global leaders, on-boarding, and other critical topics. You'll take away best practices, practical ideas, innovative approaches, and lessons learned that will guide you in your efforts to use high-impact leadership development to help your organization achieve its strategic objectives through exceptional leadership talent.

How is this book organized?

Section One: Forces and Trends in Leadership Development covers highlights from our 2004 and 2005 trends surveys of executive and leadership development conducted with one hundred organizations and previews many of the topics covered in the rest of the *Annual*. Section Two: Leadership Development Strategies, Systems, and Programs deals with case examples of effective leadership development efforts, including those at UBS, Humana, Rexam PLC, Sony Electronics, and the U.S. Navy. Section Three: Learning Methods reviews the most powerful methods for developing leaders that were identified in Section One, including leaders as teachers, coaching, business simulation, job assignments, peer networks, and military battleground experiences. Section Four: Special Challenges and Opportunities covers a broad range of formidable issues such as gaining management buy-in, high-potential development, developing global leaders, metrics, learning from experience, and applying learning back on the job.

About Pfeiffer

Pfeiffer serves the professional development and hands-on resource needs of training and human resource practitioners and gives them products to do their jobs better. We deliver proven ideas and solutions from experts in HR development and HR management, and we offer effective and customizable tools to improve workplace performance. From novice to seasoned professional, Pfeiffer is the source you can trust to make yourself and your organization more successful.

Essential Knowledge Pfeiffer produces insightful, practical, and comprehensive materials on topics that matter the most to training and HR professionals. Our Essential Knowledge resources translate the expertise of seasoned professionals into practical, how-to guidance on critical workplace issues and problems. These resources are supported by case studies, worksheets, and job aids and are frequently supplemented with CD-ROMs, websites, and other means of making the content easier to read, understand, and use.

Essential Tools Pfeiffer's Essential Tools resources save time and expense by offering proven, ready-to-use materials—including exercises, activities, games, instruments, and assessments—for use during a training or team-learning event. These resources are frequently offered in looseleaf or CD-ROM format to facilitate copying and customization of the material.

Pfeiffer also recognizes the remarkable power of new technologies in expanding the reach and effectiveness of training. While e-hype has often created whizbang solutions in search of a problem, we are dedicated to bringing convenience and enhancements to proven training solutions. All our e-tools comply with rigorous functionality standards. The most appropriate technology wrapped around essential content yields the perfect solution for today's on-the-go trainers and human resource professionals.

Pfeiffer
www.pfeiffer.com *Essential resources for training and HR professionals*

The Pfeiffer Annual Series

The Pfeiffer Annuals present each year never-before-published materials contributed by learning professionals and academics and written for trainers, consultants, and human resource and performance-improvement practitioners. As a forum for the sharing of ideas, theories, models, instruments, experiential learning activities, and best and innovative practices, the *Annuals* are unique. Not least because only in the *Pfeiffer Annuals* will you find solutions from professionals like you who work in the field as trainers, consultants, facilitators, educators, and human resource and performance-improvement practitioners and whose contributions have been tried and perfected in real-life settings with actual participants and clients to meet real-world needs.

The Pfeiffer Annual: Consulting
Edited by Elaine Biech

The Pfeiffer Annual: Human Resource Management
Edited by Robert C. Preziosi

The Pfeiffer Annual: Leadership Development
Edited by James F. Bolt

The Pfeiffer Annual: Training
Edited by Elaine Biech

James F. Bolt, EDITOR

The *2007*
Pfeiffer
ANNUAL

LEADERSHIP DEVELOPMENT

Pfeiffer
A Wiley Imprint
www.pfeiffer.com

ISBN-10: 0-7879-8074-9
ISBN-13: 978-0-7879-8074-0
ISSN: 1046-333-X

Acquiring Editor: Martin Delahoussaye
Director of Development: Kathleen Dolan Davies
Developmental Editor: Maryanne Koschier
Production Editor: Dawn Kilgore
Editor: Rebecca Taff
Manufacturing Supervisor: Becky Carreño
Editorial Assistant: Julie Rodriguez
Composition and Technical Art: Leigh McLellan Design

Printed in the United States of America

Printing   10 9 8 7 6 5 4 3 2 1

Contents

Acknowledgments

The creation of a work such as this *Leadership Annual* is an enormous undertaking. I'm indebted to so many people for their contributions. Most important, of course, are the authors, as without them there would be no *Leadership Annual*. My sincere thanks to each of you:

Nicole Drake

Eve Dreher

Michael Dulworth

Joseph A. Forcillo

Barry Frew

Marshall Goldsmith

Vijay Govindarajan

Alice Heezen

Gordon Hewitt

Andrew McK. Jefferson

Betty Kovalcik

Robert W. Mann

Val Markos

Jeff McCreary

William J. Morin

Annmarie Neal

Harold W. Nelson

Dan Parisi

Charles Presbury

Barbara Reyna

Julie Staudenmier

Chris Trimble

Fons Trompenaars

Raymond Vigil

Mark Whitmore

Warren Wilhelm

Peter Woolliams

Ashley Keith Yount

There is one person whose contribution is of such magnitude that the *Annual* would not exist if it were not for her extraordinary effort and skills: Nicole Drake. Nicole was my project manager. Among many things, that included the unenviable task of keeping the authors, including yours truly, on target with our due dates—now I know where that "herding cats" expression comes from. Nicole also assisted in editing, formatting, writing, and many other critical tasks, including things such as keeping a positive attitude when this mountain looked way too steep to climb.

I'd also like to thank Alan Shrader for his assistance in analyzing the surveys referenced in the chapter I wrote, "Mapping the Future of Leadership Development," and in preparing that chapter as well.

James F. Bolt
Editor
August 2006

Introduction
to *The 2007 Pfeiffer Annual: Leadership Development*

Wherefore art thou, competitive advantage? It's certainly not to be found in the traditional sources. Patents run out much quicker than they used to (and there are some pesky competitors who don't seem to play by those rules), technology can be bought or copied awfully fast, product life cycles are measured in months instead of years. So look in the mirror! Yes, it's *you* and the other high-quality talent that makes the difference now (and for the foreseeable future). And the one thing that has the biggest impact on talent is leadership. And (you know where this is going) that makes leadership development the hot topic of the day. Pretty much everyone agrees that the organizations with the best talent will win, so that's the focus of this *Leadership Development Annual*—read on!

The readers of this *Leadership Development Annual* will benefit from understanding how the *Annual* is organized, and that is the purpose of this Introduction. Please note that, while there is logic to the flow and sequence of articles, and I recommend reading the first one first, readers will also find value in going directly to individual articles that appear to be of interest.

Section One: Forces and Trends in Leadership Development

"Mapping the Future of Leadership Development" is the only article in this section and includes highlights from a comprehensive survey conducted by Executive Development Associates (EDA) of trends in executive and leadership development conducted with one hundred major organizations in 2004. It also includes the results of EDA's 2005 survey, which updates progress since the 2004 survey and explores new ground not covered previously. This is a suggested first-read since it sets up the rest of the *Annual* by discussing many of the issues covered in subsequent articles, such as leadership development strategy and systems, learning methods, high-potential identification and development, integrated talent management, and other critical leadership topics.

Section Two: Leadership Development Strategies, Systems, and Programs

Section Two covers a variety of organizational cases and other examples of effective leadership development efforts.

"The UBS Leadership Institute: A Case Study in Strategic Alignment" is an example of a comprehensive, overall Institute approach to leadership development—from strategy setting leadership conferences to leadership development programs—and one that is specifically aimed at developing the capabilities needed to achieve the business strategy.

"Linking Senior Leadership Development to the Mission of the U.S. Navy" describes an interesting approach to engaging senior military officers in a challenging educational experience and then the next generation of Navy leaders as well.

"Success Begins with Senior Management: Case Study of Innovative Leadership Development Design" describes an innovative design that combines a variety of powerful learning methods to engage senior executives in the development of leaders in a way that is mutually beneficial.

"Creating an Integrated Talent, Leadership, and Organization Development System for Maximum Impact" focuses on an all-too-common problem, key component programs or processes operating independently. The first article notes the importance of an integrated system in addressing the pressing bench strength challenge facing organizations. This one presents how to create an integrated system.

"Leadership Development as a Driver of Shareholder Value Creation" reviews the case at Humana Inc., where the leadership development effort is specifically aimed at improving shareholder value.

"Building Strategic Leadership Capabilities at Rexam PLC: A Case Study" is a comprehensive description of the process and programs developed at London-based Rexam PLC to build the specific leadership capabilities believed to be most critical to achieving its strategic objectives. The case covers not only successes but lessons learned.

Section Three: Learning Methods

This section deals with the topic of how leaders learn. It begins with articles on the learning methods that were cited in EDA's 2004 Executive/Leadership Development Trends Survey as most likely to be used in organizations over the next few years—executives as faculty and executive coaching, as examples—and then covers a variety of other critical learning methods and issues.

"Leaders Teaching Leaders" describes the way that Dell Inc. involves its executives as teachers as the primary learning mode in its leadership development programs, including tips for how to optimize the effectiveness of this approach.

"Level 4 Coaching: Everyone Has a Role" expands on the fact that no learning method has grown in popularity quite like coaching over the last few years. The 2005 Survey described in the first article notes that it is expected to continue to increase in use. This article explains that too much emphasis is placed on the coach and notes that three other variables need to be carefully considered in evaluating the potential success of coaching: the client, the co-workers, and the company.

"Creating a Customer-Centric Culture: 'Walking a Mile in the Customer's Shoes' at Texas Instruments" presents the case of how TI, working with BTS, created a custom business simulation to put its executives in the "shoes" of its customers in order to understand the need to become more customer focused and develop plans to do so.

"Optimizing Developmental Job Assignments" builds on the common knowledge that the vast majority of development takes place on the job—or better, the potential for development exists on the job; after all, that's where leaders spend most of their time. But how can we optimize the potential development opportunity there? That's the focus of this case.

"Lessons from the Battleground" deals with a method for learning about leadership that has been growing rapidly in popularity, that is, taking leaders to the scene of former military battles to study the strategy and leadership lessons to be learned.

"The Role of Peer-to-Peer Networks in Personal and Professional Development" makes the case for peer networks as a powerful way to develop as a leader, both for personal benefit and for the good of an organization.

Part Four: Special Challenges and Opportunities

Leadership development is a great place to be these days. Senior executives seem to really "get it" in terms of the bench strength challenges facing their organizations. As a result, organizations are investing more resources in development, and the profession is held in high regard in terms of the perceived value it delivers. In this section, we present a series of special challenges and opportunities we face, such as gaining top management buy-in, metrics, developing global leaders, assessing and development potential—just to keep us on our toes. We are making great progress and still there are great opportunities and great expectations:

Getting Management Buy-In

"Engaging the Board and Executive Team in Talent Development" describes how the leadership development organization at First Data found a variety of ways to engage its board of directors and most senior executives in development, one of the most interesting being the creation of a talent annual report.

"Gaining Management Buy-In: Responding to Unspoken Needs" tells the true story about how a leadership development team wrestled with the challenge of gaining true support of a single, incredibly important, top-level executive.

Developing Global Leaders

"Preparing Leaders for the New Competitive Landscape: New Mindsets for New Games" is a thought-provoking article that describes the challenge of creating leaders for a future competitive landscape with which they are not familiar.

"Developing Global Leaders: The Critical Role of Dilemma Reconciliation" describes the leadership challenges of global executives and presents the argument that the ability to reconcile value differences is the new core competency needed for global leaders.

Identifying and Developing High-Potentials

"Evaluating Leadership Potential: A Practitioner's Guide" provides approaches, methods, and advice for assessing high-potential talent and then presents the application of these assessments at BellSouth.

"Identifying and Developing High-Potentials: An Executive Perspective" presents a guide to practitioners on how to identify potential talent and predict future success, as well as what to do to accelerate the development of the best talent in one's organization. It is written as a practical guide based on the author's extensive leadership development experience.

On-Boarding, ROI, Learning from Experience, and Putting Learning to Work

"Successful On-Boarding" presents ideas and examples for the effective on-boarding of leaders hired from outside the organization or promoted to significant new senior leadership positions within. At a time when studies show that 40 percent of newly placed leaders fail in the first eighteen months, this is critical information.

"ROI Comes in Many Forms: Leadership Development at Baker Hughes Incorporated" is a case study of specific leadership development efforts at Baker Hughes and how the organization determined the value of the efforts.

"Learning from Experience: Easier Said Than Done" takes on an issue of potential great importance: Can we help leaders make every day a learning experience?

"Put Learning to Work" addresses a major shortfall in leadership development. Billions of dollars are spent on classroom programs and next to nothing is done to support leaders in applying what they learned back on the job. This article presents ways to ensure follow-through to results.

Introduction
to the Forces and Trends in Leadership Development Section

This section of the *Annual* includes only one article, "Mapping the Future of Leadership Development," which includes highlights from a comprehensive survey of trends in executive and leadership development conducted by Executive Development Associates (EDA) with one hundred major organizations in 2004, covering issues such as key leadership development objectives, critical talent acquisition and development topics, and top learning methods.

The article also includes the results of EDA's 2005 survey, which updates the 2004 survey and explores new ground, including succession management, integrated talent systems, leadership pipelines, leadership for emerging markets, and new metrics for evaluation. I suggest that you read this article first, since it sets up the rest of the *Annual* by discussing many of the issues covered in subsequent articles.

Mapping the Future of Leadership Development, by James F. Bolt

Mapping the Future
of Leadership Development

James F. Bolt

Summary

Professionals in executive development, leadership development, organizational learning, and human resources have achieved increasing visibility, stature, and influence in recent years. More than ever, they work as full partners with CEOs and senior executives in designing strategies to meet the strategic challenges companies face in today's highly competitive, rapidly changing global environment. And more than ever, CEOs and senior leaders realize that leadership talent is a significant competitive advantage. Yet challenges still remain—and learning is a constant imperative.

As chairman of Executive Development Associates, Inc. (EDA), I have long believed that one of the best learning resources for professionals in leadership development is the knowledge and experience of their peers. Approximately every two years, EDA conducts an extensive survey of trends in the field of executive and leadership development to uncover best practices, emerging needs, top priorities, and new approaches. The purpose of this article is to summarize this information to help those in the field advance together and stay abreast of critical trends in executive and leadership development.

In EDA's 2005 Survey, we sought to gather information on how companies are faring in meeting the bench strength imperative, which was identified in our 2004 Trends Survey as the top executive development challenge companies would be facing in the near future. (For background on the 2005 survey, see the box: Inside EDA's 2005 Executive Development Trends Survey.) The 2005 survey (sometimes referred to as the Pulse Survey here) was also designed to gather information on several closely related topics, such as succession management, integrated talent systems, the leadership pipeline, and leadership for emerging markets. We also zeroed in on strategies executive development professionals are using to identify and accelerate the development of high-potentials. In addition, we wanted to find out how companies are using key executive development tools and approaches, such as leader-led development, action learning, on-the-job development, and on-boarding. Finally, we inquired about the use and importance of measurement in executive development and patterns of expenditures on development programs.

Throughout this article, we will present highlights from the original survey, then show what we learned in the update (pulse) survey a year later in terms of progress being made by organizations, and finally present new information on topics not covered in the original survey, such as on-boarding.

Inside EDA's 2005 Executive Development Trends Survey

In 2004 EDA conducted our extensive survey of trends in the field of executive development, with one hundred companies responding and providing great insights into the state of the art. The purpose of this 2005 shorter pulse survey was to:

- Check progress on some of the key findings from the 2004 Executive Development Trends Survey. How are we doing?

- Include some items that respondents felt needed more coverage in that survey, such as developmental job assignments and spending per executive.

- Explore emerging issues in executive leadership development.

- Test a new approach to our traditional trends survey process. Since 1983, we have conducted a major, comprehensive (and lengthy) study on trends every two years. This pulse survey is an effort to test the idea of much shorter surveys, perhaps annually, targeted on a smaller number of topics.

If this is successful, the traditional, comprehensive survey might be done less frequently in the future.

Definitions

For the purpose of this survey, executives/leaders were defined as anyone who falls into one or more of the following groups:

- Members of the Board of Directors: the chairman of the board, the chief executive officer, the chief operating officer, and the president and all elected officers

---

- Corporate vice presidents (including functional heads): heads of/presidents of groups, divisions, business units, or profit centers and their direct reports
- All people included in your executive compensation program

Development was described as any activity that is aimed at broadening executives' knowledge and experience and enhancing their capabilities.

We received one hundred responses from Global 1000-size companies. Survey respondents included chief learning officers and heads of executive and leadership development.

The Bench Strength Imperative

As we had in previous surveys, in our 2004 survey, we asked respondents to identify the objectives that would be most important to their executive and leadership development efforts in the next two to three years. In 2004, the top priority for nearly 80 percent of companies—by far the most prevalent goal for survey respondents worldwide—was to increase their bench strength and ensure replacements for key jobs or people. This was the first time in the history of the Trends Survey that this issue has ranked as companies' number one objective. Table 1 shows the top responses to the questions from our 2004 survey.

Table 1.   Key Objectives of Executive Development in the Next Two to Three Years

1. Increase bench strength
2. Accelerate development of high-potentials
3. Communicate vision and strategy
4. Support change and transformation
5. Develop individual leader capabilities

The Continuing Importance of Bench Strength

In our 2005 Pulse Trends Survey, we followed up with a question asking whether respondents continue to see increasing bench strength as a top priority, specifically whether it had increased in importance, stayed the same, or decreased in importance. Nearly 72 percent of those surveyed said that increasing bench strength increased in importance, and 97 percent said it increased or stayed the same. This is simply amazing and clearly indicates that this issue continues to dominate the collective consciousness of organizations today. Not only was it the most important and most dominating issue identified in the 2004 survey, but also it has increased in importance more than any other issue a year later!

In comments on this question, respondents offered a variety of explanations for the continued and increasing importance of bench strength. Based on our analysis of these comments, two key drivers of this trend stand out: (1) the "age bomb" (as one respondent put it) as the Baby Boom generation nears retirement and (2) the increasing complexity, competition, and pace of business companies face today, which have combined to "raise the bar" in terms of executive performance. In other words, companies are facing a one-two punch: just as their most senior executives are contemplating retirement, the demands on their replacements will be greater than ever.

Since the leading edge of the boomer generation will just turn sixty this year, it seems obvious that increasing bench strength will remain a top priority for years to come.

Integrated Talent Management Systems

An Integrated Talent Management System brings together key programs and processes that identify, attract, appraise, develop, reward, and retain talent; ensures those activities work smoothly together; and aligns them with the organization's strategic goals. In our 2004 survey, 70 percent of respondents agreed that such an integrated system would be a top priority; yet only 40 percent said that their organizations excelled in this integrated approach. As Figure 1 reveals, out of twelve best practices in executive and leadership development, integrated talent management ranked eighth, just behind succession management, in the percentage of respondents identifying it as a program in which their organization excelled.

For our 2005 survey, we decided to dig deeper into how companies saw the issue of integrated talent management. We asked respondents how they thought their companies were performing in this area, whether they had specific goals for an integrated talent management system, and what those goals were.

The results showed progress by 40 percent, while 51 percent reported that their systems were about the same. While I suppose we should be pleased that the vast majority of respondents think that their organizations are holding their own or improving, it is not encouraging that, from this entire survey, this is the lowest rating of "improvement" of all of the questions. It seems we are least satisfied with our progress in the area of creating an integrated talent management system. This jibes with my personal experience working as a consultant with many leading companies around the world—most seem to feel they are making some progress, but still are quite a way from where they would like to be.

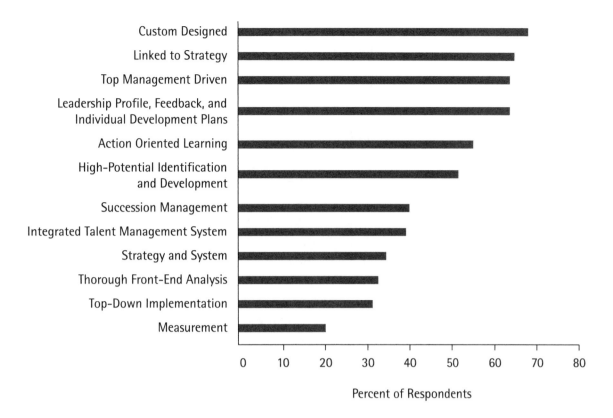

Figure 1.   Best Practices in Which Organizations Excel

On the positive side, one respondent commented, "We have a very integrated system with much more attention to rewarding our high performers with developmental assignments. We are linking strategic executive education to specific company and business strategies. Our system is better integrated today then it ever has been." Others are struggling: "The pieces are in place. Creating a mindset of how one relates to another and that together they are a system is a new idea for our organization." Still others are hopeful: "Integration of current stand-alone processes is our focus for going forward. We've made good progress on independent processes and now need to bring them together."

Goals for an Integrated Talent Management System

Fully three-quarters of respondents indicated that they have a set of goals they are working toward in the area of talent management. The goals cited tended to separate into two kinds: those who are presumably still in the process of trying to implement an integrated talent management system cited process-oriented goals involving setting up such a system; those who presumably have a relatively robust system in place cited goals involving the results they expected the talent system to achieve.

In the former category, typical goals include integration of talent management systems with succession planning; subsequent development of leadership competency models, integrating both talent management and competency models; use of technology to track talent; and better alignment of talent acquisition, development, and assessment.

Goals that relate to the results talent management is expected to achieve include an increase in bench strength and flow of talent across the enterprise; attraction of more diverse talent; retention and accelerated development of high-potentials; and enhanced leadership continuity. The breadth and scope of these results-oriented goals clearly demonstrate that many respondents have high expectations for their talent management systems. They expect real and demonstrable results that make a strategic business impact—and they clearly see a talent management system as an effective means for increasing bench strength.

Succession Management

An effective succession management process is the foundation of an integrated management system. Therefore, it was dismal news indeed when the 2004 Trends Survey indicated that only 40 percent of respondents thought their organizations excelled in succession management. Our 2005 survey followed up with this question: How would you rate your organization today in your progress on Succession Management?

The good news is that fully 60 percent of respondents see their companies as improving in succession management. This bodes well not only for succession itself but for the possibility of having an integrated talent management system, since you can't have an effective total system if the core processes like succession are not strong. However, their comments on this question indicate that many still think they have a long way to go. As one person commented, "We . . . targeted this practice area five years ago and continue to work on this." Another respondent, much further along, observed, "We are getting better year by year. The use of assessment centers, objective data, high-potential discussions, and the difference between assessing performance and potential have all helped in this endeavor."

The Leadership Pipeline

Another way to assess the bench strength issue is in terms of the leadership pipeline. The good news is that 44 percent of respondents see real progress in filling their organizations' leadership pipelines with capable talent. Less encouraging is that 38 percent see no progress, while 16 percent actually think their leadership pipeline is less strong than it was two years ago. Of all the questions in the survey, this is the one on which respondents indicate the most backtracking, that is, where they have somehow managed to do worse than a year ago. It doesn't quite fit with the other survey findings in that we seem to be saying we are making great progress in all of the systems needed to fill the leadership pipeline, but it is not getting better as fast as we might expect. Of course, the programs and processes that we are considering here take time to take hold.

The perception of those who see their leadership pipeline as weaker may reflect the "raising of the bar" in terms of leadership needs we discussed above. As one respondent observed, "We have excellent content knowledge and excel at doing what we have always done. This may not be the skill needed to take us forward. The leadership being weaker is a reflection of growing awareness. The new CEO is expecting and demanding (rightfully) a different type of leader. This is very different from what was rewarded previously. Those who thought they were strong leaders a year ago may not be perceived that way in the future." This comment doesn't necessarily reflect a broader shift in perceptions, but it is suggestive. In fact, several articles in this *Annual* discuss the changing skills and capabilities of leaders in the global marketplace. See, for example, "Preparing Leaders for the New Competitive Landscape: New Mindsets for New Games" and "Developing Global Leaders: The Critical Role of Dilemma Reconciliation."

And what are those needs going forward—and what gaps in meeting those needs do organizations foresee? We asked respondents, "As you look down in the organization at the next generation of leadership talent (the ones who are most likely to fill executive level positions in the next three to five years), what capabilities, skills, knowledge, attitudes, competencies, etc., are most lacking?" Table 2 provides their responses.

More than half the respondents cite all of the top four next-generation gaps. And they all involve abilities that might be described as *complexes* of skills, capabilities, and attitudes, many of which are *soft* rather than technical—abilities that are not easily taught. Respondents across the board showed less concern about more technical aspects of executive performance—indeed just 4 percent were concerned that the next generation of leaders understand the technical side of the business.

Leadership for Emerging Markets

As globalization becomes ever more dominant, companies face the need to fill their leadership pipelines on an international basis. Respondents were asked to choose the two or three countries/areas where they had the biggest need to develop leadership talent to support the company's strategy. The results are shown in Table 3.

It is not surprising that China is far above any other country or region in its need for developing leadership talent. The potential size of China's market, and hence the potential opportunities for companies that invest in that market, dwarfs all others.

We also inquired about the strategies and methods companies were using to develop leaders for emerging markets. Judging from the responses, companies take a wide variety of approaches in responding to this need. Many companies have taken leadership for emerging markets very seriously, given a lot of thought and attention to

Table 2.   Gaps in Next Generation's Capabilities

Ability to create a vision and engage others so they feel ownership and passion about achieving it	58 percent
Understand the total enterprise, how the different parts work together to leverage their collective capabilities to serve customers/clients better than the competition	56 percent
Strategic thinking	55 percent
Cooperate and collaborate with other parts of the business to (1) optimize the operations of our business and (2) to leverage our collectives capabilities in the marketplace to identify and serve customers/clients better than competition	54 percent
Leadership	46 percent
Ability to attract, develop, and retain the quality of talent needed to achieve the business objectives	42 percent
Ability to inspire	32 percent
Understands global business, markets, cultural differences, etc.	30 percent
Business acumen	27 percent
Interpersonal skills	24 percent
Financial analysis and management, understand and manage the P&L	19 percent
Communication skills (oral and written)	12 percent
Understand the technical side of the business and our products and services	4 percent

Table 3.   Greatest Emerging Market Leadership Development Needs

China	77.9 percent
India	42.9 percent
Other Country/Area	29.9 percent
Eastern Europe	24.7 percent
Russia	15.6 percent
Brazil	11.7 percent
Mexico	6.5 percent
Middle East	5.2 percent
Africa	3.9 percent

the issue, and developed specific programs designed just for emerging market leaders. Others bring emerging market leaders into the regular executive development process and programs. Some have customized their regular executive development programs for specific areas. And a few companies have not really addressed the issue.

Rotational assignments were the most commonly mentioned approach. Of those companies that have developed programs specifically for executive development in emerging markets, some examples include:

- Using leader led training with action learning (we could argue that this isn't unique or specific to emerging markets, but it was mentioned as such)

- Hiring of in-country nationals who are developed through an international development program

- Assigning executives to roles in headquarters and smaller emerging markets prior to significant emerging markets

- Creating a comprehensive leadership development plan modeled on the firm process, but geared culturally to their needs

- Preparing for expansion in China by recruiting Chinese students in China and other worldwide universities, including the United States, and placing them in thirty developmental positions around the world

Developing High-Potentials

As Table 1 at the beginning of this article shows, the second-highest priority for executive development revealed in our 2004 Trends Survey was "accelerate the development of high-potentials." Identifying and developing high-potentials (executives who seem to have the potential to fill positions on the top management team reporting to the CEO) is clearly a key piece of the bench strength imperative.

Progress in the Development of High-Potentials

For our 2005 survey, we asked, "How would you rate your organization today in your progress on High-Potential Identification and Development?"

Although 35 percent said that their progress had remained about the same, a clear majority (62 percent) of those surveyed think that they are making good progress in this area. Comments that accompanied this question indicated that many companies take the development of high-potentials very seriously. One responder indicated his company's level of commitment by saying, "Elaborate processes [are] in place and all senior leaders are actively involved, daily." Another observed that high-potentials are a "major focus" of the CEO.

Still, much work remains to be done, especially as companies grow more complex and deal with the impact of globalization. Many of the comments offered suggest that companies are having a difficult time developing company-wide high-potential systems outside of lines of business, geographic areas, or other company "silos." As one respondent put it, "We need information that helps identify and track high-potentials on a worldwide basis, not just within geographic regions."

Identifying and Accelerating Potential

We asked two open-ended questions to uncover the processes companies use to identify (1) high-potential executives (current executives who seem to have the potential to fill positions on the top management team reporting to the CEO) and (2) emerging leaders (younger leaders lower in the organization who seem to have the potential to fill executive level positions in the future).

The systems and processes companies report for identifying high-potential executives range from the unstructured and informal to the highly structured and formal. On the unstructured side, one respondent frankly observed that his/her company uses "judgment and wild guesses." At the other extreme, a representative comment was that the company uses "a rigorous, global identification system using common language and quarterly meetings to assess potential." Many companies use some form of talent review process on at least an annual basis. Others incorporate the identification of high-potentials into the succession management process or add it to the performance appraisal process. Many assess executives against some form of competency model. Common tools include assessment centers, 360-degree feedback, psychological tests, interviews, and the use of outside executive development firms. Regardless of how elaborate and formal the process or the kinds of tools that are used, executive judgment regarding the potential of their reports seems to play a large role.

For identification of younger, emerging leaders, the approaches used vary just as widely. The use of more informal methods seems more widespread for the identification of emerging leaders than for those higher up in the executive ranks, although many respondents claimed that the processes were the same in both cases.

We also asked what processes respondents found to be the most effective in accelerating the development of high-potential executives and emerging leaders. Most respondents cited a combination of developmental activities that they deemed effective. The most common methods mentioned included:

- Job rotation
- Stretch assignments

- Formal education and training
- Mentoring and/or coaching
- Exposure to top executives and/or the board
- Action learning
- Feedback through 360-degree assessments and other means

Executive Development Tools and Methods

For our 2005 survey, we wanted to assess the state of the art in executive development learning methods in order to uncover the tools and methods executive development professionals consider most effective in enhancing learning and development. We asked about leader-led development, action learning, executive coaching, on-the-job development, and on-boarding.

Leader-Led Development

As you can see in Figure 2, in our 2004 Trends Survey, the use of senior executives as teachers—or leader-led development—was the most preferred method of development, cited by 75 percent of all respondents as a learning method they would be emphasizing, followed closely by action learning.

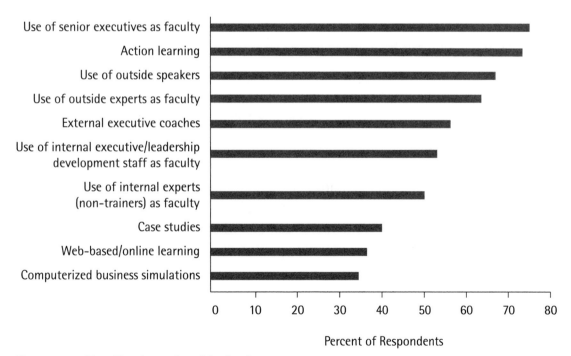

Figure 2.   Top Ten Learning Methods

For the new survey, we asked whether the use of senior executives as teachers in development programs had increased in importance, stayed the same, or decreased in importance. There was virtual unanimity, almost 96 percent, that leader-led development has stayed the same or even increased in importance. Most importantly, 43 percent said it had increased. We are seeing in practice that more and more are emphasizing this in their executive and leadership development programs, since they feel that it is beneficial for the participants in the learning programs to hear first-hand from their own executives (especially about company-specific issues such as vision, strategy, values, business challenges, and priorities, etc.) and that the executives who teach learn a great deal as well.

Those who place a major emphasis on leader-led development expressed strong satisfaction with results. One respondent commented, "We constantly hear back from participants that this is the most meaningful aspect of our programs." Another said, "This approach has clearly played a role in the high level of support for our development programs."

Of course, leader-led development requires executives who are *willing* and *able* to participate. Many respondents expressed frustration on this score. Leader-led programs "are very desirable," one respondent said, "but executive time is at a premium, and often programs are 'at risk' due to changing executive calendars." Another noted, "The difficulty actually getting the senior execs to do this is increasing." Another problem relates to executives' teaching ability: "We are finding that many executives don't have the skill set to teach in the programs. We really need to do some 'facilitation training' before putting them in the classroom."

In spite of the difficulties, however, many respondents said they are committed to strengthening leader-led development efforts.

Action Learning

Close behind leader-led learning in our 2004 survey came action learning (working in teams on real business problems or opportunities for development purposes), with nearly as many respondents (73 percent) citing it as a preferred development tool. Action learning differs from standard taskforces or projects in that the primary purpose is the development of the participants; there are typically clear developmental goals established at the onset, and there is an explicit educational component. And it differs from typical off-site team-building exercises in that participants focus on real business problems.

We found that 96 percent of our respondents think the importance of action learning is increasing or staying the same. Despite the fact that this has been the biggest fad in leadership development in the last five years or so, it still is seen as increasing in importance by a substantial 41 percent of the respondents. Many expressed plans to leverage action learning in high-potential programs and to either continue or increase the use of such a learning methodology.

Those who saw action learning as staying the same or decreasing in importance had a varied level of commitment to this developmental tool. Some saw it as competing with demanding business challenges, while others said it was hard to make practical in their fast-paced and changing environments.

Executive Coaching

In the 2004 survey, the use of external coaches was in the top five learning methods used and was *the* most frequently used method for senior executives and vice presidents. Here again, we asked respondents to our 2005 Survey whether this learning method was increasing in importance, staying the same, or decreasing in importance. Keep in mind that, even though action learning may be the "biggest fad" in leadership development over the last five years, nothing can compare to executive coaching over the last two to three years. While it used to be a dirty little secret to have a coach—it meant you were in trouble—now, it is a status symbol.

We found that use of executive coaching is still favored by organization, with 89 percent reporting that the use has increased (51 percent) or stayed the same (38 percent). In my mind, the fact that more than half see executive coaching increasing is phenomenal! However, I was surprised to see that the value of coaching had decreased for 9 percent of the respondents, some citing lack of resources or a structure to support the interaction or a reluctance by executives to use it.

Finally, when you compare the responses for leader-led learning, action learning, and executive coaching, you get another interesting perspective on coaching.

Looking at Figure 3 you can see that executive coaching showed the highest responses for "increased in importance" *and* "decreased in importance." This might indicate that executive coaching still seems controversial in some quarters.

Developing on the Job

On-the-job development continues to be a major component of organizational efforts in virtually all companies. Indeed, the classic Lessons of Experience research at the Center for Creative Leadership estimated that 70 percent of executive learning takes place on the job. In our 2005 survey, we asked respondents to "describe your most effective use of on-the-job development, i.e., your best, most effective, or most innovative use of development on the job."

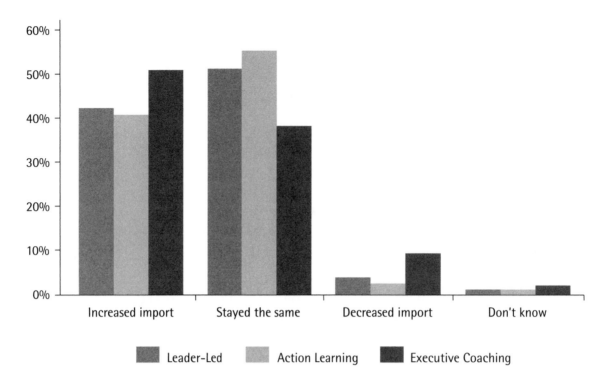

Figure 3. Relative Importance of Development Methods

We received a wide range of responses. Many mentioned job rotations, stretch assignments, assignment to cross-functional teams, overseas assignments, and other practices. Some of the more interesting and unusual practices mentioned included these:

- We provide special assignments for key talent where they are able to join a team for twelve weeks and act as a consultant to another sales region. They consult in areas similar to their own regular assignments.

- People in leadership programs are assigned a "proven business leader" to act as a coach and mentor while on the job and to help them transfer their newly acquired skills into the workplace.

- We placed an executive on a board of directors to gain an enterprise/policy level view of leadership.

- Sending a high-potential executive to run a smaller Canadian subsidiary, prior to his being promoted to run the U.S. division of the company.

- We form [and place an executive] on a team to develop a business strategy and plan for a new market area.

- Bringing in high-performing field/line leaders to do a headquarters assignment, which requires them to lead a cross-functional team with only informal authority.

Challenges in On-the-Job Development

We also asked respondents to describe "the biggest challenge you face in optimizing on-the-job development. How do you deal with or overcome that challenge?" While many responded with frank assessments of the challenges they face, unfortunately, few provided positive solutions to those challenges. While varied, the challenges mentioned generally fell into four categories: (1) no time for or appreciation of development; (2) executives who are unwilling to give up top talent; (3) lack of developmental job slots; and (4) difficulty in actually making a development experience developmental.

Making Learning a Day-to-Day Experience

Is it possible to make learning on the job a day-to-day experience? We asked for suggestions on what could be done to make every day a more effective learning experience for the typical executive. Encouraging feedback was the most mentioned suggestion, followed closely by mentoring, coaching, providing time for reflection, and learning journals. A number of respondents also suggested that leaders who foster a culture that values learning and development could make a real impact. Representative comments include:

- FEEDBACK! We have a feedback-adverse culture (no feedback means you are doing a good job). It is a challenge to get people to be open and share ideas, thoughts, and feedback. We would see exponential change if we did this because it is so foreign to us.

- Stop and ask what we learned and what could be done differently.

- I believe that executive coaching really helps. Also having a strategic and skilled HR partner to give candid feedback on situations and meetings can really make a difference.

- Time commitment and a process to reflect on individual learning [such as a learning journal], receive consistent feedback and coaching, and apply new skills/behaviors.

- A greater cultural expectation of daily development—accountability and recognition for development well done.

- We find that when our senior executives talk about development as part of their regular communications, it helps to maintain focus. All it takes is a few well-chosen words.

On-Boarding

On-boarding can help ensure the success of leaders making critical and difficult transitions, where failure rates can be high and costly, and accelerate their "time-to-effectiveness." On-boarding can be particularly crucial for executives hired from the outside into the organization and leaders moving into the executive ranks from lower levels in the organization. Yet far fewer than half those surveyed said that their organizations had a formal on-boarding process, with just 35.4 percent responding positively to this question in our 2005 survey.

Of those organizations that have a formal process, we asked respondents to identify the key components of the on-boarding program. Some organizations have elaborate and multi-faceted programs for new hires in the executive ranks. Here are the components of one company's program identified by a respondent.

- Pre-hire assessment

- Executive welcome kit

- Personalized orientation session

- Formal immersion plan

- Feedback

- 360-degree feedback

- Peer coaches

- New leader orientation forum with CEO and top executive team

- External executive coaches

Some companies focus more on the soft side of on-boarding, stressing socialization, networking, and relationship-building. Others take a more technology and information-oriented approach. Here is a sample of the on-boarding methods respondents mentioned:

- Formal on-boarding process, checklist, mentoring for executives. We also use *The First 90 Days* by Michael Watkins as a framework.

- Pretty standard: assigning a mentor; induction workshops for the latest batch of experienced hires (globally); get to know one another; spend time explaining our business principles and company values; high-level descriptions of our company and its current issues; lots of practical "Where do I?" stuff.

- High touch. Formal introduction of executive development coach at start of employment, understanding basics of the business, and networking with key stakeholders. We are in the pilot phase of this project.

- Executive on-boarding toolkit is mailed out to the incoming executive. Toolkit is divided into first thirty days, thirty to sixty days, and sixty to ninety days, with specific activities associated with each timeframe. A template is provided to help them create a ninety-day transition plan to review with their managers and teams.

Executive Development Operations

For our 2005 survey, we focused on two aspects of executive development operations: the use of metrics, or measurement and evaluation, and expenditures on executive development.

Metrics

In the 2004 Trends Survey, 52 percent of respondents said the "use of systematic measurement/evaluation to measure the impact of your efforts" was an area they would "highly emphasize" over the next two to three years (second only to developing an integrated talent management system), yet less than 20 percent of the respondents rated it as a "best practice" in which they excelled (the lowest out of twelve practices; see Figure 1). We found this result to be surprising and noted, "Few companies have yet cracked the code on quantifying the impact of executive development."

We decided to try to obtain the underlying assumptions that executive development professionals have about measurement and evaluation. We asked them whether they agreed with one or more of the statements shown in Table 4; the results are shown to the right.

While some of these statements may seem to be contradictory, in fact, as the percentages show, at least a few respondents apparently agree with both statements A and C. A very few respondents apparently disagreed with all statements. It is not surprising that respondents would have differing views about the beliefs and attitudes of senior executives toward executive development efforts and their measurement.

Table 4.   Attitudes Regarding Measurement of Impact of Executive Development

A. It is critical that we measure the impact/results of executive/leadership development activities to prove the value of our work to key stakeholders.	51 percent
B. It doesn't matter whether we measure the impact/results. They have obvious and intrinsic value. It is a waste of time and money.	5.2 percent
C. Senior executives either believe in the value in their gut or they don't. The most elaborate metrics, such as ROI, won't convince those who don't believe, and those who do believe don't care about them.	53.1 percent
D. It doesn't matter whether senior executives need or want the metrics; we need them to make key decisions managing the executive/leadership development department.	45.8 percent

However, we did find it puzzling that less than half agreed with the statement that metrics are needed *for their own decision making.*

Respondents offered some perceptive comments on this issue. Several discussed how hard it is to determine measures that account for leadership variability. One respondent, however, told how his organization was measuring the impact at the individual level using six factors, for example, developing potential successors, and using that data for merit compensation. Another acknowledged that senior management was looking for the language of measurement, while others said that their senior teams viewed training and development as an investment. For example, feedback from business groups on changes in participants was more credible than numerical cost/benefit analysis for one organization. As you can see, the conversation regarding metrics continues. In this *Annual* one of the articles, "ROI Comes in Many Forms: Leadership Development at Baker Hughes Incorporated," further discusses measurement.

Expenditures Per Executive

In the 2004 survey, we found that the average company was spending approximately $7 million (U.S.) annually on executive development (formal classroom and other development such as coaching, developmental job experiences, etc.). However, many felt that this amount was understated. Also, well over 30 percent did not know what they spent. We were frequently asked what the average spending per executive was, but we could not determine that from our survey, so we followed up with that question for our 2005 survey. First, we asked respondents to estimate annual expenditures per executive on *formal classroom training* (external activities such as university executive education programs or internal programs, including executive education, workshops, and action learning). Then we asked for expenditures on *non-classroom development*

Table 5. Annual Expenditures Per Executive on Formal Classroom Activities

Number of Responses	52
Minimum	0.00
Maximum	$900,000.00
Median	$5,000.00
Mean	$6,864.67

Table 6. Annual Expenditures Per Executive on Non-Classroom Development Activities

Number of Responses	46
Minimum	0.00
Maximum	$100,000.00
Median	$5,000.00
Mean	$11,757.64

such as coaching, mentoring, developmental job assignments, and the like. Tables 5 and 6 provide a summary of the data obtained.

Because only about half the respondents offered estimates here, we need to be cautious in placing much weight on the figures. One particular note of caution: When someone entered zero, we don't know whether that meant that there was no budget for spending or that the organization was not spending anything (highly unlikely in the case of non-classroom development activities).

All in all, looking at the responses on metrics and expenditures, we have a long way to go in measuring the effectiveness of developmental efforts.

Summary of Survey Results

As we noted in our report on the 2004 Trends Survey, "It's crystal clear that increasing bench strength and accelerating the development of high-potential managers will be critical objectives." The results of our 2005 survey only amplify that point. Not only was the bench strength imperative the most important and most dominating issue identified in the 2004 survey, but it has increased in importance more than any other issue a year later in this 2005 Pulse Survey. Three key elements that need to be in place to meeting the bench strength imperative were addressed in our 2005 survey: (1) integrated talent management systems, (2) succession management, and (3) the development of high-potentials. Summarizing the responses to our questions about progress on these crucial programs, it seems that a clear majority are making progress on the development of high-potentials, while only four out of ten are seeing improvement in their organizations' ability to implement an integrated talent management system (see Table 7). Conversely, as Table 8 shows, fully 9 percent of respondents think that their organizations have actually become worse on this crucial issue.

Clearly, many companies are making good progress in meeting the bench strength imperative, while others seem to be struggling.

Table 7. Percent Reporting Progress in Improving Key Programs

Development of High-Potentials	62 percent
Succession Management	60 percent
Integrated Talent Management System	40 percent

Table 8. Percent Reporting That Key Programs Had Become Worse

Integrated Talent Management System	9 percent
Succession Management	6 percent
Development of High-Potentials	3 percent

Conclusion

What does all this mean to you, your company, and the leadership development challenges you face? I encourage you to sit down with members of your team and assess your own responses to the issues presented here. How far along are you in developing an effective and integrated talent management system? What are the obstacles you face? Where are the gaps? Is succession management a top priority in your organization? What about the development of high-potentials? And are you bringing new people into the executive ranks with programs and activities that pave the way to success? How is the health of your leadership pipeline?

Also look at the development methods you are using, both in the classroom and out. Are you making good use of leader-led development, action learning, and coaching? Do your on-the-job development efforts actually aid in development, or do they just teach people to sink or swim?

Look as well at the information you gather and analyze in your leadership development activities. Do you have the information you need to make sound decisions? As I noted above, it is indeed shocking that fewer than half our respondents agreed with the statement that metrics are needed *for their own decision making*.

Virtually every organization has clear strengths as well as areas that are problematic. Whatever your assessment is of your leadership development efforts, this *Pfeiffer Annual* is designed to provide you with up-to-date, action-oriented information and specific tools you can put to use to strengthen your programs.

James F. Bolt *is chairman and founder of Executive Development Associates, Inc. (EDA), a leading consulting and networking firm specializing in the strategic use of executive development. EDA develops custom-designed executive development strategies, systems, and programs that ensure clients have the executive talent needed to accelerate strategy execution. EDA also supports the success and effectiveness of executives through powerful peer-to-peer networks and conducts research that supports network members. EDA's clients have included half of the Fortune 100 companies and many other leading organizations around the world. Mr. Bolt was recently selected by the* Financial Times *as one of the top experts in executive/leadership development. Linkage, Inc., named him one of the top fifty executive coaches in leadership development in the world. He is an online columnist for* Fast Company *magazine.*

Introduction

to the Leadership Development Strategies, Systems, and Programs Section

This section presents a variety of organizational case studies, which offer a wide variety of effective leadership development efforts, ranging from corporations to the U.S. Navy and from classroom programs to integrated talent systems.

The UBS Leadership Institute: A Case Study in Strategic Alignment, by Robert W. Mann

Linking Senior Leadership Development to the Mission of the U.S. Navy, by Barry Frew

Success Begins with Senior Management: Case Study of Innovative Leadership Development Design, by Warren Wilhelm

Creating an Integrated Talent, Leadership, and Organization Development System for Maximum Impact, by Julie Staudenmier

Leadership Development as a Driver of Shareholder Value Creation, by Raymond Vigil

Building Strategic Leadership Capabilities at Rexam PLC: A Case Study, by Alice Heezen

The UBS Leadership Institute
A Case Study in Strategic Alignment
Robert W. Mann

Summary

This article describes the role of the UBS Leadership Institute in the strategic development of one of the world's leading global financial services firms from the perspective of the Institute's head, Robert Mann. It illustrates how leadership development may become a key means of driving and aligning corporate strategy and culture, moving beyond more traditional views of the role of development, education, and learning. Key programs and processes are outlined and positioned within the strategic and operational context of the UBS growth strategy.

When I was given the mandate to launch a UBS Leadership Institute back in 2002, I saw it as a unique opportunity to help develop a more strategically aligned senior management team for a leading global financial services company. My accumulated experience of over twenty-five years in various marketing, business, and development functions at large corporations, as well as with UBS, left me with the conviction that an integrated and coordinated senior management team is one of the key enablers for creating sustainable shareholder value in the long term. This case study demonstrates how the UBS Leadership Institute helped accomplish this goal by providing results-focused learning experiences through the development and delivery of programs clearly aligned with UBS's vision and values, strategic business needs, industry issues and trends, and practical leadership challenges. Since its inception, the Leadership Institute helped build and communicate a common UBS identity across the organization and equipped senior leaders to become corporate ambassadors for the UBS vision and values.

UBS arrived at a critical juncture in its development as a global financial services powerhouse at the beginning of this century after a succession of mergers and acquisitions. The acquisition of O'Connor and SG Warburg, followed by the UBS-SBC merger in 1998 and the PaineWebber purchase in 2000, laid the groundwork for a top-ranking global institution. Comprising more than 66,000 employees, UBS had now established itself as one of the world's largest wealth managers, a premier investment bank, a key global asset manager, and the market leader in Swiss retail and commercial banking. Figure 1 shows the corporate structure.

In early 2002, following the expansion of the UBS Group Executive Board (GEB) and Group Managing Board (GMB), the firm's new president (now group CEO), Peter Wuffli, and the senior leadership team were considering how best to accomplish their vision, while retaining the diversity of opinion that had historically been so vital to the firm's success. Figure 2 shows the leadership structure.

The question facing the GEB and GMB was how to promote cultural and strategic unity among the strong component parts of the firm, each with unique legacies, capabilities, and perspectives. This group of senior leaders would have to achieve a delicate balance, nourishing the success that came from the diverse backgrounds of the

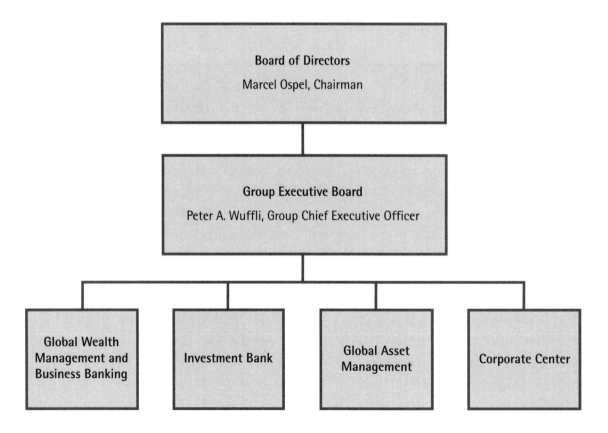

Figure 1.   UBS Corporate Structure

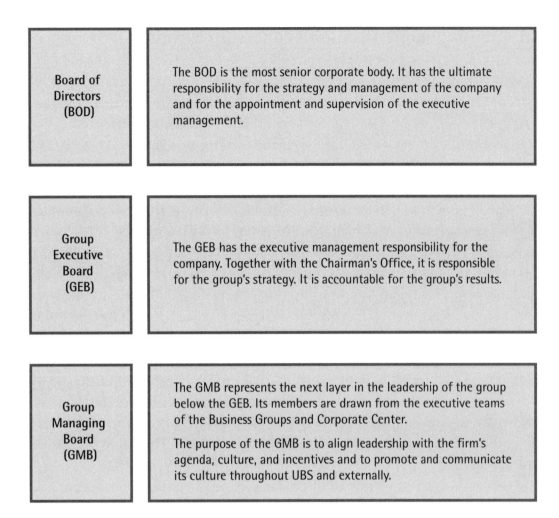

Figure 2.   UBS Leadership Structure

acquired units while aligning their creative energy toward common strategic goals. Their ultimate aim was to leverage these capabilities toward achieving the larger UBS vision: "to be recognized as the best global financial services company."

While each of UBS's business groups offered best-in-class capabilities to its individual set of clients, the GEB felt that the value of UBS should be greater than the sum of its parts, and that, if so, the firm would offer even greater value to clients and shareholders. As UBS shifted its focus from expansion through acquisitions to an integrated business model driven primarily by organic growth, greater synergies became possible. As Peter Wuffli stated, "UBS creates value for its clients by drawing on the combined resources, relationships, and expertise of our individual businesses. This integrated business model is driven by the strength, depth, and alignment of the senior leadership team."

Strategic Alignment Through Leadership Development

Peter Wuffli and the GEB believed that the best way to achieve strategic unity and alignment was to define a clear vision and set of values while concurrently developing the kind of exceptional leadership talent that would embody them.

It was for this reason that the UBS Leadership Institute was launched in 2002. As part of UBS Corporate Center, the Leadership Institute's mandate was to help develop an integrated senior leadership team focused on executing a "one-firm" business model. The firm's organic growth was to be promoted by a focus on the three UBS core values of *client focus, entrepreneurial leadership,* and *partnering for organic growth.* Wuffli described the Leadership Institute's mission as follows: "to develop our most senior leaders as a means to directly align with and in support of our firm's vision, values, culture, and identity and to support them in promoting the critical elements of UBS identity and strengthening the culture required to achieve accelerated and sustained growth throughout UBS." Simply said, our goal was to help grow the business by better aligning and developing the senior leadership team of UBS.

From the outset, we all took the position that the UBS Leadership Institute would not be a bricks-and-mortar institution, but rather a highly visible global team with a distinctive value proposition for its clients, which included the chairman's office, GEB, GMB, and the six hundred most senior leaders worldwide. The value proposition is shown in Figure 3.

The Leadership Institute's mission went far beyond the traditional concept of management education and training. Positioned this way, it became a powerful and not easily replicated competitive advantage.

The UBS Leadership Institute will support our UBS vision of becoming the best global financial services company by:

- Facilitating the development of critical strategic and leadership capabilities that reach across all UBS business groups

- Ensuring that these critical capabilities are embedded in the UBS culture and are continously refined to a world-class edge

- Providing a common understanding and sharing best practices to ensure strategic alignment and effective networking among the senior leadership team

- Serving as strategic catalyst and providing a forum for leaders in UBS to influence critical issues for the firm's growth

---

Figure 3.   UBS Leadership Institute's Value Proposition

Creating the Vision, Establishing the Partnership

Historically, the GEB and GMB (approximately seventy leaders) convened at an annual face-to-face meeting to review strategy and current challenges facing the businesses. One of the first challenges presented to me was to have the UBS Leadership Institute team redesign the event and make it a more effective strategic conference. To symbolize this transition, the meeting was renamed the "Annual Strategic Forum" (ASF), with the first such event held in 2002 based on the theme *Creating Our Future*.

In the run-up to the first ASF, a draft version of the new UBS vision and values, as formulated by the GEB and board of directors, was distributed to the GMB for their feedback and revision. During the forum, participants in working teams and plenary sessions reviewed, discussed, and analyzed the consolidated feedback on the vision and values, which amounted to some 140 pages of commentary. By the end of the forum, the top seventy senior leaders in the firm had crafted a new UBS Vision and Values for Action. The exercise had itself helped to instill a shared agenda and a common mission at the topmost levels of the firm. It was also at this 2002 ASF that the momentous decision was put in motion to move from a cluster of separate brands to a single brand reflecting the new UBS integrated approach, as shown in Figure 4.

Building the UBS Identity

Rolling out a single brand was but one aspect of establishing the larger UBS identity, namely, the internal and external attributes that comprise the one-firm integrated business model. The concept is shown in Figure 5.

The UBS Identity Framework was developed by the Leadership Institute as a matrix of characteristics that connected the UBS vision, values, and brand. This became a powerful tool to communicate and illustrate the one-firm culture senior leaders

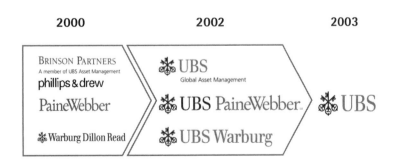

Figure 4.   Branding Diagram

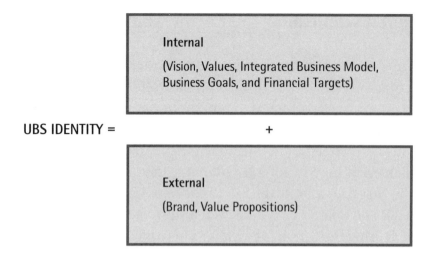

Figure 5.   The UBS Identity Concept

were striving to cultivate. It was recognized that the brand could only be truly effective when it was demonstrably consistent and integrated with the vision and values. The model is shown in Figure 6.

The ASF brought home to UBS's senior management the importance of living the UBS vision and values and of promoting the UBS identity throughout the firm as part of their leadership responsibilities. The challenge was now to get this message out to a broader audience. To help cascade the message down through the organization, the Leadership Institute developed the UBS Identity Workshop: Vision & Values. The workshop was delivered by all GMB members to their respective teams between October 2002 and June 2003, with support from the Leadership Institute. This had the result of involving an additional one thousand senior leaders in the process. Workshop participants discussed and identified solutions to the key challenges that would be faced in executing the UBS strategy. From these workshops, the Leadership Institute reported important trends and themes back to the senior leadership team. Insights from the workshops were also used to guide development of the next generation of Leadership Institute programs that were soon to be developed.

Another important initiative launched at the ASF 2002 was a mentoring program whereby GEB members served as mentors for the GMB. The program, managed by the Leadership Institute, was expressly designed to build relationships across business groups and regions with a view to generating business-focused results in the service of the one-firm integrated model. The engagement of senior leaders in building relationships also yielded long-term benefits in enhanced communication, alignment, talent mobility, board evaluation, and succession planning.

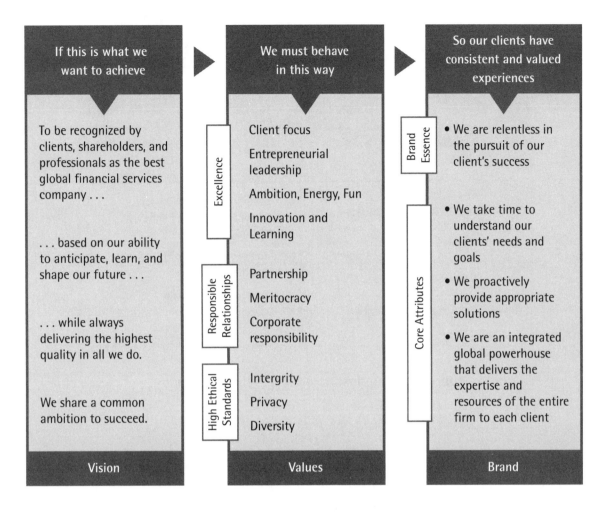

Figure 6. UBS Identity Framework: Vision, Values, and Brand

The GEB-GMB mentoring process was considered so beneficial that the process was subsequently cascaded down. As a result, GMB members were assigned as mentors to between one and four upcoming talents in the next level of leadership. This mentoring program, linking the top 250 leaders in UBS, led to a greater integration of activities across business groups through knowledge sharing, partnering on business project execution, and improved cross-business communication.

Value Delivery System— Building the Core Leadership Development System

The momentum generated by the ASF, UBS identity workshops, and senior leadership mentoring established the UBS Leadership Institute as a critical force in building understanding, alignment, and execution around business strategy among the firm's top

Figure 7.   UBS Leadership Institute Value Delivery Systems

leadership. The Leadership Institute's Value Proposition and Value Delivery System specify how the Institute will continue to support the UBS vision (see Figure 7).

The Value Delivery System comprises a series of core leadership development programs aimed at the top six hundred managers, plus the high-potential leaders. Starting with the Annual Strategic Forum (ASF), and continuing with the Senior Leadership Conference (SLC), the Global Leadership Experience (GLE) series, and the Accelerated Leadership Experience (ALE), these programs, as described below, serve collectively as the backbone of senior leadership development at UBS. Each of the programs addresses specific objectives, while at the same time reinforcing key strategic messages and addressing UBS-wide business challenges.

Annual Strategic Forum (ASF)

As described above, this is an annual meeting of the seventy most senior leaders, with a focus on building alignment among the leadership team through strategic engagement sessions, with networking and relationship building as an additional benefit of the process. The first ASF in 2002 is frequently referenced as a milestone in the UBS strategic change process, and the program continues to evolve with the changing needs and strategic focus of the firm. The ASF 2003 was based on the theme of *Leadership for Growth*, while the ASF 2004 focused on *Partnership for Growth*.

Senior Leadership Mentoring

As described above, this is a mentoring program for senior leaders in which the Group Executive Board (GEB) mentors the Group Managing Board (GMB) and the GMB mentors a cross section of the next level of senior leaders.

Senior Leadership Conference (SLC)

Following the success of the first ASF in 2002, the Leadership Institute was asked to redesign and deliver another senior management event that would ultimately reach an even larger segment of UBS's management population. The Senior Leadership Conference (SLC) was a biennial gathering of the top six hundred global leaders across UBS, traditionally held in Interlaken, Switzerland. The redesigned event was to be significantly broader in scope, providing a unique forum in which senior leaders from across the business groups and across the globe could together build unity, alignment, and capacity for execution of the UBS strategic agenda.

The first SLC in 2003 proved to be groundbreaking in more than one respect. The SARS outbreak at the time made it impossible to bring participants together in a single location, as we had originally planned. As a result, the Leadership Institute was asked to redesign the SLC concept on short notice and find a way to deliver the same strategic results without bringing the senior management team together in a single location. As a result, the event was launched on time, but in a completely new format. Instead of convening in one location, senior managers interacted with their colleagues around the globe via a ninety-minute satellite broadcast and three-hour local events that took place concurrently in New York, London, Zurich, Tokyo, Singapore, Sydney, and Hong Kong. The theme of the event was *One Firm . . . One Brand . . . One Future,* and it was designed to generate excitement and understanding around the launch of the single UBS brand. It was so successful that it was subsequently decided to hold the SLC conference every year instead of biennially, alternating between a single location and a global broadcast via satellite to multiple locations.

The SLC continues to be a cornerstone of senior leadership development at UBS, as well as an important tool to build unity and cascade important messages through the ranks of the firm's senior managers and beyond into the organization. The 2004 SLC was based on the theme *Building on Our Success . . . Broadening Our Horizons* and was delivered by satellite to seven locations around the world. In 2005 the event was held at a single location, in Montreux, Switzerland. This SLC focused on building the "relationship glue" among the top six hundred by focusing on "understanding, commitment, and trust." This theme reflected the belief that much of the conceptual understanding and alignment had been achieved and that increasing emphasis would be placed on establishing cross-organizational relationships key to building integrated business opportunities.

The GLE and ALE Programs

Besides reframing existing events such as the ASF and SLC, the UBS Leadership Institute has also expanded a stand-alone leadership development program that had been running since 1999 into a family of three distinctive programs, the Global Leadership Experience I, II, and III, as outlined in Table 1.

Each Global Leadership Experience (GLE) is custom-designed to align with the firm's strategic agenda.

The GLE programs combine internal and external experts with program project work. The UBS chairman, CEO, and members of the GEB and GMB nominate senior leaders to participate in the program, and they themselves participate regularly as program sponsors, as role models, and as faculty.

GLE programs evolve continuously to reflect strategic challenges, industry best practice, and learning. Faculty and program design adopt new technologies, simulations, and post-program coaching and measurement tools as appropriate. The GLE programs each extend over three and one-half days and currently run twelve times a year. To date, more than one thousand UBS senior leaders have participated in a GLE, and the programs continue to be highly regarded throughout the firm.

GLE I: Understanding the Total UBS Enterprise

The purpose of GLE I is to develop a deeper understanding of the entire UBS organization and stimulate collaboration among business groups in order to leverage the firm's total capabilities.

GLE II: Building and Leveraging Organizational Capabilities

GLE II helps participants delve more deeply into the businesses and to develop a common view of the current key strategic issues facing UBS. They analyze and develop specific organizational actions and measures to enable UBS to strengthen client focus and integrate capabilities from the whole firm to drive sustained organic growth and foster entrepreneurial leadership behavior.

GLE III: Building Leadership Capabilities

The purpose of GLE III is to build the personal leadership capabilities needed to execute the firm's strategic agenda. Focusing most closely on the "personal effectiveness" dimension of leadership development, participants apply leadership concepts, tools, and techniques to specific business challenges seeking sustainable performance results.

Table 1. Outline of the Global Leadership Experience

Program Title		Strategic Objectives	Design Principles	GEB/GMB Role
GLE 1	Understanding the Total Enterprise	Provide overview of all UBS Business Group products, services, successes, and challenges Facilitate cross-business integration through networking and identification of integrated business model opportunities	External faculty presentations Internal UBS business leader presentations Case studies Simulations Leadership challenge course	Open/close program Deliver presentations about their business groups' challenges, opportunities, and successes
GLE II	Building Organizational Capabilities	Enable participants to articulate their value propositions so that they can construct a more client-focused value delivery system Enable participants to become entrepreneurial leaders to support organic growth	External faculty presentations UBS business leaders serve as facilitators Group work Success story presentations	Open/close program Present business case for entrepreneurial leadership and organic growth at UBS Discuss examples of entrepreneurial leadership and organic growth at UBS
GLE III	Building Leadership Capabilities	Challenges participants to examine their leadership behaviors and effectiveness and create a plan for resolving a critical business challenge	Focused on business challenge 360-degree feedback UBS business leaders serve as teachers Action learning External executive coaches Peer coaching teams Post-program: mini-survey, coaching Technology-supported follow-up activities	Open/close program Teach the four UBS leadership capabilities upon which the course is built Share personal leadership stories Present business case for leadership development

Objective: Ensure senior leaders have capabilities (mindsets, knowledge, and skills) needed to win in the marketplace, achieve the vision, live the values, and execute the strategic agenda.

Accelerated Leadership Experience (ALE)

The Accelerated Leadership Experience (ALE) is the newest offering in the Leadership Institute's suite of leadership development programs. ALE is aimed at the firm's high-potentials, building leadership capabilities in the next generation of UBS senior leaders and focusing on building cross-business capabilities in support of the one-firm approach. The program includes preparatory work, as well as completion of a number of 360-degree feedback instruments and professional coaching and mentoring for participants, both during and after the program.

Participants in ALE enter the mentoring program approximately three months after completing ALE. This is complemented by an increased focus on each participant's individual development plans, which are carefully designed and monitored to ensure that they are continuing to develop in ways that are aligned to their goals and the requirements of UBS.

The ALE and the GLE programs provide a complementary set of strategic leadership development programs that occur at key junctures in an individual's career and are incorporated into broader development plans, which include on-the-job, cross-organizational, and other developmental experiences. These programs provide a corporate structure or cadence to leadership development that complements development programs and processes within the individual business groups.

Extending the Impact

As a direct result of its continuing work in the areas described in this chapter, the Leadership Institute has become increasingly involved in more consultative projects, working directly with the business groups to achieve specific strategic and business objectives. These engagements have come as a direct result of the various programs described above, such as the GLE, which have stimulated participants to request support from the Leadership Institute in implementing and executing strategic initiatives.

The Leadership Institute has achieved internal recognition at senior levels for its efforts in creating a highly integrated development and strategic alignment system with significant impact. The expansion of the Leadership Institute's mandate, combined with senior management's continuing involvement in many aspects of its programs and processes, points to the Institute's continuing relevance in helping shape the strategic direction of the firm.

The Leadership Institute has also garnered external plaudits. It was recognized by the Corporate University Xchange in 2004 for the "best launch of a corporate university" and further recognized in 2005 for "best practice in furthering corporate goals through learning and development efforts" and "excellence in implementing high-impact programs targeted to managers, high-potentials, and senior executive leadership." Additionally, UBS and the Leadership Institute were selected by their peers as one of the "top ten companies in executive development" in 2005.

Sustaining the Vision

The UBS Leadership Institute has gone beyond traditional leadership development to play a critical role in shaping the firm's culture and enabling organizational change in support of the organization's strategy. UBS's leaders believe that the strongest impact will result by ensuring the firm-wide integration of business effort around a common culture and a shared vision clearly aligned with strategy. Strong relationships and continuous communication among the firm's senior leaders support ongoing success. UBS has already made tremendous progress toward achieving its vision. The UBS Leadership Institute remains focused on maintaining alignment with the firm's strategy and is committed to supporting UBS in its drive to become recognized as the best global financial services company.

Robert W. Mann, Ph.D., *is a member of the UBS Group Managing Board and managing director, Global Head Learning and Development at UBS. In this capacity, he heads the UBS Leadership Institute and has responsibility for senior leadership development programs, talent management and succession planning, and integrated learning and development activities across UBS. Dr. Mann began his career with UBS in the Investment Banking Division and has since held a number of senior positions in the United States, UK, and Switzerland with the Investment Bank and Corporate Center business groups. Prior to joining UBS in 1996, he held a number of senior executive positions in various global businesses both in the United States and abroad. He earned two master's degrees and a Ph.D.*

Linking Senior Leadership Development to the Mission of the U.S. Navy

Barry Frew

Summary

How do you facilitate a change in mindset and behavior of individuals who have been successful in their careers and who have worked in an organization that has rewarded the behaviors that you want to change? In this article, I describe the design, development, and approach of two educational programs aimed at creating a mind-shift about rules, processes, and thinking about how to best support and enable a new war-fighting strategy called network-centric warfare. I discuss the target groups from the Department of Defense and the military services, the barriers to program implementation, and the results for the U.S. Navy, including an offshoot presentation and program for senior executives.

The first program was a two-week event for senior-level officers, and the second was a four-week program for mid-grade junior-level officers. Both programs were modeled after the best private industry programs and implemented at the Center for Executive Education, located at the Naval Postgraduate School in Monterey, California. The center focused on helping provide a growth experience for Navy admirals, Marine Corps generals, and Senior Executive Service (SES) civilians (the three groups are of similar stature, although two are in military uniform and one consists of senior civilian employees of the Navy department), but also involved all of the military services in the execution of these two events.

The idea for this executive education program occurred during a 1997 conversation between the author and a vice admiral known to be the "father" of the Navy's Network Centric Warfare, Vice Admiral Arthur Cebrowski. He shared his growing concern that the Navy was moving too slowly to adapt to a network-centric culture and business model, a shift from the traditional platform-centric model. A network-centric warfare environment, according to Cebrowski and Garstka (1998), is "driven and dominated by co-evolutional changes in society, economics, and technology." This new model is linked by three themes:

- The shift in focus from the platform to the network

- The shift from viewing actors as independent to viewing them as part of a continuously adapting ecosystem

- The importance of making strategic choices to adapt or even survive in such changing ecosystems

Conceptually, the argument was that, if the Navy chose to adopt this new strategy, we would need to modify how they trained, organized, and allocated resources.

Target Audience

Since most of those decisions are made by the most senior leaders within the Navy, they were identified as the target audience for these events. The Navy had no existing development program for the most senior ranks and positions. The idea was to provide an education venue for admirals, generals, and their civilian counterparts, senior executive service (SES) civilians, which could create a sense of urgency to adopt a network-centric mindset and to adjust their training, organization, and allocation behaviors. This new mindset, in turn, could support a more open mind and allow for the serious consideration of radically new ideas, rules, processes, tools, and filters.

These executives were an even tougher audience than were the school's excellent graduate students—our second target audience—who normally had good academic and thinking skills, along with very good performance ratings in a variety of settings over a ten-year period before being selected for graduate education. The graduate students at the Naval Postgraduate School, junior-level officers, truly represented the best and brightest the military services had to offer. The senior leaders introduced to the "experience" were the best and the brightest executives the services had to offer.

My observation of participants, especially the senior officers, indicated that they were smart, learned quickly, had short attention spans, were used to being treated differently, and had a long history of successes in several roles within the naval organization that led to strong intuitions about the "right thing to do." My hypothesis in approaching this challenge was that *in order to get these folks to behave differently, they had to fundamentally think differently.* Changing the minds or the fundamental underpinnings of anyone is tough, but with the individuals of this group it was even more difficult. After all, why should they change what they had been thinking and doing? It had led to success over a consistent and long period.

Potential Obstacles

While designing the curricula and the intervention itself, we faced many challenges. Executive education at the most senior level was new to the Navy and considered countercultural. The idea that the most senior leaders might require additional skills via education had not been thought relevant or important or had not been seriously considered. The Navy's culture of history, tradition, individualism, and leadership is strong. The concept that a higher self-awareness could be realized by using high-quality assessment tools for thinking, personality preferences, and performance capabilities, as well as behaviors, was thought to be useful only for remedial cases, rather than peak-performing senior executives. Finally, the idea that the most senior peak-performing leaders need to do anything differently than they had to achieve their status was counterintuitive to some. The most successful leaders, those who have shined through a history of success, often feel that their intuition and experience were all that were necessary to continue that string of success. There is lots of evidence that this is not the case, according to Clayton Christianson, based on his research of disruptive ideas.

Approach and Design

The Center for Executive Education's support staff was a diverse mix of knowledge and experience, tied to a fundamental set of shared values of trust, dedication, passion, integrity, and personal responsibility. The amount of innovation that was generated by this small band of talented and dedicated individuals was amazing. There was a high level of passion among them and a dedication to excellent results that was unmatched by any group I have led in my life.

The practice of asking provocative, yet relevant questions of participants was used liberally throughout both programs. It was extremely important for the two-week senior program. For example, we asked that senior officers consider whether vertical integration was a failed strategy for moving forward into the information age and a rapidly changing and unpredictable future, or whether it was time for them to focus on horizontal integration. We asked that they consider the intended and unintended outcomes of flattening hierarchy and dismantling bureaucracy. We asked that they balance the need for generating and managing innovation with the need to stay within the rules and the law. We asked them to consider the impact of moving from an "up or out" human capital strategy to one that invites experimentation, failure, and a much longer career pattern. Finally, we openly addressed the possibility that the world's greatest Navy could be irrelevant to some particular national defense threat. This dialogue was much more difficult to have prior to planes being driven into the twin towers in New York, which provided a stark and real example.

These questions and the idea of facilitating dialogue around these issues drove the rest of the design, although we also used valid assessment tools for thinking intentions, personality preferences, leadership, and resiliency tendencies to bring data and reality to individuals. We chose an immersion experience for participants, to increase any chance of shifting their mindsets and helping move the Navy strategy forward. We settled on a two-week course. The two-week version was long enough to raise their level of receptivity and short enough to capture their attention. One result of the courses was the formation of deeper bonds among attendees, which generated a new culture-shifting language and altered expectations. The content and speakers had to be carefully selected and had to have compelling stories, as well as be able to communicate and resonate with seasoned professionals.

The two-week format worked for a variety of reasons. It had great content, which provided thought-provoking questions that supported a robust dialogue among attendees. It captured the timely ideas that were relevant to participants' most pressing and complex issues. It was not held in Washington, D.C., where it would have been difficult or impossible to capture a participant's full and uninterrupted attention. Participants dressed and lived differently while attending a course, which helped them begin to think differently and to create innovative ideas, tools, and ways to make dramatic progress and transform. It was a safe environment for truth and conjecture without penalty or attribution. The enthusiasm and passion of the staff at CEE was infectious and had a great influence on the learning environment. In addition, the Center, its leadership, and the staff had absolutely no tolerance for mediocrity, and their consistent drive toward excellence provided the necessary high energy for speakers and participants alike.

Revolution in Business Practices (RBP) Event

After the initial thrust of providing more technological literacy to the senior leaders, the Center for Executive Education turned its attention to providing better business literacy. Frequent program discussion topics included:

1. The idea that more rapid change should be expected rather than less.

2. The environment would be impacted by more frequent disruptive ideas.

3. The future would be more unpredictable than the past.

4. Continued globalization would radically affect the world economies.

5. Technology would play an increasing role in business and national defense.

Participants were peak performers—the top 1 percent—who had risen to the top of the rank structure. They had achieved, along the way, a very strong intuition about the "right" thing to do. This was strengthened by a history of success over their careers. This strong pattern of success over a long period of time led to strong egos. The Navy has a strong "up or out" culture and hires only at the entry level, so the senior leaders were survivors in a non-forgiving promotion system. Technically, attendees were very competent (best in the world) and had strong levels of agreement among them as to what was needed when it came to fighting wars, but not when it came to making business decisions. Their perception of the war-fight was beginning to make the shift—from platform-centric thinking to network-centric thinking—but they had not translated that to any other piece of the organization. The strong "leadership from the top" mindsets made leading from all levels within the organization more difficult. Many senior leaders were comfortable with the culture and the professional development processes at play within the organization. Although they recognized that those processes had "warts," they were unaware of anything better. Many program participants reminded us frequently that the U.S. Navy was "not a business" and could not be managed like one! This program was all about bringing improved thinking and more awareness and more openness to alternative approaches by expanding boundaries, comfort zones, and perspectives. This program was about bringing positive change in thinking and behaving so that the Navy could be much more business-like as they executed their main mission of national defense.

An intense learning environment tires executives and facilitators easily. The degree of energy expended in assessing new thinking and engaging in provocative dialogue surprised most attendees and facilitators until it was experienced. We found that matching some time to tire the body somewhat balanced out the tiring of the mind. Likewise, recovery time was necessary for both mind and body. We tried teaming events like ropes courses and team problem solving, which received mixed results. Many of these warfighters had experience with serious obstacle courses; many had jumped out of planes and had team-training events that led to a crucible or life-changing perspective-shifting result. The successful events included new experiences and new challenges for the group. Rock climbing with problem solving and introspection interwoven into the event worked well. A long, challenging hike in Big Sur was a big success. We failed to add value when we used off-the-shelf team-building experiences with low levels of challenge. Both the hike and the rock-climbing experience had additional value because they gave many of the leaders a message that they had stopped giving enough priority to personal health, which led us to add that type of module to the program, with some assessment data to put their personal health in context (life balance).

The content was designed to challenge their mental models and the status quo. It was integrated with the Chief of Naval Operation's reading list, intended for all admirals, generals, and senior leaders. We thought the program would be more successful and lead to better outcomes if the duration was longer than a week. Their culture and their self-perception of being gone for two or more weeks was a challenge. They were convinced that one week was the maximum time they could sustain "away from the job." This was the start of the paradigm shift that was to occur. The push back of suggesting that they consider the possibility of achieving a new and more valuable perspective to take their execution and performance levels to a new high was not a compelling argument to them. Through observation, time and again, we observed that the dialogue took a different tone during the second week. The facilitator recognized it, as did the staff and outside speakers, who had been in each part of the course over a period of time. A few participants attended the program multiple times, and it appeared to occur there as well. When asked whether the second time was different, each told me that it was easier and even more valuable. Why? Because the robust and honest dialogue was easier, and it was easier to put their own beliefs on hold while listening to understand the story or perspective being presented because they had had practice doing these things the first time. It is my belief that being willing and able to put your beliefs on hold is a critical component of changing your mind.

Our faculty was made up of the best thinkers and practitioners available. It included several leading executives:

- Dr. Eric Schmidt, CEO of Google

- Larry Ellison, CEO of Oracle

- John Chambers, CEO of Cisco Systems, Inc.

- Jaime Hewitt, Transformation VP at IBM

- Carly Fiorina, former CEO of Hewlett Packard

- Ray Lane, general partner at Kleiner Perkins Caufield & Byers

- Raphael Benaroya, CEO of United Retail Group, Inc.

- Nick Donofrio, senior vice president at IBM

- Michael Crooke, CEO of Patagonia

- Robert Eckert, CEO of Mattel, Inc.

- Robert Buckman, CEO of Buckman Laboratories

- Alfred Berkley III, CEO of NASDAQ

- Jim Staley, president of Roadway Express

- Judy Estrin, CEO of Packet Design

- Bruce Claflin, CEO of 3Com

- Scott McNealy, CEO of Sun Microsystems

Also included were thought leaders such as:

- Dr. George Labovitz, author of the *Power of Alignment*

- Dr. Karen Stephenson, social network expert

- Dr. Frank Barrett and Dr. David Cooperrider, appreciative inquiry founders

- Walker White, chief scientist at Oracle

- Watts Wacker, author of *The Visionary's Handbook* and *Deviant's Advantage*

- Dr. David Henderson, economist, editor of *The Fortune Encyclopedia of Economics, The Joy of Freedom: An Economist's Odyssey,* and *Making Great Decisions in Business and Life*

- Dr. John Gage, chief scientist at Sun Microsystems

- David Breashears, author of *High Exposure,* movie documenter, and Mt. Everest climber

- Dr. John Kao, author of *Jamming,* CEO of the Idea Factory, and a terminal innovator

- Steve Uzzell, an award-winning photographer, whose work has appeared in *National Geographic, Newsweek,* and *Time.*

This course, according to the Chief of Naval Operations, Admiral Vern Clark, "effected fundamental change to the professional development and growth of a generation of flag officers and members of the SES . . . its profound influence will shape the Navy's executive leadership well into the 21st century."

30-Something Event for Mid-Grade Junior Officers

The "30-Something" course was an annual four-week educational immersion exercise that created an environment in which young mid-grade military officers could share their ideas for the future of the Department of the Navy and the Department of Defense with senior leadership. The course was created in response to a need expressed by The Honorable Jerry M. Hultin, Under Secretary of the Navy, whose "Revolution in Business Affairs" initiatives were breaking new ground and generating considerable enthusiasm for change in the military. Developed, managed, designed, and facilitated by the director of the Center for Executive Education at NPS, the event was modeled after the Center's flag-level officers' event that focused on innovation, positive change, and mindset shifts. Secretary Hultin emphasized that creativity, as well as critical thinking, was necessary to solve military problems and that the combination should not be the purview of senior management alone. As in private industry, often the middle management provides solutions to emerging problems or creates better paths to improved outcomes.

Exciting speakers and concentrated group work in the course provided an opportunity for mid-grade junior officers to think about issues that will affect the military of the future and to generate recommendations that might otherwise not be captured from young officers. Throughout the course, students spent time learning from forward-thinking military and civilian executives, futurists, and experts in the field of creative thinking. Speakers and readings in the various topic areas were designed to stimulate critical thinking, but the weight of the responsibility for course outcomes was placed on student participation. Students were encouraged to actively pursue learning through questioning, discussion, and debate.

Students formed groups based on passion for the outcome to work on projects that addressed significant challenges faced by the Department of Navy and the Department of Defense. Using classroom resources and their own experiences, students worked to generate innovative ideas to address the challenges that the military would face in the future. At the end of the course, the students briefed the Navy Under-Secretary and other senior leadership on their recommendations.

The mission was to build a military leader who is a broader and more reasoned thinker and an excellent decision maker. Its scope would be to stretch the comfort zones and the thinking boundaries of these high-potential junior officers. The task was to consider some of the thorniest problems their organizations faced. Many attendees described their deepened sense of commitment and life-changing experience to the mission as a result of being a participant of 30-Something. This course allowed young military and civilian minds to explore innovative ideas about learning to begin a growth process in an intellectually supportive environment with sufficient resources to support the process. The increased value to the organization was realized in the additional skills and awareness of information pitfalls and values obtained from this course and put to valuable use throughout an officer's career. For some attendees, this event was described as "life changing."

At the conclusion of the first "30-Something" final briefing, the Under Secretary of the Navy, Honorable Jerry Hultin, simply said, "Wow!" The audience did not know what to expect, but all agreed that what was presented far exceeded their own expectations. All of the participants had similar comments and agreed that perhaps the most important outcome of the event was simply that it even happened. It should send a strong message to everyone that the military's senior leadership wants its young leaders involved in its future.

What drove the establishment of this experience was similar to Jack Welch, former CEO of GE's, idea that, "If the rate of change on the outside is greater than the rate of change on the inside, then the end is near." The rate of change in the military is increasing, and people within the military can either ride this wave of change or be overcome by it. We stated it a little differently: "So what happens if the world's strongest Navy is irrelevant to the threat?"

As the graduates of this first 30-Something course can attest, you don't have to be an admiral or general to make a difference. To achieve "2020 today" is a challenge to which everyone can contribute. This inaugural group moved from questioning their ability to help, to solving easier-to-conceptualize pieces of the problem, and then to putting it all together to form a coherent and compelling vision.

They provided a creative summary by delivering a very provocative "day in the life" of a typical sailor in 2020. Pieces of this part of the presentation began to show up in admirals' presentations throughout the Navy and can still be found today. Some of their thoughts have also made it into doctrine and presentations. The powerful image of turning the Navy's "rhetoric into reality" worked for some. The compelling picture of becoming an "employer of choice" rather than an "employer of least resort" has become the focus of recruiting efforts for future recruits.

Mixing 30-Something with Revolution in Business Practices for Executives

One noteworthy innovation that occurred was to combine the 30-Something learning event with the Revolution in Business Practice course. The 30-Something group picked a small group of representatives to tell the story of what they did and what they concluded might be useful as we think about the Navy of the future. There was a very high-impact moment during the inaugural session when the 30-Something presentation to the RBP suggested that the Navy should become a meritocracy. One of the admirals questioned what he meant. It was his impression that the Navy already *was* a meritocracy. The young mid-grade officer was ready with several examples of how the organization behaved differently than a strict meritocracy would behave and included things like pay banding and promotions being based on performance for those in the band, but the bands were based on longevity with the organization; many of the ribbons and awards have rank and seniority attached to the award along with merit. This suggested that often the merit was comparatively inconsequential.

Both groups left the experience with a heightened sense of the skill set of the other. The admirals were impressed with the energy, passion, and analysis of the younger group. You could hear their respect in comments like, "smarter than we were when we were their age" or "our future is in good hands." You could also hear the 30-Somethings' respect for what their leaders had done and continue to do and for how well the leaders understood the real issues facing this organization. Some flag officers began institutionalizing the use of mid-grade working and focus groups when considering major organizational, alignment, training, and allocation change initiatives.

CEE established a website that provided a brokering place for new ideas with no other way to emerge from within the Navy organization. It was called "Outliers." Strong ideas that had rigorous analysis and good write-ups were presented on this site. The material was passed through an editorial board of Naval postgraduate professors, and the papers were blind-referred.

It was clear that the collective actions of all members, all levels of leadership, will be necessary to make the difference and that these forums were changing the language, the expectations, and the behavior of the Navy leadership.

> "Never doubt that a small group of thoughtful, committed citizens can change the world. Indeed, it's the only thing that ever has."
>
> Margaret Mead

Sample Outcomes Resulting from the Two Offerings

Here are some of the significant outcomes from the two programs:

- Helped propel organizational rhetoric into reality

- Contributed to changing the target audience for leadership training to include individual, team, unit, and organizational levels

- Put forth the idea of distributing accountability and redefining the role of commanding officers, leading to the possible future of manning ships by using two complete, dynamic teams (crews) for each ship and unprecedented individual access to information; smart racks (bunks) would be integrated with "windows from home," allowing voice and video via high-speed web access

- Led to testing processes for liberating innovation from hierarchy by unbinding it from rigid bureaucratic rules, such as providing virtual detailing (job assignments), performance evaluations, and e-promotion boards

- Established a sense of urgency for replacing the culture of buying systems with the concept of buying capability and for people-focused platforms, i.e., manning the person, rather than the equipment

- Expanded the practice of outsourcing non-core competencies, taking advantage of commercial expertise and doing so by using intranets and extranet-based industry exchanges for e-business directly

- Put forth a serious way of paying for performance versus just rank, based on professional qualifications, education, and certifications (no more "up or out")

- Generated prototypes for pay and retirement plans (401[k]) that are more portable and flexible

- Detailers becoming "talent managers" who balance individual career choice with Navy and industry partnerships

- Shifting to win-win versus win-lose paradigm and providing more service member input to trade off decisions regarding benefits and pay

- Initiated seven task forces, each led by a senior admiral, to address the most complex issues facing the Navy and integrating senior civilians on these teams and in all venues that had previously been for admirals only

- Hosting a leadership conference combining the use of large numbers of people (250 from a cross section of the Navy, from admirals to seamen and civilians) and appreciative inquiry technique

- Challenged the Navy to become an employer of choice, rather than an employer of last resort

- Initiated a policy wherein executive education alumni were promoted more frequently than the non-participant part of the flag officer population

Special One-Week Version of Program: Achieving Alignment with the Navy Mission

The original task was simply to make senior leadership more aware of the imperative that information age ideas should be applied innovatively to the way the Navy fights wars and to the way the Navy conducts business. This message was in alignment with the messages from the Secretary of Defense (SECDEF), The Honorable William Cohen, the Secretary of the Navy (SECNAV), The Honorable Richard Danzig, and the messages from the Chief of Naval Operations (CNO), ADM Jay Johnson. Follow-on CNO, ADM Vern Clark, and follow-on SECNAV, The Honorable Gordon England, continued the direction of transformation and modernization and both became strong supporters of the groundbreaking work performed at the Naval Postgraduate School's Center for Executive Education.

When our sponsor called and asked for a special one-week version of the Revolution in Business Practices Course for a select group of four-star admirals (the Navy's most senior position; only eight exist in the Navy), it was obvious that the next head of Naval Operations was in this group. As it happened, the individual selected, ADM Vern Clark, had a great understanding of the compelling case for change and for the great leverage that a top-notch executive program would provide. His position was "in times of conflict, our Navy and our nation depend on . . . intellectual capital . . . it is about a challenge to examine every assumption that we face today . . . now is the time for bold and innovative thinking—thinking that will be vital for us to achieve victory."

Admiral Clark identified his top five issues early in his tenure as the Chief of Naval Operations, which formed an articulate and compelling foundation for our intellectual program to challenge assumptions and challenge the thinking of the most senior members to affect progress toward the CNO's goals. Clark's goals included:

1. *Manpower*—Navy and Marine Corps starts with the Fleet. All our efforts must lead to a better Fleet. Our ability to recruit and retain is critical to the future. We are about Service! It is what sets us apart—our dedication to service;

2. *Current Readiness*—Committing to giving the people of the Navy the tools to succeed;

3. *Future Readiness*—Providing real numbers regarding total costs of operations or ownership;

4. *Quality of Service*—Managing better the quality of work; and finally,

5. *Alignment*—We must be about speed and agility if we are going to survive in the future. We must extract every ounce of utility out of every dollar we have.

These core mission areas were routinely addressed by our primary focus on ideas and tools emerging externally from the naval organization. We relied heavily on bringing in ideas from emerging thought leaders and stories from seasoned veterans in challenging positions who had found tools leading to success or failure. Many of the speakers from the private industry addressed being able to use real numbers for total costs that were imbedded in their company intranets; in financial systems that allowed overnight closure and reconciliation of the books; and in integrated systems that aggregated costs in supply chains, human capital, and complete product or service life cycles.

Lessons Learned

I think the story of these two programs for the military illustrates two counter-intuitive lessons. The first is that real shifts in important and long-existing impediments to change can be generated, even for seasoned leaders. Giving these leaders compelling reasons to question their own beliefs simply by getting them to "put their beliefs on hold" long enough to seriously consider alternative ideas is a very powerful way to overcome resistance to new ideas. If I were building a program today, I would focus principally on making it easier for executives and peak performers to put their beliefs on hold.

The second lesson was that senior leaders can step outside their leadership roles and fully participate in learning events, even though they dismissed the idea as impossible in the beginning.

Those two lessons and the lessons that follow are the result of continued follow-up with participants six months and one year after attending. Attendees were asked to write letters to themselves at the completion of the course, and they were mailed back to them at three- or six-month levels (it started at six months and evolved to a three-month period). They were also asked to submit narratives that described significant learning events in which they had changed foundation beliefs. These narratives were broken down to better understand the characteristics involved that led to changed mindsets. The data collected revealed that the principal characteristic in the changed mindsets was their ability to place strong beliefs on hold—no narrative resulted in changed a mindset when that characteristic was present. Several other characteristics were present in many configurations in narratives that did not describe significant learning. The only narratives that included significant new models without placing beliefs on hold were life-threatening emergent events that happened fast and resulted in some fundamental lesson without consciously putting beliefs on hold. Other lessons taken from participant descriptions include the following.

A third lesson had much stronger impact than originally thought, but it probably should not have been such a surprise. This third lesson is how much more powerful outcomes result when these educational interventions integrate senior and mid-level leaders in the same provocative dialogue, creating much more robust and diverse ideas than when each group is isolated in a homogeneous way. The *multiple generational views* produce a much more compelling case and a better path for improvement to both groups. Without credible outside thought leaders who could communicate clearly with attendees, many participants would have been incapable of putting their beliefs on hold. Without a strong facilitator who linked the material and used concrete examples of success using these sometimes new or once rejected ideas, attendees would be less willing to place beliefs on hold.

Conclusion

These two programs provided senior executives and high-potential managers with globally relevant frameworks for addressing today's issues and practices and thereby adding value toward accomplishing the Navy's goals. By facilitating leaders to become more change ready, it had positive and immediate impact on their own organizations as well as the larger Navy. The impact was both at the individual level and at the organizational level. Nothing is more rewarding than making a positive difference and impact on people's lives and on helping good organizations get better. It was the best time of my professional life!

References

Cebrowski, A.K., & Gartska, J. (1998, January). *Network-centric warfare: Its origin and future.* Annapolis, MD: U.S. Naval Institute.

Christianson, C. (1997). *The innovator's dilemma.* Cambridge, MA: Harvard Business School Press.

Christianson, C. (2003). *The innovator's solution.* Cambridge, MA: Harvard Business School Press.

Dr. Barry Frew *served in the U.S. Navy from 1968 to 1988, deployed to Viet Nam three times, and was a crew member on the USS Hornet during the Apollo 11 crew recovery. He remained with the Navy for an additional fifteen years as a civilian faculty member and received academic tenure at the Navy's graduate school in Monterey, California. After a successful stint at the Naval Postgraduate School (NPS) as the first dean of computer and information services, Dr. Frew founded the Center for Executive Education (CEE) in 1998. CEE was an immediate success with senior Navy leadership and was featured in* Fast Company *and* New York Lawyer *for the non-traditional approach to executive education. He started his own firm, Frew & Associates (www.frewassociates.com), in 2002, focusing on executive development and education forums for organizations attempting alignment and change initiatives. Additionally, he serves as an emeritus professor at the Naval Postgraduate School and has joined Executive Development Associates (EDA) as a senior consultant and serves as the executive director for the Public Sector Learning and Development Network (www.executivedevelopment.com).*

Success Begins with Senior Management
Case Study of Innovative Leadership Development Design
Warren Wilhelm

Summary

Too often, line leaders and executives assume the development of their subordinate leaders is the job of the learning professionals in their organization—the CLO, head of training, vice president of corporate education, or whatever he or she may be called. In fact, this could not be further from the truth. In organizations known for their effective development of leaders, it is the senior leaders themselves who take primary responsibility for growing their subordinates.

However, for many leaders, development of their subordinates is not a natural task. They may be consumed with achieving their own success, not want competition from emerging leaders below them, or simply be too busy to attend to development of those who report to them. For these leaders, it may be necessary to structure a process by which they can effectively develop those below them. This article describes such a process, which puts the primary responsibility for developing subordinate leaders squarely in the hands of senior leaders.

Top-Down Leader Development

The process described here was developed for a specific company, but the principles upon which it is based are universal. In fact, a similar process is used for leadership development in one of the world's largest energy companies. The company for which it was created, however, is a major consumer goods company. It wished to instill in its leadership population an enhanced understanding of the principles of effective leadership and enhanced skills to lead the company to profitable growth. The company aspired to be "a premier consumer products company," with significant top line growth, top quartile earnings performance, at minimum 14 percent annual growth in earnings per share, and a stock price/earnings ratio in the 30 to 40 range. It looked to its upper leadership population of approximately three hundred people to drive it toward these goals.

The company asked us to design a learning process to help its leaders acquire the knowledge and skills necessary to lead most effectively. Its CEO specifically asked that the learning design not be a traditional approach, but instead one custom designed for the company's learning needs and the individual professionals who make up the company's leadership core. The resulting design takes into consideration desired learning results, resources available, timing, internal versus external "teaching," and other key factors.

This learning design is built on several beliefs:

1. The learning must have a *results focus.* Leadership learning should deliver balanced results, that is, customers, employees, shareholders and the organization itself must all benefit from the improved leadership.

2. The training should be *innovative,* designed specifically for the learning needs of the organization for which it is intended.

3. It must be *CEO-owned* and delivered by the CEO and his or her "Top Team" (in this case, the top ten executives).

4. It will *focus on the future,* not the past.

5. It will use *action learning methodologies* and real application projects.

The Learning Design

From the group of approximately three hundred potential candidates for this learning, the company would select the first "class" of thirty. Candidates will be selected based on leadership potential, importance of current job, "teachability" (openness to learning), and ability to provide feedback to help further refine this learning process for subsequent classes.

The first class meeting will last three days, to establish the learning process and give it initial momentum. It will be held in or near corporate headquarters to facilitate attendance by the top ten executives (the Top Team). Each of the first three mornings will be learning about a topic crucial to company leaders, presented by a world-class expert. The topics in this case included strategy, business acumen, and organizational capability. The Top Team will participate in the morning sessions as "students," along with the thirty class members. The purpose of the morning sessions is to introduce solid, new intellectual content, which can then be used in other parts of the learning process. The Top Team attends so they know what the participants are learning and can reinforce that learning.

Beginning with the first afternoon, and continuing for the next two, the Top Team (including the CEO) become one-on-one coaches to the class participants. Each of the Top Team members is paired up with three of the participants. In ninety-minute individual coaching sessions, the Top Team members coach their assigned participants as they work on a real business problem or opportunity important to the business.

The business problems to be solved, or opportunities to be exploited, have been identified prior to the beginning of this learning process by the participants and their managers on the Top Team. Each problem or opportunity is chosen in part because of its importance, and in part because its success can be measured. Metrics for evaluating the success of the solution are established and set as one of the goals for this leadership learning process.

After the initial three-day kickoff session, the learning continues in the form of individual coaching of the participants by their respective members of the Top Team. Coaching sessions are held regularly every two weeks, and last anywhere from ninety minutes to two hours. An administrator, either internal or external, is appointed to schedule these sessions and follow up to be certain they are occurring as scheduled. The learning design is shown in Figure 1.

The individual coaching centers around the problem or opportunity each participant is working on. Coaches use this real-life behavior and experience as the vehicle to coach participants about their approach to solving the problem, their leadership behavior, delegation of responsibility, and all the other aspects of effective leadership.

If Top Team members have questions about how to coach more effectively or need other information about either the participant's business or other related issues, a "coach to the coaches" is available to assist. Obviously, learning in this design doesn't go just downward, as the coaches learn as well.

If, during the course of the coaching, the original problem is solved or the opportunity is successfully exploited, a new issue is identified to be worked on with the help of the coach. The intent is to build a close and valuable coaching relationship

Prior to Day 1		Day 1	Day 2	Day 3	At 2-Week Intervals	Wrap-Up Day
"Top Team" selects participants	AM	Business Acumen	Organizational Capability	Business Strategy	Individual coaching of participants by "Top Team"	All participants and coaches debrief learning from coaching experiences
Define projects and metrics for each person		Outside Expert	Outside Expert	Outside Expert		
	PM	Individual coaching on business acumen	Individual coaching on organization capability	Individual coaching on business strategy		Create continuing development plans

Figure 1.   The Learning Design

between the Top Team member and class participant; the specific issue being worked is less important.

When the coaching has continued for a period of ninety days after the initial three-day kickoff session, a final one-day class session is held. All participants and coaches attend. Its purpose is to debrief the participants' learning experiences and learn from each other. Ideas are generated that can be used by participants, depending on their individual, continuing learning needs. This final session is facilitated by an outside resource. It is the closure of the formal learning for the class participants. We can hope the coaching relationships established in this process will continue into the future on an informal basis.

When the first class is completed, another class begins immediately. With thirty participants in each class, and four classes per year, up to 360 participants could receive leadership development and coaching by the end of three years.

During the final one-day session, each participant and his or her coach design continuing leadership development plans mutually. The plans might be different for each participant, but could include a 360-degree feedback process, attendance at university-based learning programs such as "Finance for the Non-Financial Executive," "shadowing" of other leaders, prescribed reading, or individual coaching by an external behavioral coach. There are myriad possibilities that can be identified as the process continues.

Rationale for the Design

The leadership learning design described above is based on several learning assumptions. The first is that the senior leadership of the organization, including the CEO (the Top Team) are well-qualified to impart knowledge and skills most relevant to leadership in the company. The learning design makes the richness of the Top Team's experience available to the class of developing leaders.

Another assumption is that we should provide participants with a (sometimes new) set of "lenses" or frameworks with which to view the situations they face or find themselves part of. Looking at things with different lenses often produces breakthroughs in thinking that result in competitive business advantage. This is the purpose of the external experts who teach in the first three days.

We believe the most effective leaders can manage up, down, across, and within their own personal boundaries. One task of the outside facilitators is to assure that participants learn about leading in all these directions.

A final assumption on which the design is based is that it should employ several different proven approaches to adult learning. We know, for example, that adults learn best from their own informed experience. This is the basis for our choice of an action learning approach. We also wanted to include new input from world-class outside experts.

Measuring the Impact of the Learning

Many learning programs seem like they should have impact on the behavior of participants, but usually lack metrics to show whether they do. We recommend the impact of this leadership learning process be measured by the change it helps to produce in business results.

We require that, before the onset of the learning, each participant meet with his or her superior on the Top Team, and possibly the CEO. They mutually decide on a performance improvement goal or goals to be realized over the next six to twelve months, to be measured using the hard business metrics the company normally uses to assess business results. The measures might be market share, return on capital employed, revenue improvement, revenue dollars per employee, productivity improvement, return on assets, inventory reduction, inventory turns, or similar measures. The goals should be a stretch, but reasonably attainable.

Whether or not the agreed business goals are achieved then becomes the measure by which the value of the leadership learning is assessed. Tying "soft" learning to "hard" business goals serves to motivate the participants to take their learning opportunities seriously. They also know that the quality of their leadership of their business units will in large part determine whether their agreed goals can be met. They will be motivated to seek out the maximum possible learning from their participation in the leadership program.

A corollary is that each participant who achieves his or her business goals should be amply rewarded; and those who do not should be evaluated carefully to determine their ability to improve their performance. While the primary purpose of the learning program is developmental, its potential as a calibration tool should not be disregarded.

Another corollary is that, while the primary measures of the success of this learning will be business results, we are also striving for behavioral change through this process. We suggest that measures also be used to determine whether participants' behavior has been positively influenced. The best way we know to measure this result is through anonymous data feedback from co-workers, suppliers, and customers in a 360-degree format. The 360-degree feedback process the company chooses to use can be custom-designed or an off-the-shelf instrument easily available from many different providers.

How This Process Is Different

Nothing is inherently radical about the learning process described here. It simply represents a new way of combining several proven leadership learning tools and methodologies. Perhaps its greatest success lies in the strong, valuable coaching relationships it builds between today's generation of top company leaders and the generation who will succeed them at the appropriate time.

Another advantage of the process is that it builds leadership skill, specifically in the culture within which it will be used. This tightly targeted approach to leadership development is time-efficient and cost-effective. Selfishly, it also builds leaders to use their skills specifically in the company that is investing in their development, rather than building generic leaders who can easily transfer the investment to another company (perhaps even a competitor).

Finally, this process contributes to strengthening the culture of companies that use it. We know that competitive advantage accrues from a fully aligned, shared mindset culture from the book *Corporate Culture and Performance* (Kotter & Heskett, 1992). Virtually every aspect of this leadership learning process is designed to further cultural clarity and alignment.

Conclusion

Many organizations talk about developing their next generation of leadership, yet find that, without top leadership involvement and a supporting development structure, their best intentions don't materialize. Perhaps our most important role in working with organizations that want to build executive bench strength is to communicate a simple message—namely that the CEO's and other executives' hands-on involvement is the key ingredient for success.

Reference

Kotter, J., & Heskett, J. (1992). *Corporate culture and performance.* New York: The Free Press.

Dr. Warren Wilhelm *is an expert in leadership development, organizational change, and human resource management. He has been chief learning officer at both Amoco and AlliedSignal. He currently heads a network of CLOs of large global corporations, Executive Development Associates, Inc.'s, Global CLO Network. He also serves as president of Global Consulting Alliance. Dr. Wilhelm's last article, "On Being a Chief Learning Officer," was published in the online version of* CLO Magazine *in November 2004. He can be reached at Warren@Wilhelm Consulting.com.*

Creating an Integrated Talent, Leadership, and Organization Development System for Maximum Impact

Julie Staudenmier

Summary

Some of the most powerful levers that leaders can use to align an organization, gain commitment to a new direction, and execute new strategies are talent management, leadership development, and carefully chosen and well-executed organization development initiatives. The better integrated these levers are, the more effective they will be. The paths to integration may be different depending on the specific situation, but the principles that lead to better integration are similar and can be defined and practiced to the benefit of organizational transformation. This article explores common causes for a lack of integration, success principles essential to increasing integration, and how these principles can be applied from different starting points. Finally, we will explore a particular case, Sony Electronics, illustrating how these principles were applied to create a more integrated talent, leadership, and OD system.

Organizations large and small are faced with an unprecedented rate of change in technologies, customer demands, and competitive pressures. These changes compel leaders to continually transform the way their companies are organized, the way work is performed, and ways in which customers are served. To successfully achieve these transformations, leaders must clarify and achieve alignment around strategy, operations, and people and achieve integration of these elements (Bossidy & Charan, 2002).

Recent research (Antonucci, 2005; Cohn, Khurana, & Reeves, 2005) has demonstrated that better integration leads to stronger bench strength and preparedness for talent shortages, less disruption to business strategy implementation, increased shareholder confidence, and more positive analyst ratings. Indeed, in my experience, the principles that lead to better integration can be identified and practiced to achieve these benefits. So if integrated systems are so valuable and essential to organizational transformation and organizational success, why aren't they more common? What causes talent, leadership, and organization development (OD) systems to be or become dis-integrated? What increases the probability of integration?

These are important questions and in the following sections we will explore:

1. Factors that cause a lack of integration in systems;

2. Starting points in the path to increased integration;

3. Success principles that can be applied regardless of your starting point; and

4. A case study, Sony Electronics, illustrating how the success principles were applied to create a more integrated talent, leadership, and OD system.

The premise of this article is that, although we are seeking integration, perfectly integrated systems are rare, and when they do exist, they can easily become less integrated and less effective over time. Optimal integration requires vigilance on the part of senior management and their partners in talent and OD functions and a willingness to shift strategies and approaches as the business conditions change.

Reasons for Lack of Integration

If it's logical and fundamental that talent, leadership, and organization development (OD) systems be integrated, why is it that they are typically disjointed or working at cross-purposes? A variety of factors may be at play, sometimes more than one at the same time. Among the more common reasons are ad hoc development, a slow drifting away from systems that were once integrated, inappropriate or disjointed organizational structure, and individual issues of power, control, and/or personal "branding" gone awry.

Ad Hoc Development

Leadership, talent management, and organization development initiatives can be created somewhat independently of one another. I have seen this occur when resources are limited and the design and development of only one or two key programs are possible at any given time. In other cases, different leaders may become enamored of a development tactic that is used by an admired peer company and demand that their human resources or leadership development group create a similar process for their company. As successive initiatives are designed, they may include components that make sense in the abstract, and may even represent state-of-the-art or "best practice" thinking. The separate elements might have the promise of contributing to a cohesive system, yet work at cross-purposes with programs or initiatives designed at an earlier point in time. Often developed with the help of external consulting firms, they may be based on different philosophies of leadership and use different or competing models or language to address common leadership challenges. Even when the program elements are based on similar leadership and talent management philosophies, differences in terminology and emphasis may be just significant enough to leave the leaders who are the intended beneficiaries of the initiatives confused, overwhelmed, and frustrated by real and perceived inconsistencies.

Integration Drifting to Dis-Integration

Sometimes leaders provide a mandate to talent management and OD experts within their organization to dismantle ineffective practices and/or to rapidly implement closely integrated initiatives where none existed before. It's an idyllic situation for the human resource leader in one sense, as senior executive commitment is palpable and leaders are compelled to execute. The chief task in this situation is to build and constantly reinforce alignment toward achieving critical business strategies and to ensure that the organization, talent, and leadership development systems truly drive toward strategic execution.

The designers of the system need to give some consideration to what system elements should be introduced first and to determine how many new ways of managing talent and organization development can effectively be absorbed by the leaders who make up the system. When these choices are not made wisely, elements that are introduced after the first parts of the program are launched may become less and less aligned.

Structural Issues

Ideally, the organizational groups responsible for leadership, talent management, and organization development initiatives would be part of the same functional organization, ultimately accountable to a common functional leader. This functional integration increases the probability of shared accountability and integrated design. However, this is often not the case. Individuals responsible for organization development, leadership development, and talent management may report to different leaders or functions, or the functional head may not explicitly require integration, allowing or even encouraging actions and practices that are independent of one another.

Individual Issues: Power, Control, and the Desire to "Brand" Individual Efforts

Even when talent management, leadership, and organization development groups are part of the same functional organization, maximum integration is not assured. For some individuals, a drive for power and control over resources and program implementation prevents them from remaining open to the ideas of others and to the co-design of integrated systems. For some individuals, the desire to independently design a leadership, talent, or OD initiative is due simply to a desire to make their own distinct mark on the organization, to create a personal "brand" related to programs for which they are responsible.

Different Paths to Greater Integration

Every path has a starting point and a destination. While it's critical to be clear about the destination and "begin with the end in mind" (Covey, 1989), it's equally important to be clear on the starting point of the journey. In the quest for greater integration of talent management, leadership development, and organization development, the easiest path to recognize—and the rarest path in practice—is one of starting fresh. In this situation, the human resource leader may have the opportunity to build an entire talent, leadership, and organization development system from the ground up, either with a start-up organization or when working with a more established firm where virtually no systems exist.

Another path involves starting from the middle. A strong leadership development or talent management system may already be in place, but several elements of the system may still need to be built. In this scenario, some elements of the system may need to be redesigned to improve their business impact, but without total replacement of the system.

A third path is one on which a fully developed talent, leadership, and organization development system is in place in what once was a relatively stable business. Then, due to dramatic changes in business and competitive conditions, the existing system is not capable of producing the kind of talent flow and business results required in the new environment. Knowing whether you are starting in the middle, or whether you need to fundamentally start over, is a decision that will influence your direction and focus substantially. I have found that, to make that decision, business leaders need to assess whether a total and rapid shift will produce a faster ROI or whether modifying and building on pre-existing systems gets them to the desired bottom line.

Success Principles Leading to Integration

For each of the paths above, seven common principles can be applied to increase the probability of successful integration over time. Whether starting fresh, starting in the middle, or starting over, these principles can be applied to build an integrated talent, leadership, and organization development system.

Agree on Strategic Business Focus

As you embark on design or redesign, bring key stakeholders together to grapple with the realities facing the company, openly explore and debate possible solutions and opportunities, and reach commitment on the plan to address them. Spend time with key stakeholders to clarify and refine the key priorities for talent and organization development and collaborate in the development of a vision for how it will drive your business results. Then, continually revisit design and implementation decisions to ensure that all programs reinforce the company's strategic business objectives.

Align Structure

Have all teams and individuals working in the disciplines of organization development, talent management, and leadership development be on the same team and working under the same leader. This increases the probability of reaching philosophical alignment about talent and leadership development imperatives and models that are most suitable to addressing the company's strategic business challenges.

Take a Long-Term View

Most integrated systems are created over a period of years, not months. Think in terms of at least three to five years in the future, and revisit the strategic plan periodically to ensure that it is still relevant and having the desired impact. Taking this longer-term view is helpful when your team does not have enough resources to build the entire system in a short time period. It's also important because the design and development decisions you make today will have a longer-term impact on the organization, primarily because each decision will reflect on the philosophy and intent of your talent and organization development system. Another advantage of taking a longer-term view is that it helps keep trials and occasional errors in perspective.

Find the Energy and Expand It

Another ingredient for success, particularly when you are starting in the middle, is to begin with initiatives that have strong support from key stakeholders. Keep your long-term vision in mind of all the necessary system elements that need to be introduced over time, but begin with those elements that capture the imagination of business leaders, even when they are not where you initially had intended to begin. There is rarely one best place to start or one best way to redesign or totally revamp existing systems. Start where the commitment and alignment levels are highest, and then execute crisply with an eye on results.

Having top-down buy-in from the most senior executives in the company is typically a more effective and efficient way of initiating and sustaining organizational transformation. A complementary strategy is to first pilot a talent or leadership development process with a business unit or division leader who has passion for talent management, leadership, and organization development. If the strategy yields results for this business unit, the initial effort can then serve as a springboard to rolling out an integrated strategy throughout the company.

Establish Linkage Points

When senior management is aligned with and committed to a core leadership model, this model can serve as a highly effective center point for an integrated system. Other linkage points may include leadership competency models, leadership frameworks, for example, the leadership pipeline (Charan, Drotter, & Noel, 2001) or statements of values. Once these models are agreed on, they become powerful levers for system integration. Leadership development systems, the talent management system, and organization development initiatives can then all be designed to develop the competencies, clarify and reward how values are exemplified, or develop the particular type of leadership necessary to ensure that business results are achieved.

Inform, Engage, and Challenge Senior Leaders

As the strategic plan for the system is implemented, be sure to keep managers informed of signs of progress. For each successive element of the system that is implemented, supply data on how it is impacting the quality of leadership and effectiveness of organizational operations. Use data to inform leaders about organization-wide strengths, talent gaps, what's working well, and what efforts are not producing the return that was expected. Organize and share information to engage leaders in the ongoing design process, and use it to challenge them to step up to their critical roles in modeling the leadership competencies and values, and in developing the organization.

Focus on Execution and Results

The bottom line for evaluating the effectiveness of an integrated system is whether it helps the enterprise to achieve better bottom-line results, while remaining consistent with the organization's values and its vision for the future. This basic requirement requires a relentless focus on results and execution.

The kinds of outcomes that are tracked and measured make a big difference. Organizations that measure the impact of learning rather than satisfaction with a one-time experience understand this message (Jefferson & Wick, 2005). Rather than activities, for example, conducting talent reviews, launching a leadership development program, or developing an employee engagement initiative, focus on results. For example, if a company's strategic focus is on growth, measure increases in the number of leaders who have demonstrated success in implementing growth strategies or numbers of growth plans actually implemented.

Case Study: Sony Electronics

Sony in North America

Sony Electronics Inc. represents the largest single geographical operation of Sony Corporation and contributes about one-third of Sony Corporation's global electronics revenues and 22 percent of its overall revenues. Sony Electronics employs approximately 18,000 people in North America, with roughly 8,000 in the United States and 10,000 in Mexico. Operations include manufacturing and engineering, design, sales, marketing, distribution, systems integration, and customer service of electronics and recording media products for the consumer, IT, broadcast, commercial, and institutional market segments.

Sony Corporation is a leading manufacturer of audio, video, communications, and information technology products for the consumer and professional markets. Its music, motion picture, television, computer entertainment, and online businesses make Sony one of the most comprehensive entertainment companies in the world. Sony's other principal U.S. businesses include Sony Pictures Entertainment, Sony BMG Music Entertainment, and Sony Computer Entertainment America Inc.

For more than forty years, the world has had a love affair with the Sony brand. During that time, Sony has created numerous products and technologies that have helped make consumers' lives easier, more enjoyable, and more productive. At the same time, the company has earned a solid reputation for quality, reliability, innovation, and stylish design. In fact, for the sixth year in a row, a Harris Poll (2006) identified Sony as the number-one brand in America, ahead of Dell, Kraft, Coca-Cola, Microsoft, and Hewlett Packard.

However, the competitive landscape has changed, and Sony's future brand success will be determined by how the company meets the challenges of change. Sony has always led the market in terms of innovation. But in a digital networked world, products are no longer developed with just hardware in mind. The convergence of technologies—consumer electronics, computing, and telecommunications—is a reality, with new competitors, new distribution centers (such as Best Buy and Wal-Mart) forming, and consumer mind share up for grabs. For Sony, healthy growth will include more than process improvements, reductions in headcount, and other operational efficiencies. Let's see the part that talent management and leadership played in the development of new strategies for Sony Electronics.

Starting in the Middle

Leaders at Sony Electronics (SEL) were facing competitive challenges unlike any they had experienced before. As Sony has a strong belief in promotion from within, most SEL leaders were veterans of the company's high-growth years, during the years when innovations and technology advantages could be sustained for longer periods of time. The company had not invested in systemic talent management and leadership development in the past, and the available bench of leaders was not nearly as strong as it needed to be. The competencies required in this new competitive landscape were changing and needed to be developed quickly.

The state of talent management, leadership, and organization development at the time of this change at SEL could best be described as "starting in the middle." In 2000, there were several programs and initiatives in place at SEL that were beginning to yield positive results. A set of core leadership competencies had been developed and validated with key employee groups and had been successfully integrated into a web-based performance management application. These could be built on to address the talent challenge that was looming in the organization. Nonetheless, significant components would need to be added to create a comprehensive talent, leadership, and OD system.

Structurally, the leadership development and organization development groups reported to two different organizations, and a talent management function had not yet been created. There were several models of leadership being employed by the two different groups, with no alignment and commitment to a common leadership model or talent management framework. Leadership and employee development programs were offered by several different organizations, and although, individually, many were of high quality, the programs overall had an ad hoc quality to them. The quality of development available to leaders also varied widely by business unit and geography. Organization development initiatives were being implemented at the business unit and functional level, but without any true integration or sufficient connection to the strategic challenges of the business.

Sony Electronics' Strategic Business Focus

The senior management team created a North American growth strategy that focused on increasing growth, while continuing to take measures to maintain profitability. The growth strategy emphasized the expansion of core businesses through entering new market segments with existing products, developing new business focused around solutions in both the consumer and business to business markets, leveraging entertainment software as a differentiator by collaborating more closely with sister companies (Sony Pictures, Sony BMG, and Sony Computer Entertainment America Inc.), and by reaching more customers directly through expansion of online sales and Sony-branded retail stores. To ensure that profitability gains were not lost, the Sony Electronics leaders needed to maintain their focus on creating efficient and competitive operational processes, ensuring better return on assets, and to exit non-performing businesses.

Aligning the Structure

SEL's business strategy and long-term growth mission established an equally compelling need for a change in its talent, leadership, and OD strategy. As a part of an overall HR reorganization, the senior vice president of human resources consolidated leadership and organization development into one function called "talent and organization development" and charged the leader of that function with the task of building a systemic approach to talent, leadership, and organization development that was closely aligned with SEL's business strategy.

The Long-Term View

Working with limited resources, the newly constructed team came together to plan a long-term strategy to create a development system that would be worthy of the Sony brand. Key components of the strategy included:

- Establishment of a Talent Management Council of senior leaders and a determination that business strategy would drive both people and organization development strategies;

- Creation of a process for early identification of key talent through a process of nominations, review, selection, and assessment;

- Accelerated development for high-potentials; and

- Targeted implementation of competency-based development for all employees.

The first step in the strategy was the formation of a Talent Management Council of senior business leaders. The intent was to facilitate a process that would enable them to develop their own vision of how to best develop leaders in SEL's new competitive environment and to then implement a talent management system that was aligned with this vision. This type of senior-management-led leadership development team had never existed before at SEL, and it was far from universally embraced when the proposal was made. Business unit leaders were used to working independently and were skeptical about whether an integrated effort was even possible and whether it could result in lasting change. Overcoming this skepticism was the first obstacle. To meet this challenge, we found our first sponsor in the organization.

Finding the Energy and Expanding It

One leader who did not share this skepticism was the current head of the Consumer Sales Company, who had a keen appreciation of the impact of leadership talent on business results. This leader was determined to increase the caliber of talent in his organization, which was responsible for all consumer sales in North America. He wanted to move forward quickly and agreed to work with the talent management consultants to pilot a talent review and development system that could be easily adapted to the rest of SEL. He made a commitment to invest in development programs that would help close the skill gaps identified in the talent review.

He approached the creation and implementation of this process as the key organization development initiative in his organization. Each of his direct reports was directly involved in rolling out the process and for communicated about the process and the desired outcomes in regional employee meetings. At each stage of the design and development process, the talent management consultants and the HR generalist, working with the consumer sales group, challenged themselves to create a process that was broad enough to apply to other groups within the company. Within twelve to eighteen months, word of the progress and results made in this part of the organization began to spread, and other leaders became curious about the possibilities of a more integrated approach. The consumer sales leader became the most vocal champion of the need to establish a Talent Management Council and convinced the president of SEL and other key business leaders that this was an essential part of ensuring the success of SEL's overall business strategy.

Establishing Linkage Points

As I previously mentioned, a Talent Management Council had been formed and began meeting frequently to establish the principles, guidelines, and models that would govern talent management and leadership development at Sony. This council served as a key linkage point in the system. They agreed on the organizational capabilities that the system would seek to support, including an ability to articulate a clear strategic vision, to plan strategically to deliver that vision, to increase marketplace agility, to introduce breakthrough products in new or existing markets, to create a flexible culture that embraces change, and to upgrade our workforce and retain our best talent.

At future sessions, they established guiding principles for their leadership and for the design of programs that would become part of the system. The guiding principles were (1) that top talent would be considered corporate-wide assets; (2) that development would take many forms, but would always be aligned with business strategy; (3) that they as senior managers were accountable for aggressively managing talent; (4) that effective talent management required objective, balanced assessment of both performance and potential; (5) that this objective data would be treated appropriately and with confidentially, and (6) that top talent would also be held accountable for managing and maximizing their development. Most importantly, they agreed that managing top talent was a critical business initiative that must be linked to other business processes. Once these principles were established, they then adopted a simple talent assessment and development process that they followed to build these capabilities, as shown in Figure 1.

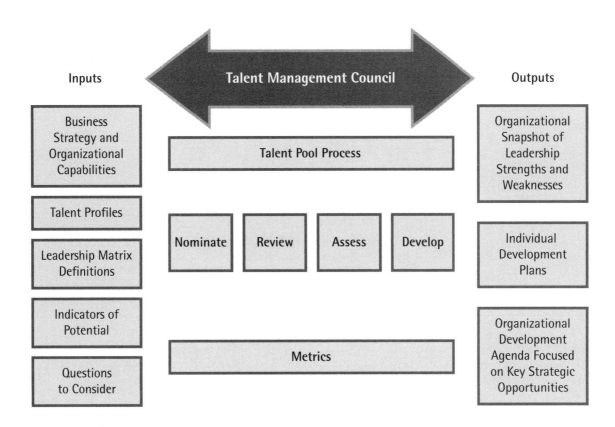

Figure 1. SEL's Talent Management Process

At about the same time as the Talent Management Council was being formed, Sony Corporation initiated the development of a set of global leadership competencies, validated across all global regions. This set of competencies served as a second link in our system. The talent and organization development team participated in the development of this model, working with senior leaders at SEL to ensure relevance to business challenges, and this set of more advanced competencies was communicated throughout the organization. The core competencies stayed in place and continue to be evaluated as part of the performance management system for all employees. The leadership competencies provided a framework for providing feedback and development planning for leaders of people in the organization, and they were integrated into the online talent management system. The competencies are laid out in Figures 2 and 3.

A third linkage point for elements of SEL's talent, leadership, and organization development system is the premise that leaders must develop unique sets of skills as they make different transitions in their careers, for example, from an individual contributor to a manager of people, from a manager of people to a manager of a functional area, or from a functional leader to a business unit leader (Charan, Drotter, & Noel, 2001). This philosophy became a critical foundation in SEL's core leadership curriculum, along with a belief that sustained application of new leadership skills is more likely when

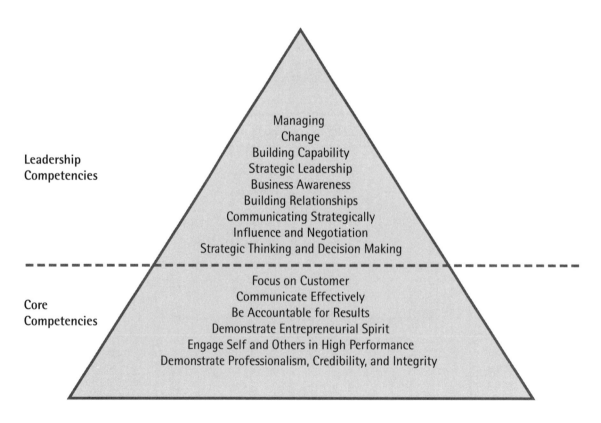

Figure 2.   SEL Competencies

Strategic Leadership	Creates a vision and persuades others to strive toward it. Motivates and empowers others by trusting in their ability to deliver results. Takes personal responsibility in ensuring that outcomes are achieved. Acts in an ethical manner.
Managing Change	Continue to learn, adapt, and perform as the organization and environment change, learning from experiences and applying new behaviors to new situations. Anticipates changing circumstances, challenging assumptions and taking calculated risks to improve on existing processes and systems.
Strategic Thinking and Decision Making	Identifies business issues and opportunities, their critical elements, inter-relationships, trends, potential risks, and implications. Generates a range of alternative solutions weighting pros and cons of different options. Takes all relevant factors into account when making decisions.
Communicating Strategically	Communicates complex information clearly, concisely, and in a timely manner, encouraging open discussion and ensuring understanding. Projects a positive, professional image of our company in all interactions, tailoring messages and communications as appropriate.
Business Awareness	Understands and aligns the structure, strategy, and overall goals of Sony with marketplace challenges and opportunities to create new business and promote the Sony brand. Considers issues in terms of costs and profits, maximizing return on activity. Promotes cross-business interactions and partnerships inside and outside of Sony.
Building Capability	Identifies and supports proper opportunities and mechanisms for the development and achievement of potential. Clarifies objectives and responsibilities, gives honest and constructive feedback.
Building Relationships	Builds relationships across all levels, business groups, and locations. Demonstrates sensitivity to other cultures, exhibiting tact and diplomacy.
Influence and Negotiation	Identifies key motivators of individuals and groups, acknowledging underlying objectives/concerns. Presents own position confidently, using a balanced set of options and logical arguments to persuade others. Explores and facilitates creative solutions where disagreement exists, aiming for a win-win outcome.

Figure 3.   SEL Leadership Competencies

learning is done over a longer period of time, with follow-up tools to ensure application of learning. Each of the series in SEL's core curriculum builds on skills developed at earlier series. Each program in the series includes an e-learning component in advance of classroom learning, and extensive follow-up on progress toward goal achievement back on the job. The process is reinforced by having participants work with small

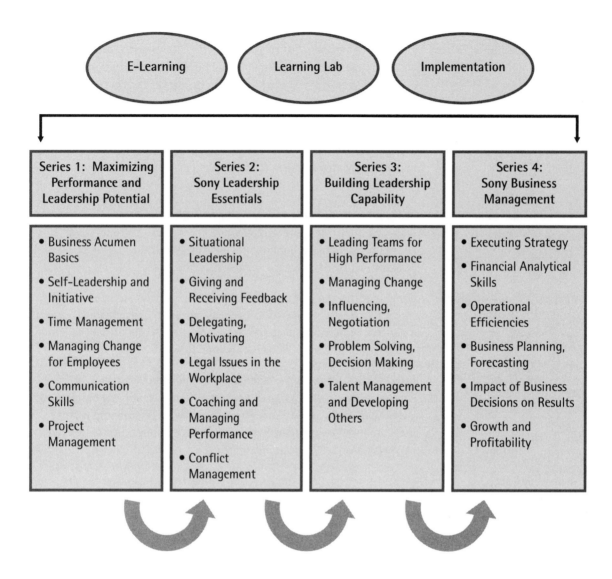

Figure 4.   Integrated Leadership Curriculum

learning subgroups throughout the process, building peer support and breaking down organizational silos at the same time. The process is shown in Figure 4.

Inform, Engage, and Challenge Senior Leaders

As the Talent and Organization Development Team continued to add new elements to the integrated system, starting with the talent review and development process for the director and vice presidential level, the senior business leaders on the Talent Management Council stayed involved and engaged through bi-monthly meetings and even more frequent written updates. Sharing and interpreting the ongoing results and learning was one purpose of these meetings, and soliciting input on design of additions to the talent and organization development system was a second purpose. Provocative data shared at these meetings drove better integration, higher impact, and increased commitment to the financial investments required to enhance the quality of leadership at SEL.

As an example, the first pool of leaders selected for inclusion in the talent pool participated in developmental assessment centers. This assessment center data helped to more finely target required development and also illuminated development needs that were common across the high-potential group, such as financial acumen and execution-focused leadership. The core leadership curriculum (see Figure 4) and leadership forums designed expressly for the high-potentials were then designed to address these needs. Based on their analysis of the assessment center results, the Talent Management Council also decided to increase investments for the development of this core curriculum to ensure greater depth of talent at all levels of the organization.

The first Leadership Forum for high-potentials included several modules led by senior executives and, in these sessions, they came to understand that many of the participants felt that the strategy needed to be clearer and that communication around SEL's vision, mission, and strategy was not comprehensive enough to fully engage employees at all level. Senior executives listened to this feedback and engaged high-potentials in developing a communication strategy to address the issue.

Results and Execution Focus

From the beginning, design of the talent, leadership, and organization development system has been focused on results. By the 2004–2005 timeframe, SEL had a stronger understanding of its leadership strengths and gaps and had taken a number of steps to close those gaps. The organization had been through a number of changes, including the startup of several new businesses, a move of the company headquarters from New Jersey to San Diego, and a new president. Throughout these changes, the Talent Management Council revisited their long-term vision for developing people and the organization and stayed true to the guiding principles established by the charter members of the council. Even though council membership has changed, which was intentional, the principles have stood the test of time and change of leadership.

The SEL Leadership Forums for members of SEL's talent pool have been particular success stories, along with the SEL Core Leadership Curriculum. These leadership development programs are designed and implemented to educate people about the company, our desired culture, and our industries and markets so that they can significantly increase their contributions to profitable growth. The programs help leaders to see the cause-and-effect relationship of their strategic and people leadership decisions on SEL's financial performance.

Participants in the 2003 Leadership Forums estimated that they were able to contribute revenue increases, cost reduction, and asset improvement activities valued at over $163 million, with over $18.6 million of those revenues directly attributable to skills and/or relationships developed at the forum. Estimated results from the first five sessions of the 2005 forum are even more impressive, with participants identifying over $430 million in growth and profitability initiatives since their participation, with $118 million directly attributable to their learning from the SEL Leadership Forum. These leaders have renewed belief in the ability of their leadership behavior to have a direct impact on business results.

Summary and Conclusions

Sony Electronics' journey toward greater integration is far from finished. The Sony Electronics Talent Management Council and the Talent and Organization Development Team are continuously refining and improving the system with each decision. In retrospect, one can present a cohesive picture of how the elements of the system came together. At the time, however, adjustments and modifications were challenging to implement, and occasionally the obstacles to overcome seemed daunting.

Keeping a long-term view can keep your organization focused and better able to weather similar frustrations. Balance the necessity of having patience with the long-term process with a sense of urgency and accountability. Understand and accept that integration and reintegration of a talent, leadership, and development system will require vigilant, ongoing attention. The results—stronger leadership and a more effective organization—are well worth it.

References

Antonucci, E. (2005). The perfect storm: How talent management integration can help your company avert looming leadership shortages. In J. Bolt (Ed), *The future of executive development*. San Francisco, CA: Executive Development Associates, Inc.

Bossidy, L., & Charan, R. (2002). *Execution: The discipline of getting things done*. New York: Random House/Crown.

Charan, R., Drotter, S., & Noel, J. (2001). *The leadership pipeline*. San Francisco, CA: Jossey-Bass.

Cohn, J.F., Khurana, R., & Reeves, L. (2005). Growing talent as if your business depended on it. *Harvard Business Review, 83*(10).

Covey, S.R. (1989). *The 7 habits of highly effective people: Powerful lessons in personal change*. New York: Simon & Schuster.

Harris Poll. (2006, July). http://biz.yahoo.com/prnews/060712/nyw079.html

Jefferson, A., & Wick, C. (2005). Ensuring transfer of learning and accountability for action in executive development. In J. Bolt (Ed.), *The future of executive development.* San Francisco, CA: Executive Development Associates, Inc.

Julie Staudenmier *is vice president, Talent Acquisition and Development, at American Express. Prior to that, she was vice president, Human Resources, at Sony Electronics. In this role, Ms. Staudenmier was responsible for Sony Electronics' talent and organization development initiatives, including succession planning, executive and high-potential development, management and professional development, and performance management. Before joining Sony, Ms. Staudenmier was a partner with Executive Development Associates (EDA), a firm that pioneered the use of executive development to align and engage executives around the execution of critical business strategies. Ms. Staudenmier has consulted with companies in a wide variety of industries, including consumer and industrial products, telecommunications, publishing, consumer electronics, forest products, and insurance. She holds a master's degree in industrial/organizational psychology from Wayne State University.*

Leadership Development as a Driver of Shareholder Value Creation

Raymond Vigil

Summary

CEOs are seeking conceptual frameworks that go beyond "an act of faith" to help them direct their learning investments and accelerate the value generated through learning. To meet CEO expectations, new conceptual frameworks must be able to identify and link superior learning/human capital practices with shareholder value.

The purpose of this article is to explore the premise that, increasingly, investments in leadership development can be best evaluated in terms of their contribution to an organization's shareholder value. Specifically, I will share how one organization, Humana Inc., evaluated its learning initiatives based on the value created for the enterprise in the form of tangible business outcomes such as new insights, innovations, and the ability of leaders to execute the company's strategy. Humana's practices and experiences provide a conceptual framework for leadership development that is worth considering as a better alternative to traditional efforts to measure ROI from event-driven transactions.

CEOs are increasingly interested in leveraging the value of human capital as they search for a competitive advantage to differentiate their companies. Learning can be a key to exploiting the "talent lever" as CEOs seek to outperform their competitors through better execution (Bossidy & Charan, 2002). Many competitive strategies such as consumerism, innovation, personalized services, or signature consumer experiences are highly dependent on having learning strategies to complement their business strategies.

As a result, CEOs are placing increasing demands on human capital initiatives to enable them to win in the marketplace and sustain their competitive advantage in the future. Simply stated, the competition for superior talent is increasing, and leadership development is a critical driver of strategic differentiation that, if leveraged, should in turn lead to increased shareholder value.

Let me describe the recent experiences of Humana Inc., a Fortune 200 health benefits company based in Louisville, Kentucky, where I am currently the chief learning officer. To realize the goal of becoming the industry leader in consumerism, CEO Michael B. McCallister declared that Humana would become a "learning organization." Under this mandate, the leadership development team built its enterprise learning strategies and leadership development initiatives on the foundation of a human capital framework that is illustrated throughout this article.

Rather than justifying the inherent value of learning, Humana's learning initiatives derive their value by being tightly linked to the strategic needs of the enterprise and specifically to the talent needed to execute business strategy. Subsequently, metrics are created to measure the results of these learning initiatives. Let's look at an example of such a measurement. At Humana, execution of strategy requires the effective engagement of cross-functional, high-performance teams coming together in a collaborative learning environment to create innovative consumer solutions—something leaders must learn how to do.

Therefore, an interim measure of the value of the learning can be viewed in terms of the variable quality of team interactions, the key metric being the quality of conversations and interactions that leaders engender as they go about implementing the strategy through cross-functional teams. In this initiative, we measured the value created by the number of new insights, innovations, and social networks that deliver greater value to consumers.

We utilized a new conceptual framework for measuring the value of learning that may provide a more useful paradigm for our leaders as they seek to make better learning investments, and we demonstrated that learning can increasingly be viewed as an untapped driver of value creation.

Outcome–Based Conceptual Framework for Learning

Humana has embraced the concept of creating a *talent mindset* as one of the key components of its enterprise learning strategy (Michaels, Handfield-Jones, & Axelrod, 2001). In doing so, learning is outcome-based rather than event-based. The metric of measure becomes the strength of the talent pool in the company and the ability to execute the company's consumerism strategy. The belief is that having superior talent that executes better than the competition will result in increased shareholder value.

Embracing this concept is not just an add-on to a learning strategy, but rather a whole new approach to talent management.

The benefit of this concept is that it creates a constellation of talent-development practices that can be recognized as either being present or not present, and, if present, they can be scored against a best-practice standard. It is worth noting that this metric is focused on results, as opposed to the previous typical measure of the quantity of learning activity. In fact, by starting with end in mind, the various methods of learning can be more appropriately evaluated, based on their ability to enhance the depth of the talent pool and the ability of leaders to execute the company's strategy.

It creates the opportunity to measure whether the desirable behaviors are currently being practiced and, if so, the extent of their impact as indicated in a "stoplight" dashboard: red indicating no activity, yellow indicating some activity, and green indicating full implementation. Humana has implemented a human capital/leadership development dashboard and conducts quarterly business unit reviews to assess progress.

A sample of the dashboard and scoring mechanism is shown in Exhibits 1 and 2.

HR Organization Assessment—SAMPLE ONLY

Organization Name:	Quarter:	Assessed by:

Assessment Levels (consider impact on people and organization when making final assessment determination)
R   Red   Insufficient Leadership demonstrated in achieving strategic intent
Y   Yellow   Inconsistent Leadership demonstrated in achieving strategic intent
G   Green   Clearly demonstrating Leadership in achieving strategic intent

Category	As evidenced by	Rating	Observations/ Recommendations
Leadership	Do the leaders of Humana demonstrate knowledge, skills, and beharorial competencies? Do leaders tell the Humana story? Do leaders act as "super coaches"?	Y	
Talent Mindset	Is the organization focused on creating the talent required to execute the strategy? Is the organization committed to developing internal talent pools to fill open positions? Do they have the right people in the right roles? Is the organization retaining its top talent? Is the organization leveraging diversity as a competitive advantage?	G	

Exhibit 1.   Excerpt from Humana Organizational Assessment Dashboard

Business Unit A						
Strategic Focus Area: Leadership			**Results**			
Activity	Status	Metric	Timing	Q1	Company Q1	Trend
Retention	Y	Overall Voluntary Turnover Rate	YTD	15.6%	16.6%	↓
		Overall Involuntary Turnover Rate	YTD	7.3%	5.0%	↓
		Leader 1 - Voluntary Turnover Rate	YTD	6.3%	16.6%	↓
		Leader 1 - Involuntary Turnover Rate	YTD	20.0%	5.0%	↓
		Leader 2 - Voluntary Turnover Rate	YTD	22.2%	16.6%	↓
		Leader 2 - Involuntary Turnover Rate	YTD	10.5%	5.0%	↑
Strategic Focus Area: Talent Mindset			**Results**			
Activity	Status	Metric	Timing	Q1	Company Q1	Trend
Leadership Talent	Y	Total # Assoc	Q	1076	25,000	↑
		# of Leaders	Q	20	300	↓
		# of New Hires Filled Internally (Promotion, Rotation, etc.)	Q	1	30%	↓
		# of New Hires Filled Externally	Q	2	70%	↓
		# with Formal Mentors	Q	3	20	←→
		# Participating in Rotational Assignments	Q	1	10	↑
		# Attending 1 or more External Seminars/Classes/Programs	Q	2	150	↓
		# Attending Leadership Training	ETD	5%	10%	←→
Recruiting	Y	# of Open Positions (Coming 2005: by Role)	M	75	1068	↓
		# of Open Positions per Recruiter	M	50	34	↓
		# of Open Positions Filled (Coming 2005: by Role)	Q	65	1013	↑
		# of New Hires Through External Search	Q	35	775	↑

Exhibit 2.   Performance Metrics Dashboard Prototype (Sample Data)

Human Capital

As I have mentioned, Humana's strategy is grounded in a growing body of knowledge and intellectual understanding of human capital, which is generating new concepts of how learning creates value (Ulrich & Smallwood, 2003; Watson Wyatt, 1999, 2001). These new concepts share the common premise that the value of learning should be grounded in superior business practices and outcomes. The stronger the linkage these outcomes have to shareholder value, the better.

Human capital concepts are more useful than traditional financial methodologies in untangling the inherent complexity of learning. Learning is comprised of a set of multidimensional and interconnected practices. To attribute value to learning, it is necessary to "connect the dots" and capture the interrelated processes and practices involved in learning initiatives.

A powerful expression of the business impact of superior human capital can be found in the "intangible" portion of the market capitalization of publicly traded firms. This view is based in part on research and findings in Thomas Stewart's book, *Intellectual Capital.* An adaptation of Stewart's concepts is depicted in Figure 1, which defines

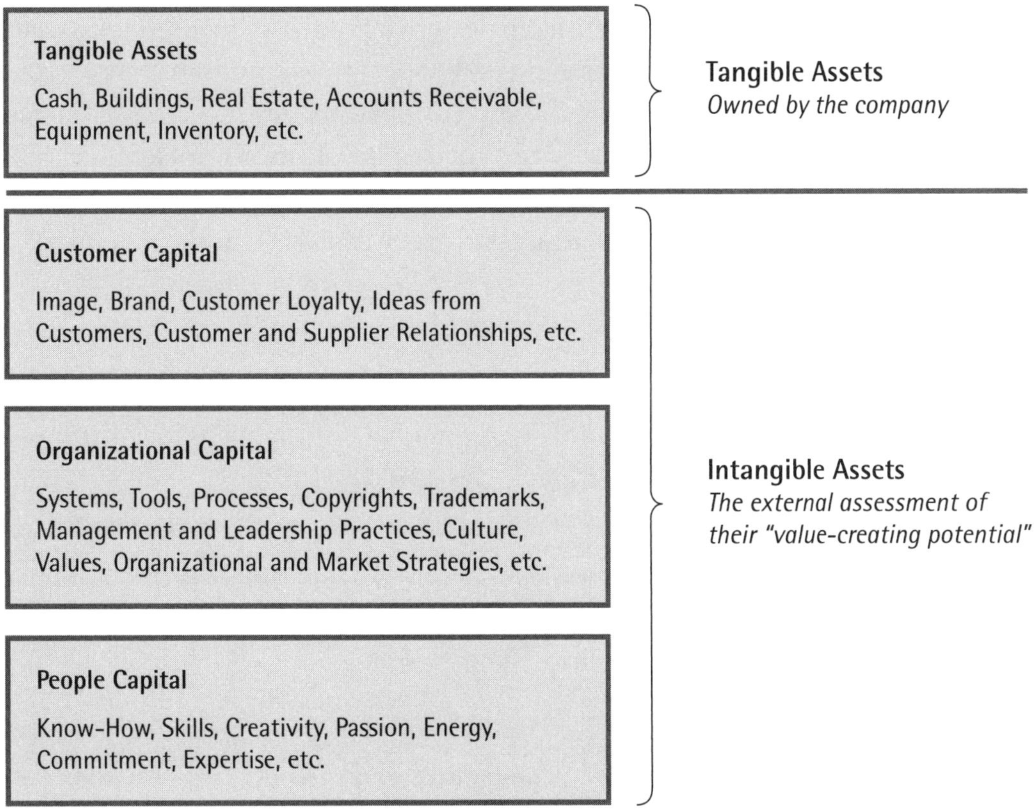

Figure 1. Market Capitalization of Publicly Traded Firms
Adapted from a presentation by Susan Burnett, Gap Inc., at the CLO Forum, October 2004.

the components of intangible assets as being social (or customer) capital, infrastructure (or organizational) capital, and human (or people) capital.

If we take Humana's case, the tangible or book value of the company has doubled over the last five years, while the company's intangible assets have increased more than sevenfold during the same period. While it is not possible to single out the direct impact that learning has had on the increase in intangible assets, we can draw on the human capital studies that identify the positive relationship that leadership development plays in shareholder value creation to conclude that learning has made an important contribution toward the intangible value creation and that it will continue to do so in the future.

Human Capital Gap

Humana's human capital strategy is the backbone of our efforts to identify the knowledge, skills, and behaviors that are required to sustain its innovation business strategy. Core to the human capital approach is the work we have done over the last four years to transform our "title/job description" structure to a much more agile and adaptable "role/competency" structure. This competency platform enables us to assess, staff, develop, and reward based on the competencies critical to the business. Assessment through regular "calibration" sessions is the key aspect of the human capital strategy. It has enabled Humana to determine the gap between the critical competencies we need to realize our business aspirations and the reality of the competencies we have as they exist today.

The human capital strategy incorporates several ways to reduce this human capital gap.

Attracting and Staffing

These are ways of reducing the gap by changing the competency mix through acquiring talented people with new competencies and developing the competencies—knowledge, skills and behaviors—we need to execute on our business strategy.

Key Measures

- Depth of Humana's leadership talent pool
- Number of leadership positions filled internally
- Speed to alignment of new leaders with the strategy of the business
- Number of qualified candidates who post for internal open positions
- Speed with which we fill key roles in the company

Leadership Development

This category focuses on growing the competencies of our current associates. We use a competency-based corporate curriculum.

Key Measures

- Number of leaders who match new competencies, as captured from calibration assessments

- Number of value-generating interactions between senior leaders and other leaders

- Number of new ideas and insights generated by leaders

- Number of value-generating new social networks created

Reward and Retention

These are ways of reducing the gap by creating a focus on competencies through a new infrastructure that measures and rewards competency attainment. Reward is market-paced, competency-based, and contribution-driven.

Key Measures

- Turnover rate of leaders

- Profile match of desired competencies with newly promoted leaders

- Rate of dissemination of best practices across the organization

- Measures of employee engagement

- Alignment with the overall strategy of the business at all levels in the enterprise

Humana Leadership Institute

The Humana Leadership Institute was formed to be the CEO's forum for transmitting his vision and conveying his expectations of his leaders. For each offering, we took into account the type of content and methodology required and worked to incorporate a variety of approaches to address the different learning styles and knowledge levels of our executive population. In a sense, it became the "compass" to balance and guide the implementation of our programs within the Institute. The programs are plotted along two continuums: content (business knowledge versus self-knowledge) and methodology (cognitive understanding versus experiential application).

The compass is also used to plot the individual development activities and experiences for the top 150 leaders of the company. In this way, the Institute helps our leaders learn more about themselves as well as the business, and our approach provides experiential application that reinforces and enhances the cognitive understanding they gain. The compass is shown in Figure 2.

In all areas of the Institute, Humana has leveraged strategic partnerships with other firms such as BTS, the George Group, and Personnel Decisions International (PDI) to provide opportunities for key leaders to close the gap on the competencies they need to execute the company's business strategy. Examples of these programs are

- The Business Simulator brings leaders together to learn the complexities of our business model: broker/customer/consumer relationships and the metrics used to measure financial performance. A second phase simulates in more detail the consumer experience and the relationships and tradeoffs that need to be considered. (Partnership with BTS)

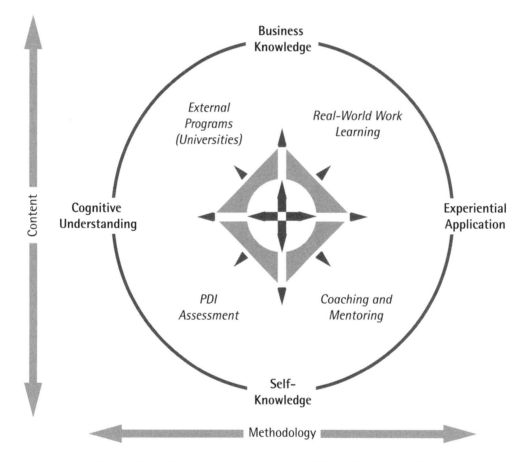

Figure 2.   Humana Leadership Institute Strategic Compass

- Action-learning programs, known as real-world work sessions. One of the first sessions was aimed at conquering complexity (partnership with the George Group, author of *Conquering Complexity in the Workplace*). The second program focused on the topic of "perfect service." The third program tackled the topic of "culture." We encourage the development of cross-functional cohort groups that have resulted in highly beneficial new social networks.

- For specific competency development, we arrange for individuals to participate in external programs offered through executive education programs at leading universities, The Conference Board, Concours Group, Institute for the Future, and others. The number of programs has increased dramatically, along with the specific focus and purpose of the development objective.

- We encourage coaching and mentoring personal development relationships to accelerate the development of strategic competencies on the part of our rising leaders. We have established an executive coaching practice as part of our leadership development program. We include having leaders teach as a component of leadership competency development.

- We offer a customized, comprehensive, two-day assessment center (PDI) to accelerate leaders' development plans. These and other assessments are used to develop highly customized individualized development plans that are owned and executed by the direct report manager.

The Leadership Institute is also highly integrated with Humana's succession management program. This connection has provided an important ability to personalize and customize robust individual development plans for high-potential future leaders of the business. This personalized approach to development has allowed the senior leaders in Humana to look at significant experiential leadership development activities such as rotational assignments, action learning assignments, and the opportunity to teach others.

A useful technique in our succession management program to engage leaders in leadership development is asking them the simple question: How much of what you know about leadership have you learned on the job versus in the classroom? Nine out of ten leaders say that experience, by far, has driven the majority of their learning. This technique focuses the leaders' attention on the importance of linking leadership development to work assignments and highlights the coaching role of leader in developing future leaders of the business.

Finally, succession management has become our data warehouse for talent in Humana. It provides the data for a key measure of our outcomes-based approach to leadership development, for example, the enhanced depth of the talent pool and the ability of multiple leaders to execute the company's strategy.

Conclusion

In an era of tightening resources and increasing competition, even enlightened leaders are under pressure to fine-tune their learning investment decisions. What should a leader do when the organization demands more structure, context, and outcomes-oriented measurement for its learning investments? And on a personal level, where do leaders turn when they need to make an informed decision about investing their own time in pursuit of executive development? We believe that Humana's practices and experiences provide a conceptual framework for leadership development that is worth considering as a better alternative to traditional efforts to measure ROI from event-driven transactions.

The Humana case demonstrates how value can be created by taking a holistic view of leadership development inputs from business unit reviews, dashboards, focus on talent mindset, integrating performance management calibrations, and competency-based leadership curricula and combining them with leading-edge leadership development practices. The result is that Humana has experienced accelerated organizational transformation toward its consumer-based strategy and has at the same time experienced significant growth in its shareholder value.

References

Bossidy, L., & Charan, R. (2002). *Execution: The discipline of getting things done.* New York: Crown Business.

Michaels, E., Handfield-Jones, H., & Axelrod, B. (2001). *The war for talent.* Cambridge, MA: Harvard University Press.

Stewart, T.A. (1999). *Intellectual capital.* New York: Currency Doubleday.

Ulrich, D., & Smallwood, N. (2003). *Why the bottom line isn't: How to build value through people and organizations.* Hoboken, NJ: John Wiley & Sons.

Watson Wyatt. (1999, 2001). *Human capital practice studies.* Arlington, VA: Author.

Dr. Raymond Vigil *is the vice president and chief learning officer of Humana Inc. In this position, he has responsibility for creating and implementing a company-wide learning strategy that is highly integrated with the business strategy. Key responsibilities include establishing the Humana Leadership Institute, the creation of a robust succession management program, and the implementation of an enterprise-wide learning consortium that centralized the core, accelerating the adoption of technology-enabled learning throughout the enterprise. Prior to joining Humana, Dr. Vigil was the vice president and chief operating officer for learning at Lucent Technologies. His previous positions have included many senior-level human resources leadership positions at Jones Intercable, Inc., US West, and IBM. Dr. Vigil currently serves as a member of the Workforce Development Advisory Board for ACT. He holds a Ph.D. in education/career counseling from the Colorado State University.*

Building Strategic Leadership Capabilities at Rexam PLC
A Case Study
Alice Heezen

Summary

Recently I was managing leadership development programs at Rexam, a £3.2 billion (British Pounds) global consumer packaging company with a vision to deliver consumer-packaging solutions for the beverages, beauty, pharmaceutical, and food markets. My mandate was to build leadership capabilities and create leadership bench strength at all levels within Rexam in order to support the company's competitive advantage. In the following case study, I will explain how Rexam is building strategic leadership capabilities through leadership, provide some historical context for the evolution of our programs, describe our design process and training program components, and share thoughts on Rexam's next steps.

In 1996, Rexam's CEO, Rolf Börjesson, wanted Rexam to become the leading consumer-packaging business in each of its chosen market segments. He was determined that Rexam should become a world leader, focusing on excellence in customer service, innovation, quality, efficiency, and profitability, and he was certain that even the most comprehensive strategy would only deliver results if it were implemented by talented and inspired managers of the highest caliber.

Vision for a Leadership Development Program

When I joined Rexam in March 2001 as group management development manager, Börjesson entrusted me with attaining the following talent development goals within a three-year timeframe:

- Improve the quality of the Horizon Program, a leadership development initiative

- Extend the business school for senior executives

- Ensure the development and implementation of Rexam's Internal Recruitment Program

For the purpose of this article, how the quality of the Horizon Program was improved will be explored, including the set-up of the Senior Executive Development Program. This exploration will give more insight into how Rexam has built strategic leadership capabilities in the last four years.

Continuous Improvements in the Horizon Program

Within Group Management Development, we identified and prioritized tasks to improve the quality of the Horizon Program. The two major tasks for Group Management Development to work on from 2001 till 2004 were

- The development and implementation of Rexam's Competency Framework and its related Rexam 360-Degree Personal Development Program (PDP)

- The development and evolution of the Horizon Program
  - Managing the Horizon Program in close partnership with a consortium of four international business schools
  - Extending the Horizon Program with the Senior Executive Development Program (SEDP)

The first task was a crucial step in improving the Horizon Program, as it identifies the basis for the design of all modules in the Horizon Program. It is critical for the success of the Horizon Program that the skills and behaviors to focus on and develop at each management level be understood.

Rexam's Competency Framework and
the 360-Degree Personal Development Program

Rexam had started to work with Aston Zoraster (a consultancy organization based in Reading, UK) in 1999 to provide 360-degree feedback to the participants in the Introduction to Management Program and asked the firm to assist in creating Rexam's Competency Framework for use in all segments in the Horizon Program. In addition, as Horizon Program participants are based in different countries around the world, Rexam commissioned Aston Zoraster (in association with Applied Information Ltd.) to develop an online Rexam 360-Degree Personal Development Program (PDP), based on Rexam's Competency Framework, so that it could be used as a measurement tool in the Horizon Program.

In the initial implementation during the second half of 2001, Aston Zoraster and Applied Information produced an intranet version of the 360-degree process based on generic competencies and behaviors. Although these competencies and behaviors focused on leadership qualities agreed by sector HR directors and members of the Group Management Committee, they were not "Rexamised." The reason was that in 2001 Rexam was still a large collection of relatively unconnected businesses.

In order to help Rexam to move to more of a single, sophisticated integrated whole and to better support the Horizon Program, the Competency Framework was then redesigned around the four key values of the "Rexam Way." These values are "trust," "teamwork," "recognition," and "continuous improvement."

After redesign, profiles were completed for various management levels. These profiles were used in the Rexam 360-degree PDP for the Horizon Program, and the executive/senior management profile was selected for the initial Rexam Way assessments. Moreover, in 2002, Rexam distributed the redesigned Competency Framework to all Rexam managers in order to further launch the Rexam Way. Subsequently, the Competency Framework has been refined, and the result is that currently we have two versions of the Rexam 360-degree PDP. The first version is for the general management population and consists of twenty-nine Rexam Way value profile statements. The second one is for the Horizon Program participants consisting of fifty-six or forty-five behavior statements, depending on level, as we want to develop the Horizon Program participants in more depth.

The management of PDPs in the Horizon Program was first carried out by the group management development manager. The PDPs were monitored and quality-checked; then half-way through the Horizon Program, the PDPs were discussed with the individuals to help them to achieve their objectives.

To help around one hundred participants on an individual basis was an almost impossible task for me as a staff on only one, but even more importantly, it created a culture of dependency. As we want our talent to take responsibility for their own careers, we needed to create the right environment to develop an attitude that they were responsible for self-development. Therefore, it was decided to put the accountability/responsibility for self-development with the Horizon Program participants and to create the opportunity for them to help one another to achieve their objectives by coaching each other during modules in the program.

An advantage was that this peer coaching could be extended beyond the Horizon Program, while the former coaching by the group management development manager could only exist during the Horizon Program. The only challenge is that peer coaching should be supported and encouraged. In the Horizon Program, this is not an issue as time is allotted and the group management development manager is physically present for support if and when necessary. Beyond the Horizon Program, the risk is that the line managers of participants don't understand the rationale behind the process and therefore don't support it.

The Development and Evaluation of the Horizon Program

To assume the role of market leader in each market segment and to grow in developing markets, our premise was that the demands of globalization and regional specialization must be reflected in the Horizon Program. We understood that exposure to other cultures would enhance the ability of Rexam's managers to gain a competitive edge through respecting cultural differences.

A Consortium of Business Schools

To accomplish the internationalization of the Horizon Program, Group Management Development realized that it had to create a consortium of business schools. Rexam chose to continue with the more internationally focused business schools and to broaden the scope of its partnerships. Rexam now manages the Horizon Program in close partnership with the following business schools: Ashridge (UK), Carlson School of Management (U.S.), ESCP-EAP (France), and Hong Kong University of Science and Technology (China). These partners also brought Rexam the flexibility to create customized programs and a high-quality tutor base.

To enable these different business schools to work together effectively, it was necessary to identify with the program directors, to set clear responsibilities, and to make each school either the leader or partner for each program. For example, the lead school for the Advanced Management Program (AMP) is Ashridge. As lead school, Ashridge identifies a core curriculum to support organizational and learning objectives outlined by Rexam and works with partner schools to draft a design of the program. Other responsibilities were carefully laid out and communicated to all parties.

This all had to be carefully managed while I was Rexam's group management development manager. Additional responsibilities for Group Management Development are

- To provide overall strategy, direction, and structure to the Horizon Programs, as well as final decision making on all programs

- To identify program participants and provide individual participant biographies

- To manage and advise the lead schools

- To measure and monitor performance of partners

- To communicate and collaborate with individual schools, as well as negotiate all contracts

- To coordinate core interactions and best practice sharing with partners

- To provide executive speakers for key subject-matter areas

Review of the Horizon Program

In 2004 Rexam introduced a yearly face-to-face Horizon Program review meeting with the program directors, which I chaired as Rexam's group management development manager. The purpose of this meeting is to identify the strengths and weaknesses of the previous year's Horizon Program and to identify improvements for next year's program. Also, we assess the Horizon Program to establish whether it is still supporting Rexam's strategy and to identify any necessary changes. Rexam's CEO attends this meeting to ensure the program is aligned to Rexam's vision and strategy and that the program directors and group management development manager understand his priorities for leadership development in the forthcoming years.

During this review meeting, the consolidated Horizon Program participants' evaluation report and the outcome of interviews, which the group management development manager conducted with some senior executives, were also used. These interviews gave insight into the desired state of the organization, key challenges, strategic context (competitive differentiators), and changes in the organizational capabilities, which then were translated into the following Rexam leadership edge attributes:

- Maintaining drive and energy

- Inspiring/motivating others

- Communicating powerfully and listening with an open mind

- Collaborating with and teamwork among Rexam employees, suppliers, and customers

- Developing strategic perspectives/vision and bringing it to reality

- Thinking out of the box and being receptive to new ideas

- Being open to feedback and challenge, leading to learning and creativity

- Being open to change from anywhere around the globe

- Recognizing no single "right" way to see the world

- Orchestrating the conflict

- Developing others/coaching

- Possessing strong business ethics

An important outcome from the two-day review meeting in 2004 was to refocus the overall purpose of the Horizon Program and to clarify the objectives of each individual program. The purpose of the program is summarized in Figure 1.

Another important result of the annual review was the renewal of the guiding principles for the design of the Horizon Program. The guiding principles for the design for 2004–2005 were

- Focus on leadership: leading people, leading the business, and leading the future

- Innovative

- Experiential

- Integrated in every aspect

- Accountability/responsibility for self-development

- Ensure relevancy to Rexam

- Link with Rexam 360 and personal development plans (PDP)

These guiding principles inspired us to consider using other development mechanisms to extend learning beyond the classroom walls. Below is the list of learning mechanisms, most of which were used in the Horizon Program for 2004–2005:

- Homework in teams

- PDP throughout and linked with supervisor

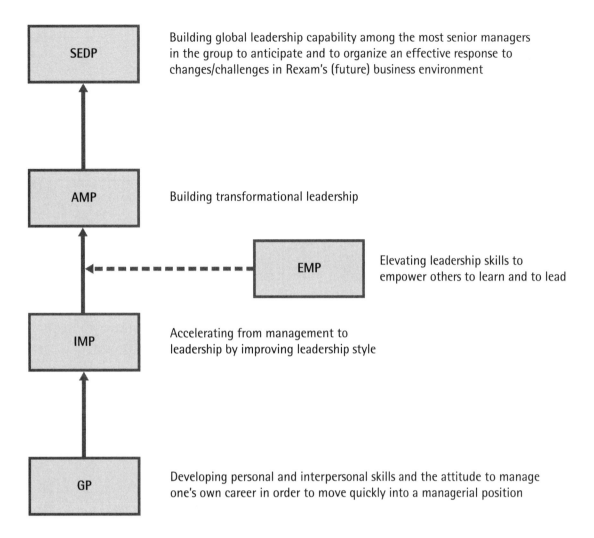

Figure 1. Purpose of the Horizon Program: Build Leadership Capabilities
and Create Leadership Bench Strength at All Levels Within Rexam

- Peer coaching in each session and between modules

- Communities of practice

- Content shift to one-third lecture, two-thirds experiential learning

- Overview plus contextual message at the start of the program and in each session as well, but then combined with Good Morning Rexam presentation, which will inform the participants about the latest news in Rexam

- Interviewing leader

- Live cases

- Rexam case studies

- Company visits

- Plant visits

- Learning journal

The program directors also realized that clear responsibilities must be identified for each faculty and communicated by them to the faculty. These responsibilities include:

- To create learning opportunities that are much more experiential (only 10 to 30 percent lecture)

- To develop content focused on leadership, much less on skill development, with more emphasis on leading people, leading business, leading the future

- To provide content linked to individual development and of overall importance to the business

- To involve executives in facilitating sessions to ensure Rexam relevance

Finally, a new Horizon Learning Model was introduced (see Figure 2). This model emphasizes that the three "leadings" are included in all programs. Some sessions in

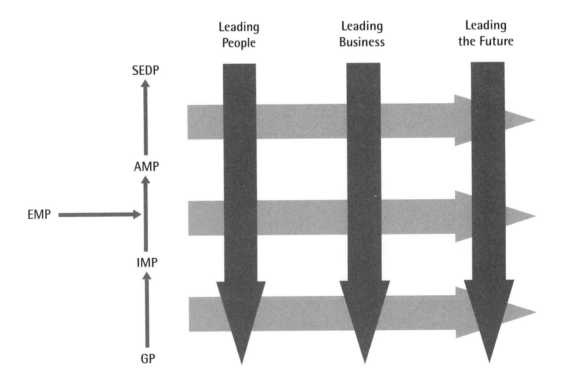

Figure 2.   Outline of the Program

the Horizon Program modules might focus only on leading people or leading the business or leading the future. Other sessions might focus on a combination of two or three areas. For example, the business game used at the end of two programs has the objective of integrating and applying all the learning in the program and is focused on all three areas: leading people, leading the business, and leading the future.

The Senior Executive Development Program

As part of the quality improvement of the Horizon Program, it was further extended to include a Senior Executive Development Program. The premise was that, by allowing the most senior managers in the group to understand, to anticipate, and to organize an effective response to Rexam's challenges, Rexam would then become better focused on achieving a sustainable competitive advantage.

The Sharing Program

In the spring of 2001 Rexam was asked to join a management development program—the Sharing program—for executives of large multinational organizations. It was a consortium program organized with a limited number of participating companies from different industries, including Renault, Schneider Electric, Usinor, Gladerbell, and Alcatel. To enrich the learning process, each company nominated five or six participants for the program, who were responsible for managing units in an international environment or an executive with the potential to be part of the executive group in the next three years.

It was a program based on sharing innovative practices on key issues among these companies, creating a learning process between the different companies of the consortium and transferring some good practices from one company to another. To a great extent this differentiated the Sharing program from typical business school programs. The program consisted of two modules of four days each, separated by a period of four to six months during which a project to share innovative practices on four to five key issues took place (four or five company visits). The first module consisted of lectures and discussions on competitive strategy. The second module was focused on developing leadership competencies for a turnaround world.

The program aimed at developing critical competencies in strategy and leadership for companies in the 21st century:

- How to manage profitable growth, both internally and through mergers and acquisitions

- How to become a boundary-less organization, sharing between functions, units, and companies to learn and develop synergies

- How to manage your "self"

- How to lead younger generation, reinvent tomorrow, to create change

One of the major competencies needed for organizations in the 21st century is sharing inside the company and with stakeholders. The sharing program was completely dedicated to the development of this competency through a study conducted by participants from different companies to identify the most innovative practices on common issues developed by the companies. At the end of the exercise, the participants shared their experiences and were able to report ideas for improvement to their own companies.

Just after the first module took place, Rexam decided to withdraw from the sharing program. The main reason was that, because of the numerous changes that Rexam had recently gone through, the company was not yet ready to participate properly in this type of exchange. In retrospect, we realized that this was a classical mistake, that is, to think that just because a program is good in itself, it should work. Clearly, it also needs to fit the maturity of the company.

Our Second (Successful) Attempt

The absence of any formal structured development activity beyond the Advanced Management Program for senior managers in Rexam had been challenged. However, our premise remained the same, namely that development experiences form part of the process of helping managers achieve higher levels of performance and better focus Rexam on achieving a sustainable competitive advantage. To address what seemed to be a leadership development gap, we decided to invite a sample group of Rexam's (senior) executives in February 2002 to discuss their views on potential senior-level development activities.

Focus Group

The focus group was structured to identify:

- Whether there should be a structured development experience for top managers in Rexam

- What form such experiences should take

- What content they should have

The two-hour discussion followed a questioning strategy of moving from a broad view of the business toward the specific nature of a development experience. The summary output from the focus group was as follows.

The Vision.   A series of points was made about Rexam becoming a more integrated corporate entity. It should have a stronger brand identity, and an identifiable culture will have emerged on a global basis, such that people will live their work lives by the same set of values. This process will not be driven by the imposition of one model, but by using the benefits of the existing diversity to extract the most effective aspects from across the company.

Growth will also be a feature, but one that rebalances the portfolio away from the current preponderance of can-making activities. In going through a period of growth, the business will become more adept at absorbing other businesses within it. A greater proportion of its business will be devoted to the provision of services, rather than pure manufacturing. The global spread of the business will also be more balanced, with Asian activities becoming a much more prevalent feature. As the business grows and becomes more unified in cultural terms, there will be a greater degree of sharing across the group and a strong desire to identify best practices will emerge.

Key Challenges for Rexam in Achieving the Vision.   A significant gap on communication processes within the company was identified, particularly those that would have an impact on engaging middle management with the strategy. It was also felt that top management behaviors could be better tied in with performance rewards.

Personal Development Needs to Help Meet the Challenges.   The majority of needs identified were behavioral. Key to the cultural unification was the development of the ability to build trust within a team and to use that trust to manage the business. Behavioral responses to change also had to be worked on to reduce the degree of fear associated with change and to reduce the reluctance to look outside current experience for fresh views and approaches.

Another major area of need was connected with developing sharing capability. This demanded both personal behavioral changes, as well as organizational ones.

Individuals had to become more open to sharing, looking outward, being prepared to communicate more widely, being less protective of their own information.

Individuals also had to develop their skills in building the processes of sharing and creating the organizational infrastructure to encourage sharing to take place.

Other reflections on personal development needs at a senior level included the ability to anticipate the future, build a vision for the business to follow, deal with ambiguity and contradictions, and a range of skills around developing people.

Effective Personal Development Methods.   A strong theme that emerged was that change was a major force in personal development. Moving to a new business, making a career change, being exposed to new people and new ideas, and taking on an international assignment were all identified as having a positive impact on this group's learning and personal development. In addition, the existence of a strong mentor, coach, or role model was emphasized as particularly helpful.

Whenever training courses have been used, they have not usually had sufficient follow-up to capitalize on the development in the Rexam work environment. In many cases, the opportunity to network with Rexam peers was seen as more valuable than the published objective of the course. In terms of style, the approach must be engaging and at a level that is relevant both personally and to the Rexam business. "Tell and do" is not an appropriate strategy for development programs.

At the end of the focus group, the crucial question was finally asked: "Do we need a Rexam top management program?" The unanimous verdict was yes, with the following qualifying remarks: It should be positioned as preparation for a more senior role in the near future and it should build on the personal qualities that will mark people out for the most senior positions in the business. A major feature should be the involvement of the "top team" to facilitate extensive exposure to the General Management Committee (GMC). Although many elements of development can be achieved by e-learning processes, it was recognized that other aspects can only be achieved with face-to-face experiences or a residential event of some kind.

Program Design

After having regained the commitment for a senior executive development program from a sample group of (senior) executives, it was time to provide the design criteria for the program. A series of interviews was held with the senior executives in Rexam, members of the GMC including the CEO, during July and August 2002. The purpose of the interviews was to explore their individual perspectives on personal development at a senior level, what issues were important to be covered, and the most effective process to deliver it.

One common theme emerged: that personal development was very important for those due to succeed the current GMC members and that Rexam, as a corporate entity, had an obligation to design an appropriate vehicle for top executive development.

Apart from this imperative, there was a surprising lack of common ground. This subject has had little exposure at senior management meetings, and individuals were not generally aware of their colleagues' views or whether their own views were generally held. This pointed to the need for further discussion (at GMC level) of the results of the interviews, to explore differences of view and gain agreement about a way forward.

The prime areas of focus for development fell into three categories:

1. *Personal leadership skills*—those behavioral qualities required to be demonstrated at top executive level.

2. *Organization development*—the competencies required to build the appropriate organization.

3. *Business understanding*—those business areas in which it is crucial for top executives to have deep knowledge.

Personal Leadership Skills.   A minority view was expressed that such behavioral qualities were present naturally in those who had risen to the top of organizations and that there was little point in devoting resources to this purpose. Most of those interviewed believed that this area was vital, but differed in what should be the primary focus.

One strongly held view was that top executives needed to develop their relationship-building capabilities, so that they were less transactional in their dealings with key customers and more focused on building long-term personal relationships.

To develop a more open, supportive, and coaching style was seen as important for the future of the business. Similarly, there were a number of mentions of the importance of being culturally sensitive, that is, having a natural understanding of what may be a cultural taboo, and building comfort in operating in a diverse cultural environment.

It was also seen as important to demonstrate a consistent focus on the end result of the business, to articulate it clearly and frequently, and be seen to be committed to it through the executives' behavior.

Organization Development.   The development of the Rexam Way is one example of a means to build a consistent set of values and supporting behaviors throughout the company. Other processes would need to be put in place to create the desired unified corporate culture, and a strong understanding of these processes was needed among top executives.

Another internal theme was the need, especially for the larger business units, to develop cross-functional capability and to build effective communication processes.

As design and service become more important in the business, there was a growing need to develop an innovative capability.

A desire for focus on change and conflict management was seen as helpful in supporting smoother passage through processes, such as the integration of new businesses. A majority view was held over the need to develop a stronger external focus, both in terms of the outlook of individuals and in the way the organization is structured.

Business Understanding.   A significant minority considered there to be some weaknesses in the senior management's understanding of issues critical to the running of the business. These were in two areas:

- A deep understanding of the strategy development process, such that the industry, the competitive position of Rexam within it, and the markets in which it operates are sufficiently well understood to develop a well-thought-out strategy for the business. This includes an understanding of the fundamental economics of the business and the dynamics among price, volume, and cost.

- An understanding of the finer points in the acquisition of businesses, particularly around the assessment and valuation of a potential target.

These findings were presented to the CEO, Rolf Börjesson, in September 2002, together with outlined proposals for a senior executive development program and its overall aim and outcome. It was explained that the program was designed to build capability among the most senior managers in the group, to anticipate and to organize an effective response to Rexam's challenges.

Sharing knowledge and experiences and exchanging ideas with colleagues, guest speakers, and faculty would accomplish this. It would touch on strategic and organizational thinking and focus on personal leadership behavioral qualities. It would allow Rexam to achieve sustainable competitive advantage. The added value for the participants would be an enhanced understanding of the leadership challenge from Rexam and its required leadership. They also would gain insights and tools needed to improve the effectiveness of their own leadership styles and to improve the effectiveness of their own teams.

Program Implementation

After having gained the commitment of the CEO and some GMC members and having received the approval from the CEO to start the senior executive development program in spring 2003, Group Management Development developed the program further with the support of the Leadership Trust, Ashridge, and the coaching firm, Pitkeathley & Partners.

We worked during the development and implementation phase with three parties because we had identified three different learning mechanisms to achieve the overall aim of the program and to address the development areas, which were identified during the interviews with some GMC members. These mechanisms were action learning, master classes, and a coaching program (using input from Rexam's 360-degree PDP). Each learning mechanism required in-depth knowledge and experience to be developed and managed during the course of the program.

During the review of the program with the participants, the CEO, and the group HR director, it became clear that the program had some considerable value for the participants' personal development. Every one of the participants recommended coaching to future SEDP participants. One of the main reasons for this was that it was perceived to be a real catalyst for personal and business improvement.

Conclusion and Next Steps for Rexam

The Horizon Program with its five programs has so far been hugely helpful in raising awareness, giving ideas and stimulation and, most of all, in bringing a sense of Rexam identity and belonging. The belonging cannot be understated in a company such as Rexam, which essentially has been built through acquisitions since 1999. The Horizon Program is an important part of the corporate glue that holds the company together.

The Horizon Program is only one piece of the total process of leadership development. We now need to move the focus of our career development system firmly toward leadership. We need to help our people to take initiative by creating an environment of leadership in which their approach is proactive and not reactive. If we want Rexam to be out front in all areas, we need to inculcate a leadership mentality in the way we think about our company and ourselves.

The Rexam Way is about how we want to run the company for outstanding performance. Our leadership style, informed by trust, teamwork, continuous improvement, and recognition, is the umbrella under which we take the whole company forward. It is the single most important factor in what we are trying to achieve.

The answer to the leadership challenge is not just about the Horizon Program, but it has to link with other elements of the career development process: appraisal, Rexam's 360-degree PDP, management review, and the Internal Recruitment Program. In themselves we generally feel these to be good processes. What is required now is better linkages between the elements.

Rexam's group director of human resources, Peter Moxom, said: "The real challenge going forward is to have a well functioning, integrated, people development system and process. This will take time. It's one thing for managers to accept and buy into the case for a new way of doing things. It's quite another to make the process a successful reality."

The Horizon Program, and the other elements of the career development process, raise career expectations. We have to meet those expectations; otherwise we will simply lose the best people to other companies. The way forward now is to be the integration of the different pieces of the process with clear, agreed objectives. Against these, we must progressively deliver over time what individuals want in career terms and deliver what Rexam needs to drive our performance to the highest possible level. We have now reached the point where this has become a "must do," not an option.

Alice Heezen has a broad range of HR expertise, from HR consultancy to strategic resourcing, talent management, leadership development, and also operational HR in different HR positions in multinationals, including BG Group, Rexam, Hay Management Consultants, EnerTel/Energis, and Andersen Consulting, currently known as Accenture. She joined BG Group in October 2005 as HR manager, group functions, after more than four years at Rexam, where she was responsible for group management development. In this role, Ms. Heezen was responsible for supporting the development of talented managers, professionals, and potentials within Rexam worldwide, both personally and professionally, by implementing leadership development programs and processes to create bench strength at all levels. She set up, managed, and integrated five major initiatives in the fields of OD and management development. One of these initiatives was the creation and management of a consortium of four business schools: ESCP-EAP in France, Ashridge in the UK, Carlson School of Management in the United States, and the Hong Kong University of Science & Technology in Hong Kong; this consortium has become Rexam's Horizon Program. Ms. Heezen received a master's degree in organizational and social psychology at Leiden University in The Netherlands.

Introduction
to the Learning Methods Section

This section deals with the critical and fascinating subject of how leaders learn. Topics range from learning methods highlighted in EDA's 2004–2005 Executive/Leadership Development Trends Survey to other innovative learning methodologies. Six articles are included.

Leaders Teaching Leaders, by Ashley Keith Yount

Level 4 Coaching: Everyone Has a Role, by Marshall Goldsmith

Creating a Customer-Centric Culture: "Walking a Mile in the Customer's Shoes" at Texas Instruments, by Dan Parisi and Jeff McCreary

Optimizing Developmental Job Assignments, by Betty Kovalcik

Lessons from the Battleground, by Mark Whitmore and Harold W. Nelson

The Role of Peer-to-Peer Networks in Personal and Professional Development, by Michael Dulworth and Joseph A. Forcillo

Leaders Teaching Leaders

Ashley Keith Yount

Summary

This article explores the increasing use of the leaders teaching leaders method of instruction in executive and leadership development programs, including how it is currently being used, critical success factors in its application, potential pitfalls, and how one company (Dell Inc.) is using it to transform its culture.

Leadership Development at Dell

In an era in which talent management and leadership development are increasing in importance and significance, for any organization to execute its strategy, leaders are being asked to contribute to the development of other leaders in a variety of ways. Conducted by Executive Development Associates, Inc. (EDA) in 2004, a survey of executive development professionals within the Global 500 and other major corporations found that the number one learning method for training new leaders was the use of senior executives as faculty. For the purpose of this article, "leaders teaching leaders" is in reference to the roles leaders can play in the delivery of formal leadership development programs.

Leaders teaching leaders provides the executive/leadership development professional a unique set of opportunities to have a significant impact on culture change efforts as well. Organizations that want to utilize this delivery approach should, at a minimum, make sure the sponsorship and leadership role models exist first. In the absence of these role models, they must create the right conditions.

It is interesting to note that, in the same survey conducted by EDA, executive/leadership development professionals also indicated the top five topics that will receive the most emphasis in the next two to three years. (See Table 1, which compares 2000 results with 2004 results.) We all know that adults prefer learning that is action oriented and associated with real work. Leaders should be involved in teaching any of the topics on the list. The topics read like an executive job description and each of them

Table 1.   Emphasis for Leaders

2000	2004
1. Leadership	1. Leadership
2. Strategy execution	2. Leading change
3. Leading change	3. Managing human performance
4. Strategy formulation	4. Strategy execution
5. Managing human performance	5. Business acumen

gives executives the opportunity to impart wisdom and the chance to help transfer learning to other leaders.

The role that external faculty and facilitators play will not be less important in the future. Rather, organizations that are investing significantly in leadership development simply have more choice in who they have deliver their programs (internal and/or external). Either way, leadership development is an investment of both time and money. For organizations in which executives teach, it is important that they know that teaching others is expected in their roles. To be done well, executive training requires significant time from both current leaders and executive development professionals.

How the Method Is Used

In the classroom, there are a variety of ways in which an executive can contribute to the development of other leaders. Development may consist of (1) advancing a leader's skills and knowledge; (2) enrolling and gaining buy-in of others to the vision, mission, and values of the organization; and/or (3) strategic intervention designed to facilitate a major initiative or change agenda. Based on a leader's experience, he or she may be asked to contribute in any of the following ways to support the executive development agenda:

- *Kick-off and/or close a program.* A senior executive will open the program by communicating the importance of the program and his or her expectations of what the participants will learn, do, and apply. Many organizations start with this method and expand later with some of the other options.

- *Teach a model, concept, or entire subject.* This method is ideal for a leader who really has command of a subject or practice and can teach it (strategy, financial analysis, coaching, etc.). The leader can share examples of how he or she has applied the model or concept.

- *Share leadership stories.* A leader shares his or her personal stories of leadership experience (those critical moments that have most influenced him or her to be a leader, etc.). The stories can also be of lessons learned (failure, hardship, or success). As long as the leader can share in a genuine way that allows others to connect with him or her, it is rare not to be successful in this role.

- *Co-teach with an external thought leader or other leaders.* A leader may co-teach with an external facilitator, who brings the broader view of the subject, while the internal leader(s) discusses how the subject applies to a particular situation.

- *Provide feedback to teams on their presentations.* Leader(s) may be asked to provide feedback on a team's presentation and critique it. In these situations, the leader will need to deliver both negative and constructive feedback.

While this list is not exhaustive, it includes some of the more common ways in which leaders may teach leaders.

Critical Success Factors

Several factors go into making a highly successful program:

- *Sponsorship.* Securing sponsorship for a program in which leaders advance the knowledge and skills of other leaders is critical. The higher the sponsorship, the stronger the signal about the level of importance this role has, not only to the leader as teacher, but to the participants.

- *Ideal role.* Identifying the type of role that is most suited to an individual's strengths and interests is also important. Consider this as identifying the "sweet spot" that will allow the person to be most successful. Putting a leader in a role that doesn't enable him or her to play to strengths puts participant learning at risk and could destroy the credibility of the leader and the program.

- *Simplicity.* When designing the session to be taught by a leader, keep it simple. Be sure to involve the leader in determining the learning objectives, key messages, and possible content. Simplicity should also be applied in how the session flows. Make it easy for the leader, without getting too wrapped up in training techniques.

- *Preparation and practice.* Preparation begins with the design of the session. By involving the leader on the front end, you gain his or her input and buy-in. Outline with the leader what the participants need to know, think, feel, and do differently as a result of the session. Talk together about ways to achieve this, make any needed design changes, and then bring the design back for the leader to review prior to delivery. Use a format that is easy to follow. Discuss with the leader how he or she will prepare and what he or she will need. Some leaders may also want to utilize their personal coaches or the HR manager.

- *Feedback.* If you plan to use a leader-teaching-leader model, consider how you will collect and give feedback to your leader. Be sure to mention that you will also be letting them know whether the objectives were met and collecting suggestions from participants for making their programs stronger the next time.

Often, specific conditions unique to the company's culture and business cycle must be considered. For example, executives may not be available to teach during the end of the quarter or sales cycle.

Potential Pitfalls

Employing the leader-teaching-leader method is not without potential pitfalls. Give careful thought to potential issues, and become adept at adapting "on the fly" in case a leader who is scheduled to teach has to cancel at the last minute. Here are some other potential problems that could come up:

- *A leader who doesn't prepare and consequently doesn't deliver the intended content/message.* Due to competing demands on the leader's time, he or she may not invest the proper time for preparation. This can have a twofold negative impact: (1) the participants do not learn what was intended and (2) it reflects negatively on the leader's credibility. In this situation, you may have to seek alternative times to teach the points that were missed. There also may be a coaching opportunity during a session break when you can help the leader get back on track, or you may want to step in and co-teach.

- *Leaders who have content expertise but lack platform skills.* In this situation,, provide some feedback to the leader and ask whether he or she would like to work on this area. An opportunity for development can be provided through some training, individual coaching, practice, and more feedback. Often, improvement in this area will have additional payback for the leader outside the classroom.

- *Leaders whose schedules change suddenly and prevent them from being available to teach.* This can feel devastating when it occurs, but can be mitigated when you have identified alternatives beforehand and have blocked time on another leader's calendar.

- *Demand for the same leader to teach other programs.* As organizations expand the opportunities for leaders to be involved, it is possible to find the same leaders being tapped again and again to teach in various programs. Consider tracking the leaders' utilization, and keep expanding your list of potential presenters.

- *Demands of the business take precedence over teaching.* If tough business conditions exist, leaders may feel the pull away from the classroom and it may be more difficult to get leaders to volunteer their time to teach. Here, one approach does not fit all. Consider many factors (culture, overall business performance, the structure of the program, the learning objectives, etc.) in determining a possible solution. It may be that the program can continue with someone else teaching it (internal or external), or conditions may be such that the program has to be postponed.

Case Examples: Dell on Dell

At Dell, leaders teaching leaders is the predominant method of delivery of our leadership programs. We have not arrived at this overnight, but through thoughtful and careful planning. Below are just a few examples of how we employ leaders teaching leaders.

Leadership Imperative

After a rapid growth phase in 1997, Dell reached an inflection point. The economy was receding and Dell was not immune. This was the most challenging time in the company's history, and we had to reduce our workforce, as did most other companies in the technology sector. But we also did something unprecedented: We announced in 2001 that we were going to double our revenue from $30B to $60B in the next five years. We realized that, in order to accomplish this milestone, we had to put the same kind of focus and discipline into developing our culture and our leaders.

Reflecting on this challenging time, Michael Dell (chairman of the board) and Kevin Rollins (president and CEO) started to discuss the need to communicate and align every leader around their expectations of being more than just a great financial institution. To sustain the growth we wanted to achieve, the company and its leaders had to come together and determine the kind of leadership and culture required to be a great company.

Therefore, "winning culture" became one of four Dell strategic initiatives, along with customer experience, globalization, and product leadership. At the backbone is the "Soul of Dell," a description of aspirational goals for the company and our values, beliefs, and commitments. It serves as a guide in many cultures we call home. The Soul of Dell has become embedded into all of our executive and management development initiatives.

The Leadership Imperative was launched in 2002 as a way to gain strategic alignment around the leadership required to live the Soul of Dell and create a "winning culture." These training sessions were leader-led and began with Michael Dell and Kevin Rollins leading sessions with their teams. Then each of their direct reports led sessions with their teams until it cascaded to every people manager in the company around the globe.

Each year we have Leadership Imperative training sessions that are targeted to teach and align our leaders around whatever leadership message we feel is most important in the execution of our business strategy. Each year it begins with the leadership at the top, cascading to the next level of leadership. It has become more than an expectation of our leaders—it is now a part of our culture.

To achieve this level of rollout requires and utilizes the support and involvement of not only the learning and development teams in our various businesses, but also our HR generalists. Our leaders are provided coaching by these groups of professionals to enable them to be successful.

The payback on this initiative has been substantial. Our senior leaders have thrived in teaching newer leaders and, through the process, have further aligned their efforts with the business's goals. They have modeled what is expected, which has allowed them to connect with their leadership teams via personal storytelling and examples. This major effort has led to other ways in which we now utilize our leaders to teach, gain strategic alignment, and demonstrate our values, beliefs, and commitments.

Leadership from the Start

Leadership from the Start (LFTS) is just one of the strategic executive programs offered and is instrumental in our new executive on-boarding. This program is required for new executives coming to Dell. During the three-day class, current Dell executives teach new executives "How Dell Wins in the Marketplace," "How Things Get Done at Dell," and "How You Will Win as a Leader at Dell." Executives share first-hand both business advice and transition advice. The executives who are selected to teach are usually leaders who are identified as key talent (those identified as high-potential). This helps to ensure our new executives are learning from sources who are considered among the best. An executive development professional facilitates the overall session and helps the participants to capture and assimilate their learning into a ninety-day on-boarding plan.

Finance for Executives

Finance for Executives is a global executive development offering co-led by Dell leaders and external faculty, who serve as the main facilitators of the program and teach financial concepts from a broad context that is applicable to many organizations. The Dell leader teaches how particular concepts work at Dell and their application at Dell. Typically, the Dell leaders have been identified as key talent from finance.

Leadership EDGE: Executive Leadership Series

The Executive Leadership Series (ELS) is our most intensive use of leaders teaching leaders. As a way of continuing to demonstrate commitment to investing in and developing leaders, Michael Dell and Kevin Rollins champion and support the development of the top level of our key talent group, known as Leadership EDGE. One component of the multi-tiered development strategy for this group is an intense ten-day leadership development program called the Executive Leadership Series (ELS).

The goals of this program are to build personal and business leadership capabilities to (1) grow the business profitability, (2) manage Dell growth and scale, (3) ensure customer market leadership, (4) build organizational capability, and (5) grow to and beyond $80B. For the first two days, Michael Dell and Kevin Rollins teach and facilitate various sessions to achieve the objectives listed above. This investment of their time signifies to the participants that they are important and that top management takes an interest in their development.

At least seven other senior vice presidents serve as faculty over the ten days to teach parts of the curriculum and to share their personal leadership stories. The participants also take part in an action learning program during which they work on a real strategic business issue at Dell and present their recommendations to Michael Dell, Kevin Rollins, and their direct reports on the last day. Approximately 80 percent of the program is dedicated to leaders teaching leaders, and the remaining 20 percent utilizes external expertise on areas that we believe are better addressed by someone outside the organization.

This level of program, with so many internal Dell leaders teaching, requires seamless integration of key messages and content. Leader preparation is critical, as well as how we align and attune the leaders before they come to deliver their parts. Flexibility is crucial in being able to work both with the learning needs of the participants and the leaders' teaching styles.

Keys to Our Success

As mentioned earlier, a critical success factor is sponsorship. Dell has been largely successful in using a leader-teaching-leader method in its leadership development programs by having clear sponsorship at the very top (Michael Dell and Kevin Rollins). Also, modeling what is expected has created significant momentum for the leadership development efforts. Sponsorship also exists from the head of HR to every senior HR leader. Support can mean anything from helping us to identify leaders to teach to actually prepping the leaders.

Second, our success lies with our talented leaders, who have stepped up to the challenges of being in the classroom to coach, teach, and mentor current and potential leaders. They are the key to us being able to build organizational capability, and they make it a high priority, putting in the time required.

We have been able to maintain this effective model over time by keeping things simple and using our leaders' time effectively. Most often, we seek the leaders' input around the key messages to be taught and posted on slides. (However, at Dell, we believe fewer PowerPoint slides is preferable.) We create a first draft of the materials to be presented and meet with each leader possibly two more times to get him or her ready to teach. We make sure the content is not in "HR-ease" and that it sounds natural.

We work with each leader to personalize his or her message with leadership stories. We recruit individuals who can give us preliminary feedback on the content and approach (for example, an HR leader or the learning and development person assigned to a leader's business) prior to giving feedback to each leader. If a leader has a coach, we sometimes involve the coach or suggest a coaching session also to prepare the leader. Because we do these preparatory steps, our leaders come away from teaching sessions feeling confident in their abilities as leader-teachers and that the time spent had high value.

Third, we are continuously looking for ways to improve, both for the leader who is a teacher and for the learning and development community. We collect feedback (formal and informal) from participants, summarize the information, and feed it back to leaders either via email or face to face. We also ask each leader for his or her perspective on what worked well and what he or she would want to do differently next time. Together, we make decisions regarding changes to the content and design—a true working partnership.

Through this process, we have all become smarter about how to make leaders teaching leaders the most effective learning experience it can be. We give and take direct feedback all in the spirit of building a winning culture.

The impact of these efforts can be seen as you talk to employees at various levels within the organization, either through focus groups or via our leadership and culture survey, called Tell Dell. We use Tell Dell to measure the progress of our management effectiveness training, holding managers accountable for improvement and making meaningful changes based on team feedback. Our line employees know that a significant investment is being made in developing their managers, and they obtain the benefit of being led by stronger leaders. Our various levels of leaders, both those teaching and those learning, are experiencing greater success with their teams. The impact of the program can also be measured as we continue to grow and reach our aggressive business goals.

Conclusion

Having leaders as teachers is by far the most advanced and challenging way to develop leaders. When the circumstances are right and leaders are poised for success, you unleash an untapped capability that cannot be compared to what happens with other methods of educating leaders. An incredible cadence occurs, and it becomes contagious for leaders to step up to the role of leader/teacher and impact not only those they teach but themselves.

Ashley Keith Yount *is senior manager in Global Talent Management for Dell, Inc. In this role she is responsible for the strategy and the development and delivery of executive development of Dell's key talent program, Leadership EDGE. In addition to these current responsibilities, she is working on advancing Dell's global talent management strategy. She also successfully developed and delivered an executive development core curriculum for Dell executives worldwide. Prior to Dell, Ms. Yount worked for NCR Corporation and SCANA Corporation. Her more than fourteen years of experience includes various roles in learning and organization development throughout the business and corporate functions. In her last role at NCR, she launched and managed the executive development and top talent programs to include formal training, 360-degree feedback, and coaching. Ms. Yount is an active member of the Executive Development Network, Organization Development Network, and the Human Resource Planning Society. She holds a B.S. in psychology from the University of South Carolina and an M.S. in organization development from the Johns Hopkins University.*

Level 4 Coaching
Everyone Has a Role
Marshall Goldsmith

Summary

Many organizations are currently using executive coaches to try to improve some aspect of an individual's results or behavior. In these instances, there is typically a great deal of interest in the coach and his or her qualifications. However, my experience has shown that a coach, no matter how able he or she may be, is not the sole factor in determining whether or not the coaching "works." In addition to the coach, the client, the client's co-workers, and the client's company, all have a role to play in a successful coaching experience.

In my work as an executive coach, my mission is to help successful leaders achieve positive, long-term, measurable changes in behavior. My success—or failure—is not determined by me or by my coaching clients; it is determined by the pre-selected key stakeholders of my clients.

I believe that I have been doing this specific type of leadership development about as long as anyone in the field. Experience is a great teacher. Over the past twenty-eight years, I have made several mistakes. While wise people learn from their mistakes, much wiser people learn from someone else's mistakes! So I hope that this article will help you learn from a few of my mistakes. My goal for this article is to help you do a great job in ensuring that leadership coaching provides real value—for both the person being coached and for the company.

Over the years, I have gone through four levels as an executive coach. At each level, I have gained a greater appreciation of how hard it is to help leaders achieve positive, long-term changes in behavior. I have also become more effective in determining when leadership coaching can help—and when it is probably going to be a waste of time.

Most of the literature on coaching focuses on one condition for success—the qualities of a great coach. I now believe that the coach is only one variable—and usually not the most important one—in determining the future success of the coaching process and in helping leaders actually achieve positive change. Three other variables that need to be carefully considered in evaluating the potential success of coaching are the client, the co-workers, and the company.

Level 1: It's All About the Coach

Early in my leadership development career, I had the hallucinogenic belief that the leaders I worked with would achieve positive change because I (the coach or teacher) was wise and could enlighten them with my profound insights, which would inevitably result in them getting better. Although this "coach-centric" (or "ego-centric") belief made me feel important, it wasn't very close to reality.

For the past fifteen years, my partner, Howard Morgan, and I have been measuring the effectiveness of a variety of leadership development activities. Six to eighteen months after participating in training or coaching, we have asked co-workers if they believe that participants have become more effective leaders. We recently published this research in a study (Goldsmith & Morgan, 2004) that involved over 86,000 co-worker respondents—who provided feedback on over 11,000 managers—in eight major corporations. Many of these managers had participated in exactly the same type of development activities, conducted by the same coaches or teachers at roughly the same time. Our findings were very clear: the key variable in producing long-term change was *not* the teacher, the facilitator, or the coach. *Leaders* who engaged in ongoing follow-up with *co-workers* were almost always seen as achieving positive, long-term change. Leaders who did not follow up were seen as improving no more than random chance.

My one-on-one personal coaching experience has also validated this research. Of all of the clients I have coached, the client who probably produced the greatest positive overall change was the client I spent the *least* amount of time with (Goldsmith & Morgan, 2005). He is also one of the greatest leaders of people I have ever met. After our time together, I commented, "I have spent less time with you than anyone I have ever coached, yet you produced the most positive change out of the coaching process." I then asked him, "What should I learn from my experience with you and your team?"

His reply explained why he was a great client and is a great leader. After pondering my question, he explained that my success as a coach is not primarily caused by me; it is primarily caused by my great clients—and their team members—who deeply want to get even better. He then went on to modestly note that his success as a leader was not primarily caused by him, but was primarily caused by the great people he has the honor of leading (Goldsmith, 2004).

As obvious as all that I have said may seem, most literature in the field of leadership coaching completely misses this point. The literature generally implies that the "great" coaches are successful because they—as coaches—demonstrate a list of noble qualities that lead to long-term change by their clients. The *coach* has years of experience. The *coach* is a great listener. The *coach* really cares about clients. Although this type of literature may be great for glorifying coaches, there is almost always no real research that indicates the *coach* is the most important factor for predicting client improvement.

On the negative side, I have also learned this lesson "the hard way." When I was young and naïve, I thought that I was so good that I could help anyone change. I will never forget being asked to work with one executive who had just scored in the second percentile in the area of "treating people with respect." When I asked him why he thought his scores were so low, he grunted, "Because they are all fools!" Rather than having enough sense to just walk away, I wasted one year of my life working with him. When I finally gave up on this assignment, I felt like saying to his boss, "Why don't you shoot him—before I do!"

I learned a very humbling lesson: I cannot make someone who doesn't care change. I have the same lesson for you—you can't either!

Many coaching organizations are very concerned with the "certification" of coaches. They want to make sure that coaches have great credentials. This implies that the credentials of the coach are the key factor in producing positive change with the clients. Both my research and my experience negate this assumption. "On paper" I am probably as qualified as anyone to do what I do. I have a Ph.D. in organizational behavior from a top school; I have been recognized by almost every professional organization in the field; and I have years of mostly successful experience in working with very senior executives. If the key variable in the success of the coaching process were me—the coach—I should have had roughly the same amount of success with every client. This has certainly not been the case!

In my own coaching network, one of my least "qualified" partners (on paper) has one of the best track records of consistently delivering results for his clients. One of his strengths is that he realizes that success in achieving change is not primarily about him, but about his clients. He is more concerned with their progress than with his own ego! To me, the best indicator of a "qualified" coach is the consistent achievement of *results* in areas in which clients want to achieve change—not an impressive bio.

Extensive research on behavioral change—as well as my own experience—finally led me to quit focusing on myself, the coach, as the key factor in determining success and to start focusing primarily on my clients, the people who actually have to make the change!

Level 2: It's All About the Client *and* the Coach

I believe that there is no such thing as a great generic "executive coach." The value of the coach depends on who is being coached and the goal of the coaching process. In my work as a coach, I only work with CEOs or potential CEOs, and I only focus on helping them achieve a positive change in behavior. I don't do anything else. I am not an expert in strategy development, strategy execution, organizational change, HR systems, life planning, values clarification, getting organized, or giving speeches. It is not that these issues are not important—it's just that I am not an expert on these topics.

Many people who call themselves "executive coaches" seem to represent themselves as being qualified to help almost *everyone* get better at almost *everything*. No one is qualified to be a coach on every topic.

Before worrying about selecting the right coach, it is better to start with the client. What does the client need? What are the client's challenges, hopes, and expectations for the coaching process?

Again, as obvious as this basic level of analysis sounds, it seldom happens. Most companies just conclude, "I think that Vice President Jones needs a coach" without a clear analysis of why Jones needs a coach, and specifically, what coach is most qualified to meet Jones' unique needs.

Given the current popularity of the coaching field and the amount of positive press that I have received, I receive frequent requests to be an executive coach. Sometimes these requests make absolutely no sense! In one case a pharmaceutical company called and said, "We would like you to coach Dr. Smith." I asked, "Why does he need a coach?" The caller replied, "Because he is not updated on recent medical technology!" I replied, "Neither am I!"

Behavioral coaching only helps leaders who want to change behavior. It doesn't turn bad doctors into good doctors or turn bad accountants into good accountants. Behavioral coaching also doesn't turn the wrong strategy into the right strategy. If someone is going in the wrong direction, my coaching will only help him or her get there faster!

Even more troubling to me than the inefficient use of executive coaches is the improper use of coaches. Some companies have actually hired executive coaches to "help" leaders who commit an ethics violation. Leaders who commit ethical violations should be *fired*—not *coached*.

Using the example of behavior coaching, let us assume that the client wants to achieve a positive change in leadership behavior. Let's also assume that the coach is a specialist in behavioral coaching and has a history of helping clients achieve positive change. The coaching process still may not be effective. In some cases, the key variable in impacting change may be the *co-workers*, not the coach or the client.

Level 3: It's All About the Co-Workers *and* the Client *and* the Coach

In my current coaching practice, more than half of my time is not spent with my clients—the people I am paid to coach—but it is spent with their co-workers. What counts in leadership is not what the leader *says;* it is what the co-workers *hear!* I am frequently asked the question, "Do your clients *really* change their behavior, or are they merely *perceived* as changing because they involve their co-workers and do so much follow-up?"

The answer to this question is that it is much easier to change our own behavior than it is to change the perceptions of co-workers. One of the most-researched principles in psychology is cognitive dissonance theory. The application of cognitive dissonance in the coaching process is very important. We all tend to interpret people's behavior in a way that is consistent with our previous stereotype of the person. In other words, if you think that I am a bad listener, you are going to look for behavior that reinforces your previously held belief that I am a bad listener.

Let me use a simple example to illustrate the importance of co-worker involvement in changing perceptions. Assume that, in "situation A," the leader, Jim Jackson, received 360-degree feedback that he made too many destructive comments about his co-workers. Jim might think, "This problem is easy to fix. I don't have to involve my co-workers or follow up. I merely need to stop making destructive comments, and the problem will go away." Now, let's assume that Jim goes seven months without making a destructive comment about anyone. Jim is still human. Like all humans, one day Jim will make a mistake. Jim gets frustrated and says, "Those idiots in finance. How do we get anything done in this company? We are being controlled by a bunch of bureaucratic bean counters!" The co-workers (who hear the comment) will probably think, "There he goes again. Jim has never changed."

Assume that, in "situation B," Jim receives the same feedback. Only now he talks with his co-workers and lets them know of his desire for change. Every month or so Jim does a "progress check" with co-workers to see how he is doing. The co-workers begin to note changes in Jim's behavior. *They* begin to see how he is changing and to give him positive reinforcement for the change. Eventually, when Jim makes a mistake—as we all will—they realize that this is just one isolated negative event that has occurred after seven months of positive behavior.

In "situation A," did Jim's behavior change? Yes. Did the co-workers' perceptions change? No. In "situation B," did Jim's behavior change? Yes. Did the co-workers' perceptions change? Yes. As was mentioned earlier, in leadership it doesn't matter what we say—it only matters what our co-workers hear!

In my personal coaching practice, I have four requests for each of the co-workers of my clients:

1. *Can you let go of the past?* My clients cannot change behavior that has occurred in the past. I have found when co-workers continually "dredge up" the past, leaders tend to give up on the process of change. If co-workers "let it go" and focus on ideas for a more positive future, the leader is much more likely to change.

2. *Can you help this leader by being positive and supportive, rather than cynical, negative, or sarcastic?* Every leader I coach has to commit to have ongoing dialogues with co-workers. If the co-workers use this as an opportunity to put down the leader, or if they make cynical or sarcastic comments, the leader will tend to abandon the follow-up process. If the co-workers are positive and supportive of the leader's efforts to change, the leader will be much more likely to continue the process.

3. *Can you swear to tell the truth?* In our coaching process, I don't get paid if my clients don't get better. "Better" is not defined by my clients. "Better" is defined by the co-workers. It would be very disheartening to work with a leader who is told that she has increased effectiveness and then have the co-workers say (behind her back), "She didn't *really* change; we just said that." I am not naïve. I realize that having people swear to tell the truth does not mean that they will tell the truth. On the other hand, I know that this increases the probability that they will tell the truth.

4. *Can you (Mr. or Ms. Co-Worker) pick something to improve?* All of my clients ask for ongoing ideas on how they can get better. When they follow up with co-workers, it is very helpful for the co-workers to also try to improve. In this way, the process of helping each other is two-way and not one-way. Another potential benefit is that many (up to hundreds) of co-workers can begin to achieve positive change, based on an initial assignment to work with only one client (Goldsmith & Morgan, 2005).

Unfortunately, it is possible to have a client who wants and needs to change, co-workers who are working hard to support this change, and a coach who is skilled in facilitating change—and still not add value for the organization. The final key variable that we will discuss is the role of the *company* in making sure that the coaching process adds value.

Level 4: It's All About the Company *and* the Co-Workers *and* the Client *and* the Coach

Sometimes the management of the company has "written off" the coaching client. In other words, no matter what he does, he doesn't have a chance. But instead of just firing this person, the company hires an executive coach, so executives can say, "See—we tried! We even hired an executive coach for this person—and he still didn't get better. We have to fire him."

On two occasions I believe that I—as an executive coach—have been used as a pawn in an executive's political process.

In one case, I was hired by the CEO to coach the CFO. I had a gut feeling that the CEO didn't really like the CFO and didn't want her to succeed. I should have listened to my gut and turned down the assignment. Unfortunately, I didn't. The CFO was told that if she improved in the area of interpersonal relationships, she would become the next CEO. The CEO assured me that the CFO was very competent in all technical and business dimensions and that her interpersonal issues were her only real limitation. I worked with the CFO for over a year. She received a glowing report from fifteen of sixteen co-workers on how much her interpersonal skills had improved. Only one person saw no improvement. Who was this? You guessed it—the CEO! After reviewing her report, which documented her great improvements in interpersonal skills, the CEO then concluded that she "lacked needed skills in marketing." This was the same CEO who said that she had excellent skills in marketing one year earlier. It was obvious to me what had happened. The CEO did not want her to get the job. He did not think that she would improve. After a year, he was planning to go back to the board and say, "Well, I tried. I got her the best coach I could. I guess she is just not the right person for the job." Eventually, she left the company, after receiving a multi-million dollar settlement. As her coach, I was happy that she got better and am glad that she can use what she learned in her new company. I am sorry that I accepted this assignment.

In a second case, my coaching client, a division head, was "written off" by human resources (HR). The executive vice president (EVP) of HR just could not stand this leader. No matter what the leader did, the EVP kept finding problems. My client's own HR staff reported to corporate HR and not to him. They seemed to relish playing the role of spy and finding out what this person was doing wrong. Eventually, the division head gave up on the company and found another job.

In both of the cases listed above, the key variable that inhibited success was not the coach, the client, or the co-workers, but the company! In both cases, the company did not really want the person to succeed and was determined to make sure that the person failed! As a coach, I have learned (the hard way) to test the commitment of the company to the leader, as well as the commitment of the leader to change.

When Everyone Plays His or Her Role, Coaching Works!

In most executive coaching relationships, the company does not do a thorough analysis to ensure that the background, skills, and process of the coach match the unique situation faced by the clients. The coach does not do a thorough analysis of the client, the co-workers, and the company to ensure that the coaching process can make a significant positive difference for all key stakeholders. This lack of analysis and understanding at the beginning of the coaching process may well result in disappointment with results at the end of the coaching process. Hard questions, honest analysis, and thorough involvement of stakeholders—at the beginning of the coaching process—can help ensure that leadership coaching produces the desired results for the company, the co-workers, the client, and the coach.

When the *company* is sincerely committed to the success of the coaching process and truly wants the person to succeed . . .

When the *co-workers* "let go" of the past, give the client a fair chance, provide supportive suggestions, tell the truth, and try to get better themselves . . .

When the *client* wants and needs to change, is willing to involve co-workers, and has the discipline to follow up on key areas for improvement . . .

And when the *coach* has a background and skill set that matches the unique needs of the client . . .

The leadership coaching process will almost invariably help leaders achieve a positive, long-term change in behavior, and then everyone involved in the process will benefit!

References

Goldsmith, M. (2004, October). It's not about the coach. *Fast Company,* p. 120.

Goldsmith, M., & Morgan, H. (2004, Fall). Leadership is a contact sport. *Strategy+Business,* pp. 70–79.

Goldsmith, M., & Morgan, H. (2005). Expanding the value of coaching: From the leader, to the team, to the company. In H. Morgan, P. Harkins, & M. Goldsmith (Eds.), *The art and practice of leadership coaching.* Hoboken, NJ: John Wiley & Sons.

Marshall Goldsmith *has recently been recognized by the American Management Association as one of fifty great thinkers and leaders who have impacted the field of management over the past eighty years. He has been described in* The Wall Street Journal *as one of the top ten executive educators, in* Forbes *as one of five most-respected executive coaches, in* Business Week *as one of the most influential people in the history of talent development, and in* The Economist *as one of the most credible thought leaders in the new era of business. He has appeared in a* Harvard Business Review *interview,* New Yorker *profile, and* Forbes *feature story. In 2005, Dr. Goldsmith was recognized as a Fellow in the National Academy of Human Resources (America's highest HR honor). His work has received national recognition from almost every professional organization in his field. He is one of a select few consultants who have been asked to work with over seventy major CEOs and their teams. Dr. Goldsmith is the author or co-editor of eighteen books, including* The Leader of the Future *(a Business Week best-seller),* Coaching for Leadership, *and* The Art and Practice of Leadership Coaching.

Creating a Customer–Centric Culture
"Walking a Mile in the Customer's Shoes" at Texas Instruments

Dan Parisi and Jeff McCreary

Summary

Texas Instruments (TI) used an innovative business simulation experience, co-created with BTS USA, to transform TI's overly product-centric culture into a more customer-centric culture. TI's senior vice president of worldwide sales and marketing, Jeff McCreary, harnessed the power of experiential learning to convert TI from an entrenched culture of technical arrogance to compelling passion for the customer. This article gives two perspectives: the perspective of the TI senior executive, Jeff McCreary, who led the change process, and the perspective of the lead consultant, Dan Parisi, from BTS USA, who collaborated with TI to create the simulation experience known as the "The Customer Loyalty Boot Camp." The article contains detail on the learning objectives and simulation methodology that was used to engage and teach over two thousand TI executives and managers. The article concludes with comments from Jeff McCreary regarding the significant impact of the training experience on TI culture and business results.

Introduction (The TI/Jeff McCreary Perspective)

Imagine you are a senior sales executive at the world's third-largest semiconductor company. Your company creates and markets arguably the most complex products on the planet—products that require a mind-boggling orchestration of the latest advances in sub-micron physics, electronics, chemistry, and engineering. Your workforce is comprised of world-class engineers, physicists, mathematicians, and scientists, who create highly differentiated products.

Your company is also experiencing unprecedented revenue, margin, and stock price growth. Innovative products, growing margins, bigger employee bonuses—what could be wrong with this picture? It turns out that a lot can be wrong, especially when formerly loyal customers begin calling to tell you they are switching from your company to your nearest competitor's.

By any benchmark, you know your product is great. Your technology is superior to the competition. Why would customers leave?

On closer inspection of your financial data, you realize that market share trends support the anecdotal information you are hearing from defecting customers. While your revenues are increasing in your high-growth markets, market share is slipping against your direct competition.

More of your best customers are consciously and systematically embracing your competitor's solutions. Why is this happening?

You begin to drill beneath the surface. You dialogue with defecting customers. You begin to hear things about your corporate culture you do not want to hear. Customers tell you the following:

- Your culture has become overly product centric.

- Your people are too inwardly focused.

- Your workforce radiates a sense of technical arrogance.

- Your product has truly become king, and your customer service has slipped.

Sure, many of these characteristics are representative of your entire industry. However, it has become clear that you are among the worst of the offenders. You realize you can't fix this market share problem with a better product. This won't be cured by a better business model either. This is a culture problem. Do you take on the monumental task of trying to change a deeply embedded corporate culture?

This is the exact situation I found myself in as the senior vice president of worldwide sales and marketing at Texas Instruments at the close of 2000. The rest of this article is about how we used a dynamic business simulation training experience created by BTS USA to kick off a broader corporate change process at Texas Instruments.

The Simulation

Texas Instruments (TI) co-created with BTS USA a dynamic simulation experience to begin changing an overly product-centric corporate culture. The simulation experience, called "The Customer Loyalty Boot Camp," allows TI managers to "walk a mile in the customer's shoes." The simulation puts TI managers in charge of running a business profiled to mirror some of their largest customers. Participants manage a digital consumer electronics company whose success is deeply linked to the support from their semiconductor solution providers.

While "walking in the customer's shoes," TI leaders begin their experience committed to purchasing semiconductors from a vaguely familiar sounding chip supplier, "Terrific Instruments." We specifically coached the BTS/"Terrific Instruments" facilitators to operate with many of the same overly product-centric traits of the real TI (late delivery, technical arrogance, execution missteps, lack of responsiveness to customer demands, and more).

The simulation experience is designed to have an emotional/visceral impact. It is also designed to teach what we had identified as four key drivers of customer loyalty:

Execution:	Must keep promises to customers
Knowledge:	Must establish intimate knowledge of the customer's business (system and product specification knowledge are not enough)
Responsiveness:	Must consistently demonstrate responsiveness to customers in order for them to feel valued and respected
Long-term view:	Must demonstrate a long-term view with customers

Further, it reinforced the essential requirement to have the customer's perspective at the core of our decision-making process.

Besides the customized, computer-based business simulation of the customer's business, the experience also includes human simulation (role playing), videotaped customer interviews, mini-case studies that analyze how TI missteps impacted its customers' business in the past, and Q&A/storytelling by senior TI executives.

Results

The simulation experience was designed to be the first step in our broader change process, which included changing corporate metrics, structurally changing the sales organization, modifying/simplifying our key performance metrics with the sales force, reinitiating a formal customer satisfaction measurement process, and making other essential improvements. But, as in all change efforts, the first step (engaging hearts and minds) is often the most important and the most difficult. This simulation experience was initially delivered to three hundred of the most powerful leaders inside our company. After the first year, it was deployed more widely and has been delivered to over

2,500 TI executives and managers in six countries. It has become clear that this simulation experience has been integral in turning TI from a product-centric to a customer-centric culture and has been a key element in turning around our decreasing market share problem.

Why Simulation? (The BTS/Dan Parisi Perspective)

In a presentation, Michael Schrage, MIT's leading expert on the economics of innovation and author of *Serious Play: How the World's Best Companies Simulate to Innovate*, stated that many corporate executives fall into a common communication trap. Many of them implicitly believe in the following equation:

Change in Information = Change in Behavior

Schrage states that many executives think that a better-formulated strategy presentation or more clearly articulated change initiative can begin to effect change. He says that, regardless of message content, adults are resistant to change unless they have a chance to "persuade themselves." He also says the most effective way to drive behavior change is through experiential learning. Therefore, he modifies the equation:

Change in Information + Simulation = Change in Behavior

The addition of "simulation" into the equation is critical, as it allows adults to experience key issues, challenges, and scenarios and persuade themselves as to why they should change. Without the self-persuasion element, attempts to change behavior by transferring new information can be empty intellectual exercises.

Senior TI executive Jeff McCreary knew that he would have to do more than just "change information" to drive change at TI. In fact, he noticed that others in TI had attempted to convince TI employees to change by using the following communication vehicles:

- A well-designed PowerPoint slide presentation, which clearly showed the economic impact of TI's lack of customer-centricity. The slides even showed how it would impact share price—and ultimately TI employee wallets.

- Videotaped interviews with TI customers. These videos contained frank messages from TI customers exhorting TI employees to improve execution.

As well designed as these communication tools were, the messages "bounced off" the well-entrenched product-centric culture. People nodded in agreement with the logic of the PowerPoint slides, but the messages did not seem to stick. A few days after the "PowerPoint extravaganza," people were not behaving differently. In response to seemingly convincing customer videos (who can argue with "the voice of the customer"?), some engineers were overheard saying, "Those customers just don't understand that we're on the leading edge of technology. They need our products, and they'll just have to put up with our problems."

Clearly, the people designing these change messages were not giving TI employees a chance to "persuade themselves." Jeff knew TI employees with rigorous scientific backgrounds were inherently skeptical. He knew that he could leverage the impact of his message if he could take advantage of the fact that the TI culture was responsive to learning situations in which they could "tinker" with cause and effect, play out multivariate scenarios, and assess quantitative impacts. He also knew he needed to create a profound learning experience that would break down resistance and get into people's hearts and minds—an experience that impacted them both intellectually and emotionally. Jeff also knew the participants would respond with serious effort and a real commitment when placed in a competitive team environment. That is why he turned to BTS USA to build a customized simulation experience. The resistant product and engineering managers were now going to have a chance to "persuade themselves" to change overly product-centric behaviors by "walking a mile in the customer's shoes."

The Customer Loyalty Simulation

Realism, Relevance, and Applicability to the Job

BTS began a three-month-long customization process in which the simulated customer company, called Streavo, and the 2.5-day event would be created. The event itself was called "The Customer Loyalty Boot Camp." The simulated customer needed to appear realistic enough to engage employees' imagination, yet simple enough to execute three years of running a simulated company over the 2.5-day training event. By co-designing the simulation closely with TI engineering and marketing managers, the products being simulated paralleled the products of many TI "real-life" customers.

- The simulated products are highly dependent on the "Terrific Instruments" semiconductors inside the product.

- The simulated products are sold into very competitive markets, where time to market, cost, and differentiation are critical.

A case study (pre-work received one week before the event) was created that communicated to the twenty-five TI managers invited to each program what kind of company they would be running during the simulation. They were told that they would be broken into five teams of five managers and that each team would be in competition against the others. They were also told that they would be measured by which team could build the most revenue and profit while running the customer's business over the simulated three years.

Of course, there was a catch. To execute their strategies over the three simulated years, their simulated company (Streavo) would be highly dependent on a sometimes difficult semiconductor supplier named "Terrific Instruments."

The Visceral Simulation Event

BTS uses a discovery learning process that has been refined over the last two decades. While senior TI executive Jeff McCreary created the customer loyalty framework (execution, knowledge, responsiveness, long-term view), BTS provided the learning process shown in Figure 1 (on page 136).

The following section briefly describes each of the key components of the learning process.

The Customized Simulation Experience

The simulation was designed to create a high-pressure, competitive environment in which teams never seem to have enough time or data. The TI managers are tasked with running their customer's complex product development process, including being responsible for the customer's market launch dates, revenue/profit growth, and employee satisfaction. Once the TI managers were in the simulated "customer cockpit," they needed to select various combinations of semiconductor speed, power, and functionality to drive their handset product. They also had to begin the "design in" process, whereby they begin to allocate resources around embedding the semiconductor into the guts of their wireless handset product. Critical interdependencies were simulated between semiconductor and handset product image quality, feature richness, battery life, and ease of use.

Each simulated year lasts about 3.5 hours. About 2.5 hours into the first simulated year, teams are asked to hit a "supplier commit" button in the simulation. This freezes the contract between the simulated company and its supplier's (Terrific Instruments) chip specs and puts the customer business (Streavo) at the "point of no return." That is, in the last hour of the simulated first year, you are totally dependent on the chip supplier to deliver the cost, performance, and delivery date promised. Once "commit" is pressed, you can only manage the non-product variables of the customer company.

But there is a problem . . . and it begins with the product manager from Terrific Instruments knocking on the first team's breakout room door. The first of six consecutive Terrific Instruments' execution failure messages are delivered. The first one reads:

Dear Streavo Management Team:

Allow me to report on the progress of the handset chip you ordered.

At Terrific Instruments we think we are . . . well . . . Terrific, but sometimes we can also be a little late. The bad news is that the chip will be twenty-one days late. The good news is that you might get it in roughly the quarter you expected it.

We think this is pretty good. It could have been much worse. Count your blessings.

As you know, we work on the bleeding edge of technology and things like this are bound to happen.

Regards,

Dee Lay
Terrific Manager

This seemingly minor delay is then input into the simulated company's product development parameters in real-time. Suddenly, the chip arriving twenty-one days late prevents the managers from launching the product in time for the "back to school" high-demand season. Streavo's revenue forecast has to be adjusted downward. With revenues off by 25 percent, gross margin has dropped to zero.

After the next few messages from Terrific Instruments (impacting promised chip cost, quality, and performance), a perfectly optimized product development process is in tatters. The managers are quickly running out of time to deal with the Terrific messages. The managers running the simulated customer company demand a response from Terrific Instruments. Their business has been materially impacted by Terrific's execution problems. They are going to be competitively disadvantaged in the market. They are upset. They want answers. Message back from Terrific: "Sorry, we are too busy visiting an important customer and can't meet with your company today . . . maybe tomorrow." Yes, there is some hyperbole in the messages and the approach. However, it is so close to what the participants have really seen happen in the past that the impact is enormous. In every simulation we ran, you could find folks expressing the fact that these delays and execution and communication failures were consistent with things TI had done to customers in the past.

I have delivered this simulation over fifty times at TI, and it never fails to have a visceral/emotional impact on the TI managers running the simulated customer business. The fact that Terrific Instruments lacked execution, lacked intimate knowledge

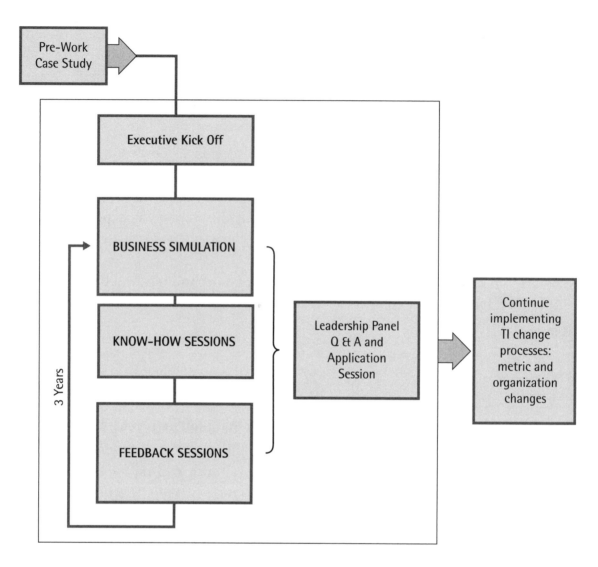

Figure 1.   The TI Customer Loyalty Boot Camp

of its customer, was not responsive, and lacked a long-term view of this growing customer's business is an experiential learning "coup" around Jeff's four key customer loyalty learning objectives.

Instead of listening to a PowerPoint presentation on why customers defect, the TI managers are "walking a mile in the customer's shoes," a painful mile they will not soon forget.

In year 2, the TI managers running the Streavo customer business are offered an opportunity to switch away from Terrific Instruments to another supplier. They can switch to Terrific's simulated chip competitors who happen to resemble TI's real-life arch-competition (with names changed to protect the innocent). All teams end up switching to Terrific's competitors. A key learning point: the competitors don't necessarily have superior technology, but they offer a superior customer experience. The

TI managers running Streavo switch because the competitors offer better execution, more intimate knowledge of their business, more responsiveness, and a longer-term view. Besides the high irony of TI managers switching to simulated versions of their own real-life competitors, Jeff's customer loyalty learning objectives are once again driven home.

The Know-How Sessions

As you have read above, it should be clear that the simulation provides a high-impact, experiential, emotional learning experience. We knew we could reinforce the experiential impact on skeptical, analytical TI managers with other methods as well, and know-how sessions were one of those—the goal being that the cumulative effect of several different learning methods would create an irrefutable impetus for change at TI.

The know-how sessions contain mini-case studies from specific TI examples, which "dollarize" the impact of poor execution on TI customers and on TI itself (lost revenue/profit and reputation impact). The know-how sessions also contain videotaped interviews with major customers. Interestingly, these were the same videos we mentioned earlier—the videos that, when presented in isolation, were easy for engineers to rationalize about or ignore.

For the know-how sessions, teams leave their breakout rooms (somewhat shell-shocked from the simulation experience) and gather in a large conference room. The experience is debriefed. They are asked to explain how they feel (feelings are not commonly discussed in a data-driven, engineering culture) about Terrific Instruments. They responded with descriptions like angry, betrayed, and eager to switch suppliers. They described Terrific's arrogance and product centricity and the fact that they lost trust in Terrific as a supplier. They were shocked by Terrific's lack of responsiveness.

Then we played the customer videos. The customers echo many of the same sentiments, only this time they are talking about the real-life Texas Instruments. When the stop button is hit on the video, you could hear a pin drop in the room. One manager described "feeling it in his stomach." Suddenly, the videos that were once ignored are now hitting home emotionally and personally. Why? The answer is simple: prior to the simulation the videos were only "change in information." This time, we expanded the equation to include "change in information + simulation"—we added the experiential element that allowed managers to "persuade themselves."

The final know-how session consists of a leadership panel hosted by three senior TI executives. We knew the subject matter of customer loyalty was equal parts art and science. To discover the "art" of customer loyalty, we knew that executive "storytelling" would be a powerful learning method. The three senior executives answered challenging questions from the audience and also shared their own compelling stories about how they handled difficult customer loyalty tradeoffs over their careers.

Feedback Session

For those managers in the room who love data and evidence, we turned to the highly quantitative feedback sessions, which contain data generated from the annual simulation results. The objective data is overwhelming: a chip company's smallest execution missteps can have enormous "domino effect" impacts on a customer's business. Poor execution by a chip supplier can hobble a large customer and put a small customer out of business. And most importantly, now they know what it *feels* like to run a customer's business that is on the receiving end of this poor execution. The feedback session also updates managers on the simulated competition, thus further engaging them in the simulation process.

Application Session

On the last half-day of the 2.5-day experience, managers spend time dialoguing with key leaders and committing to actions they will implement back on the job. Teams take time to reflect on the learning and prepare presentations to the senior executives. Executives question and clarify commitments during the final presentation. Plans are taken back to the workplace and followed up on with managers in semi-annual review meetings.

Lasting Impact

One of the most important impacts of the customer loyalty simulation experience was that it created a milestone cultural event and a new language for over 2,500 managers at TI.

At the end of the simulation experience, we give out baseball hats with "Terrific Instruments" written across the front. We told TI managers that, if they ever witness other TI employees acting overly product-centric, technically arrogant, or inwardly focused, they should just place the hats on their heads and stand there quietly until others notice. We heard from many managers that this simple action went a long way to getting the message out. When managers who had attended the simulation experience saw another manager place a hat on his head, they immediately "got the joke" and realized they were slipping back into some old, bad habits. One senior executive went as far as giving his most important customer the "Terrific Instruments" baseball hat with the following instruction: "If a TI employee is acting in an overly product-centric manner, please place this hat on your head; the employee will immediately 'get your point' and correct the behavior." The customer has used the hat several times—to great effect.

In the end, the Customer Loyalty Boot Camp was the critical first step in a broad TI change initiative. Jeff McCreary was able to capture the hearts and minds of thousands of executives and managers. Since the Customer Loyalty Boot Camp started rolling out in 2002, TI has seen improvements across the board, from market share to improved execution. Most important, customers notice the difference, and loyalty has increased.

We know that it would be naïve to credit only the Customer Loyalty Boot Camp, but the fact is that, since initiation of this simulation experience, the company has had four years of consecutive market share growth in its three most important and highly targeted markets. Anecdotal evidence, once again collected in the form of videotaped interviews with customers, also supports the perspective that Texas Instruments is making clear and impressive progress in becoming more customer-focused. Combined with the record profitability that TI has been delivering in recent quarters, it all adds up to a vastly improved enterprise.

Dan Parisi *is a BTS USA partner and the general manager of BTS San Francisco. Throughout his ten-year career at BTS, Mr. Parisi has pioneered the application of customized business simulations for leading Fortune 100 clients such as Hewlett Packard, Texas Instruments, Cisco, and others. He is passionate about making business learning "come to life" through simulation and strives to make learning business concepts fun, memorable, strategically relevant, and highly applicable to the job. Besides innovating how companies use business simulations to develop leaders, Mr. Parisi spends much of his time as a senior facilitator. He has led over 7,000 executives and managers through simulation experiences focused on aligning management teams to corporate strategies and initiatives. He received his MBA in finance from New York University.*

Jeff McCreary *recently retired from Texas Instruments as a senior vice president and the worldwide sales and marketing manager. He was responsible for TI sales and account management, field technical support, and channel marketing strategies around the globe. A twenty-three-year TIer, Mr. McCreary was named a vice president in 1995 and a senior vice president in 1998. He led the turnaround of TI's worldwide military semiconductor business in the early 1990s, resulting in record sustained profitability. He also managed TI's highest volume business, Advanced System Logic, and held assignments in product development, sales management, and technical sales. Prior to joining Texas Instruments, Mr. McCreary held engineering and strategic marketing positions within the Bell System. He earned a B.S. in electrical engineering from the Rose-Hulman Institute of Technology and an honorary doctorate of engineering from the Institute as well. He currently serves on the Rose-Hulman Board of Trustees and the Board of the Global Wireless Engineering Consortium (GWEC).*

Optimizing Developmental Job Assignments

Betty Kovalcik

Summary

Identifying and developing high-potential employees has become a hot-button issue when addressing sustainable growth and success. Stocking a talent pipeline is a critical factor for all businesses, but not necessarily intuitive to all managers responsible for providing the optimum development to high-potentials, ensuring that they live up to their full potential. This article provides usable and practical processes that can be implemented by all managers to address their increasingly important bench strength shortages.

Few companies would argue that developmental job assignments are not valuable, when done correctly. The challenge is to successfully implement them in a way that serves both the individual and the organization. This article provides a glimpse into how one organization, Navy Federal Credit Union, learned to successfully leverage developmental job assignments. While the approach used at Navy Federal may not be directly applicable to every organization, I believe that the insights gained at Navy Federal form the basis for successful developmental job assignments in all companies. As the head of Executive Development and Talent Management for Navy Federal, it has been extremely rewarding to see the developmental job assignments we use impact not only the individuals rotating, but also the organization as a whole. The case study outlined here helps to illustrate the approach that made this possible.

Why Developmental Job Assignments Are Important

The need to develop leaders continues to increase. In a 2005 Executive Trends Survey conducted by Executive Development Associates, leadership bench strength jumped to the top of the corporate agenda. Research is consistent that learning on the job has the most impact and most Executive Development practitioners are familiar with the 70 percent, 20 percent, 10 percent rule, where 70 percent of the development should occur on the job, 20 percent should be other activities, such as mentoring and coaching, and 10 percent should be in the classroom. Developmental job assignments are and will continue to be an important vehicle for developing future leaders.

In addition to developing future leaders, developmental job assignments are becoming increasingly important as a competitive advantage for companies. As the world continues to change, with its shifting demographics, emerging markets, and increasing demands for innovation, companies are desperately in need of leaders who can effectively navigate these changes. This skill set is best developed through experience working in different disciplines, cultures, and geographic areas.

Being successful in these new environments requires that individuals think about things differently. Cross-functional knowledge and collaboration will continue to grow in importance. The successful individual who stays in one functional area and builds strong content expertise will not have as much success in the future, as his or her exposure is too narrow. Michael Treacy, author of *Double Digit Growth,* says it brilliantly: "All ideas within the functions have been identified; now all good ideas sit at the intersection of the functions." Without an appreciation for what others bring to the table, innovation cannot occur.

Job assignments, by their design, help to cross-pollinate the organization by exposing the moving employees to new concepts, new people, and new leadership styles. Conversely, the new employees provide exposure to new perspectives and new styles. This integration helps seed the appreciation and understanding that allow for innovation to occur. In his book *The Art of Innovation,* Tom Kelley shares the story of how IDEO instills an environment of creativity and innovation within the company. As he notes, "The difficulty most companies have when they try to innovate is that they have trouble getting out of their own shoes." He goes on to write about how expertise can hurt innovation: "Expertise is great until it begins to shut you off from new learning." In the June 2000 issue of *Fast Company,* an article written by G. Pascal Zachary states that "to win in a global economy, it takes a commitment to mixing people, experience, and ideas." The article goes on to say "companies that use this mix to stimulate creativity will be the ones that own the future. The ability to apply knowledge to new situations is the most valued currency in today's economy." Developmental job assignments are a powerful tool for creating the environment in which creativity and innovation can thrive.

Success in Optimizing Developmental Job Assignments

A lot of organizations have developmental job assignments and frequent career moves as an expectation within their cultures. Historically, this was simply the price one paid for getting ahead. For many companies, an individual knew that he or she would move every three to five years, as a part of a natural career progression. I remember one executive at BellSouth telling me years ago that his family stopped hanging their pictures when they relocated because they knew another move would be coming soon. This is changing in many companies. In Executive Development forums, practitioners talk about the challenge of getting people to take job assignments and the trend toward high-potentials saying "no thanks" to developmental moves that require relocation and hardship to them and to their families. Although some of this occurred earlier, the changing priorities of individual workers (especially since 9/11) and the changing demographics of the workforce are creating an environment in which this rite of passage is being actively challenged. Additionally, career paths are no longer as clear as they once were, and individuals are not certain about the benefits of taking developmental job assignments. Today's future leaders know they have choices inside and outside their companies, and they are less inclined to accept these interim steps to advancement if they have options elsewhere. In a *Wall Street Journal* article titled "Timing the Time Abroad: Overseas Work Assignments Are Getting Shorter," Erin Stern, who is the senior vice president of GMAC Relocation Services, states, "At one time, overseas was considered a plum assignment. You were doing a favor for the company, and your status within the company would rise. Now all of a sudden, people aren't making more money, and they don't necessarily see the need to sacrifice their family life for three to five years. They would just as soon switch jobs."

Developmental Job Assignments as a Catch 22

In some ways, developmental assignments are a Catch 22. We are faced with the value of developmental moves *and* with the reluctance of employees to engage in them. I have learned, as a practitioner, that companies have to be clear on the critical parameters of setting up developmental job assignments. They should ask four key questions before a program is set up: (1) What is the objective for making the moves? (2) What will our culture support? (3) How do we set realistic expectations? and (4) How do we establish a support system that maximizes the chance of success for the individuals and for the organization? Let me first briefly describe these parameters and then illustrate how we applied them at Navy Federal.

Getting Clear About the Objective

The objective drives the type of developmental assignment and determines what makes the most sense for the individual and for the organization. Some companies have learned to use moves in a strategic manner as a strong developmental vehicle for both the individual and the organization. Conversely, some companies use moves primarily to address organizational needs, such as a turnaround situation, or to address performance, burnout, or retention issues. Neither objective is good or bad—they are just very different, and the organization must clearly understand the distinction.

Understanding What the Culture Will Support

Regardless of all the best practices in the world, if your organizational culture will not support the optimal approach, do not try to implement it. The reality is that developmental moves will not work if they place too high a burden on the organization. This burden can be in the form of pulling needed expertise from an area or creating a system that is so complex that it takes too much time to manage. Forced moves will consistently fail, as will your opportunity for a second chance. Instead, the goal should be to do only what will be successful within your culture, will still reap some benefits, and will positively set the stage for future developmental moves.

Setting Realistic Expectations

The individuals moving to a new position and the area accepting them need to be clear about their expectations of each other. If not, this can quickly derail the benefits of any developmental move.

Establishing a Support System

In order to maximize the chance for success, developmental job assignments cannot be treated as an insulated event. Cultures are too strong to have the moves taken out of context. For example, the benefits of being able to leverage the new perspective are quickly lost if the individual moves into an area where there is no tolerance for making change or proposing different ways of doing things. It is critical that the person moving into the position feel supported and have space to learn and grow. If done as a standalone, the prevailing culture will "teach" the individuals to do things as they have previously been done, and the fresh perspective of the individuals moving into the position will be lost.

Providing opportunities for individuals to reflect on what they are learning is also critical. In a May 2000 position paper by Boston University's School of Management titled *The Role of Agility in Executive Learning*, Kent Seibert's chapter on "Reflection-in-

Table 1. Work Conditions That Create a Reflective Environment

Reflection Condition	Definition
	An immediate work environment that offers:
Autonomy	Ample freedom and discretion to structure one's work as one sees fit
Feedback	Information on the results of one's actions (note: performance appraisals were not listed as a source of feedback that contributed to reflection-in-action)
Interactions with other people:	
• Access to others	• Encounters with skilled and knowledgeable people
• Connection to others	• At least one caring interpersonal relationship
• Stimulation by others	• Encounters with people that provide new ideas and perspectives
Pressure:	
• Promotive pressure	• Significant performance demands resulting from time limitations and/or large amounts of new information
• Directive pressure	• Significant performance demands resulting from the visibility and importance of the work
Momentary solitude	Periodic, brief occasions at or away from work to process new information alone

Action, Tools for Cultivating On-the-Job Learning Conditions" contains five different work conditions that create an environment conducive to individuals reflecting and learning on the job (see Table 1).

Developmental Job Assignments in Action

Company Background

Navy Federal Credit Union is a seventy-three-year-old not-for-profit organization, with approximately five thousand employees worldwide. We currently have 109 branch offices around the world and a facility in Pensacola, Florida, that will eventually house around 2,500 employees. Currently, the majority of our employees are centrally located, at company headquarters, and, with only a few exceptions, all of our executive-level positions are based at headquarters. There is low turnover at and above the executive manager level and little movement across functions at this level. Vacancies at this level typically result from retirements and are filled by individuals in the same functional area following a natural job progression or with retired military personnel.

Several years ago, we put into place an executive development program to proactively develop future leaders. The program was primarily designed to develop mid- to high-level executive managers, with the goal of developing a cadre of people who could potentially move into positions as vice president. The executive development program has seven components, one of which is a job rotation. The other six components, which I describe later in this article, consist of academic modules, action learning projects, mentoring, attendance at board and committee meetings, networking with peers and senior leaders, and exposure to our branch offices via a two-week trip working in multiple branch offices serving members. It is important to note that the rotations are the last part of this executive development program.

Navy Federal, like all companies, has its own unique culture. The culture that exists at Navy Federal was born out of its military roots. The organization's employees, many of whom have military connections, have a strong loyalty to the company and a passion to serve our members around the world. Seniority and hierarchy historically defined much of what was valued, and the company is steeped in history, policies, and procedures. Individuals performing jobs were expected to be experts in those areas, and for years this drove promotions within the same career path and relatively little movement across the organization. In spite of our unique culture, I believe that many of our critical success factors translate across other companies, regardless of industry, size, and culture.

Our success factors were developed by answering the four critical questions mentioned earlier:

1. What are our specific objectives for the job rotation?

2. What will our culture support?

3. How can we set realistic expectations?

4. How can we establish a support system that maximizes the chance for success?

Our Specific Objectives for the Job Rotation

We knew that the primary objective of our job assignments was the development of the individual. The development could take many forms and was unique to the individual. A second objective was to expand the participant's understanding of the broader organization, and a third objective was to break down the functional silos that had developed over time.

What Our Culture Would Support

Navy Federal employees have a long tenure, and the organization places a high value on people's content knowledge. In addition, Navy Federal had limited experience in job rotations and had only done a few many years ago as part of a new hire process wherein employees were rotated through multiple functions for a short period of time. The objective of these past rotations was more to gain exposure than actually having the individuals accountable for the work.

Within this environment, we knew developmental assignments would be challenging. We felt that permanent moves or job swaps would seem too extreme for our culture, which expected deep content knowledge. Additionally, we realized that permanent moves would not foster the culture that we were trying to normalize, that is, the concept of job changes as a natural way of running the business. As a result, we opted to implement a single job rotation for a defined period. We wanted to do an official rotation, versus simply having job shadowing, because we felt that the accountability for results was an important factor in the individual's development.

We also had to assess what length of rotation would be acceptable. This is where we had to break with best-practice research. Most such research shows that rotations are the most valuable when they are between twelve and twenty-four months. The exception is when the goal for the rotation is building managerial skills. In these cases, most experts agree that these rotations should last thirty-six months.

While we were aware of the best-practice research, we knew that a culture with limited experience in job rotations was not prepared for rotations lasting between twelve and thirty-six months. To minimize the complexity and increase our odds for success, we defined a nine-month window for our job rotations. Because none of our moves required relocation to a different city or country, this timeframe was logistically doable and felt acceptable to the organization.

Setting Realistic Expectations

The components of our executive development program are widely communicated throughout the organization. Each individual going into the program knows that there will be a job rotation. The management of that area also knows that, by endorsing someone for the program, they are committing to fully support a job rotation in their area.

Unlike many accelerated executive development programs, we use an application process. Interested employees with at least three years of Navy Federal service must write an essay, complete a lengthy application process, and solicit recommendations from one to two senior leaders. They are then selected for the program by a senior-level committee that makes the selection decisions—and later the rotation decisions. This has worked exceedingly well for us. By having to officially apply for the program, individuals enter the program with an additional level of commitment and understanding of the expectations of the program. The rigorous selection process done by the senior leadership team, coupled with the required letters of recommendations from senior leaders, also works to reinforce the senior leadership commitment to the program and sets expectations among the senior team about job rotations and the senior leaders' role in supporting them.

Establishing a Support System That Maximizes the Chance of Success

As I mentioned before, the job rotation is one of seven components of our two-year accelerated executive development program. The other components provide the infrastructure around the rotations by expanding the individuals' thought processes, by increasing their understanding about the organization, and by building relationships at all levels prior to the rotations occurring. The entire program is outlined in Exhibit 1.

- Four three-day academic modules via a partnership with the University of Virginia's Darden School of Business. Three modules in Year 1. One module in Year 2.

- A formal two-year mentoring relationship between each participant and a senior leader.

- Rotating attendance at board and strategic committee meetings over the course of the two years in the program.

- A strategic project in Year 1. We use strategic projects as our action learning component of the program. The topics are proposed by the senior team and selected by the CEO. There are five team members and a sponsor for each project. The projects last six months. At the end of the six months, each team produces a written proposal and does a formal presentation to the senior team. The individuals cannot be placed on a project for which they have expertise, for which the sponsor is the senior leader of their organization, or for which their mentor is the sponsor. This is designed to build multiple relationships with senior leaders.

- Networking activities throughout the two years for the current class (which also includes interaction with the previous class and senior leaders).

- Exposure to the branch offices by working in the field for two weeks. The full class travels together and, as pairs, they are assigned to work in various branch offices over the two-week period. This occurs in Year 2 immediately prior to the rotations.

- Job rotations in second year.

Exhibit 1. Components of the Two-Year Executive Development Program

In addition to the surrounding infrastructure, several support mechanisms are put in place to increase the likelihood of successful rotations:

1. *We confine the rotation to the group of twenty in the accelerated development program.* We have twenty high-potential participants in our accelerated development program, and we seek to move them within these same twenty organizational areas. We base our rotational moves on the participant's developmental needs, regardless of level, office, compensation, and so forth, of the position into which he or she is placed. The participant moves into the incumbent's office for the nine-month period and carry the title of the rotational position, regardless of their previous levels. Our guiding principle is that, if we can make the moves within the twenty, we will do so and, if not, we will have the latitude to look elsewhere in the organization. So far, we have been able to contain the moves to the twenty program participants. By confining the moves to the group, we maintain an overarching support structure for the individuals involved in the rotations.

2. *Keeping the program flexible to accommodate unique situations.* While the expectation is that all of the participants will rotate, we also remain flexible if developmental objectives are being met otherwise. For example, if an individual is promoted into a new position in a different area within a couple of months of selection for the rotation, we do not put this person in the rotation mix, because he or she is being developed in the new assignment.

   We also try to remain flexible in cases in which a rotating employee is selected for another job during the rotation. Because we still use a posting system throughout the company and because we have limited openings at the executive level, we do not stop someone from applying for a job when it may be his or her only opportunity. Eventually, as we implement a more integrated talent management system, executive positions may be filled differently. For now, we address these moves as unique situations and do our best to minimize the impact on the others rotating.

3. *Giving others input into the rotational decisions.* Decisions regarding rotational moves occur in the fourth quarter of the first year of the program. By this time, the twenty participants have learned a lot about different parts of the organization. They have had nine months to get to know each other and what others do, nine months with their mentors, several months on their action learning projects with their senior-level sponsors—addressing a strategic organizational issue—and nine months attending board and committee meetings, gaining exposure to different areas of the company.

   Because the relationships have been built within the program and because the participants have had a chance to learn more about the organization, we give the participants, the mentors, the participants' senior leadership, and the project sponsor a chance to have input into the rotational moves. This feedback is collected and used as input into the senior-level rotation committee, which ultimately makes the rotation assignments for the nine-month period.

As a part of the input, we place the primary developmental objectives into three categories: (1) supervisory experience, (2) experience working in an operational area, and (3) exposure to a different functional area. We then solicit input regarding what the primary developmental driver for this individual should be during the rotation. In 2004, we also allowed individuals to recommend specific roles for the individuals rotating. A form we use for this purpose is shown in Exhibit 2.

Participant Name: _____

Your relationship to the participant (please place an "X"):

_____ Self

_____ He/she is in my organization

_____ Mentor

_____ Project sponsor

Please place an "X" by the primary opportunity that you would like a rotation to address for the participant. (If more than one area, please prioritize, with "1" being the most important.)

_____ Exposure to a different functional area

_____ Increase operational knowledge

_____ Managerial/supervisory experience

_____ Other, please specify:

In your opinion, what rotational position (see participant list) would benefit this individual the most?

_____

Based on your understanding of this individual's current position, which of the participants could you see being placed in this individual's current position as his/her rotation (see participant list)?

Exhibit 2.   Rotation Input Form

4. *Clearly communicating the individual advantages that a rotation provides.* Many participants see the rotations as a way to build their skills and experience base, thus increasing their chances of being selected for different jobs in the future. While no guarantee, the rotations are serving as a way for the participants to be viewed beyond their functional expertise and for many of them to gain experience that they had never had previously. In 2005, for example, we moved the executive manager of our 24/7 Call Center Operation, which has three hundred employees, to become the public relations director, working with the media and the senior executive team.

5. *Leveraging networks with each other and senior leaders.* The rotational employees have a built-in support network while they are on rotation. They have the support of their previous leadership, their new leadership, their mentors, their project sponsors, and the employees who previously graduated from the program. This is in addition to the network of support that they provide to each other. Because the group is in rotation status at the same time, they have shared experiences and can support each other.

6. Preparing the organization for the job rotations. We encouraged and congratulated incumbent managers on their participation in the program and communicated the following metrics of a successful rotation:

   - How well they embraced the new role and maintained a high standard of performance;

   - How well they prepared their existing areas for accepting the rotational employees who would be moving into their roles; and

   - How well they prepared the rotational employees to move into their roles.

   These expectations helped incumbents release their previous positions to program participants and encouraged the groups to support each other. We also involve these incumbents in the final evaluation of the rotational program.

   At the end of the rotation cycle, we solicit input from the senior team at the location where the individual rotated. We ask these incumbents to share:

   - Two strengths they saw in the individual rotating;

   - Two areas on which they would encourage this individual to continue to develop;

   - Unique perspectives that this individual brought to the organization that allowed him or her to do things differently; and

- Ideas the senior team has for how the program could have supported the individual better in preparing for the rotation.

7. *Setting expectations about returning to previous positions.* All of the participants rotating know that they will return to their previous positions at the end of the rotation. Any moves that occur are handled outside of the program boundaries in order to keep the rotation process clean.

Conclusion

As I am writing this, I cannot help but ask myself, "What would the individuals who have rotated as a part of the program say about the things I am writing?" I feel certain that they would talk about the rotation as a rewarding and positive experience, agree with the philosophies of the program, and agree that the rotations—although not always perfect—affected their confidence in themselves, their perspectives, and the loyalty they felt for the organization.

From my perspective and from the perspective of our senior team, the job rotations have been a tremendous success. The individuals rotating gain a new perspective, learn new skills, and, in some cases, discover new strengths they had never considered before, such as a love for management.

From an organizational perspective, the job rotations are creating a powerful, yet subtle shift in our culture. As I talk to current employees in the program, who will be rotating in 2007, they talk about how they are working with their direct reports to build their skills so that they can support and learn from the person rotating into their soon-to-be vacant positions. They also talk about who should rotate into their areas. It is fascinating to listen to them as they move beyond "It needs to be someone who knows content" to "What is the next growth area for this group, and who has the skill that can take this group to that next level?"

As I talk to senior leaders and other vice presidents, they are beginning to acknowledge that there is value in having their employees work for people with different leadership styles. They also talk about the excitement of working with the incoming rotational employees, who are eager and excited to learn, and how this, in essence, has caused them to become learners again. One of the most important successes of the job rotations is that we have organizationally made it acceptable to say, "I don't know" and to allow a few mistakes along the way as individuals are learning their new roles. These cultural changes will be critical for us in the future as we continue to grow and operate in an external environment that is experiencing great change.

References

Kelley, T. (2005). *The art of innovation.* Palo Alto, CA: IDEO.

Seibert, K. (2000, May). Reflection in action: Tools for cultivating on-the-job learning conditions. In position paper titled *The role of agility in executive learning.* Boston, MA: Boston University School of Management.

Stern, E. (2001). As quoted in K. Voight, Timing the time abroad: Overseas work assignments are getting shorter. *Wall Street Journal.* www.gmac.globalrelocation.com

Treacy, M. (2003). *Double digit growth.* New York: Penquin

Zachary, G.P. (2000, June). Mighty is the mongrel. *Fast Company.*

Betty Kovalcik *is associate vice president—executive development for Navy Federal Credit Union, headquartered in Vienna, Virginia. She is responsible for executive development, including talent management and succession management.*

Prior to joining Navy Federal in 2001, Ms. Kovalcik was a senior manager with Ernst & Young, LLP, in their organizational development/change management practice area. She also worked for BellSouth in various marketing and human resources positions. Her executive development program at Navy Federal was featured in the July 2005 edition of Credit Union Management *magazine. Ms. Kovalcik received her BS/BA from the University of North Carolina at Chapel Hill and her MBA from the Goizueta School of Business at Emory University.*

Lessons from the Battleground

Mark Whitmore and Harold W. Nelson

Summary

This article reviews the use of battlegrounds and history as a useful tool to study leadership development and organizational issues. The reasons why these experiences create such an impact on participants are explored. A number of battlegrounds are surveyed, and learning points are identified. Some of the more profound learning experiences are presented. The process for developing a retreat is outlined, and tools used for enhancing the learning experience are discussed.

Each year hundreds of organizations, public, private, and from all sectors of industry, visit battlefields for the purpose of leadership development. In our current roles as a human resources executive and professional historian (and former Brigadier General) we have worked with many of them to design their programs. For some readers, however, this approach may be a new one, and you may be asking yourself, Why visit a battleground to learn lessons about leadership? Or you might ask, What is the value of learning from history, particularly when the events occurred many decades or centuries ago? How can these things be relevant to us today?

In this article, we will describe principles and concepts that can be used to create a meaningful and valued leadership development experience. Specifically, we will look at the use of history and battles as effective business metaphors, explain the importance of actually visiting the site of the battle, describe some of the significant learning that has occurred during these battleground retreats, describe the process to create a memorable leadership development experience, and introduce a useful tool to reinforce the learning and transform learning and experience into meaningful actions back in the workplace.

Visiting former battlegrounds as a learning opportunity has been a technique used by military organizations dating back to antiquity. Some of the more popular battles to study have been the battles of Antietam and Gettysburg in the Civil War and the D-Day invasion of Normandy in World War II. In the 1980s and 1990s, the Army War College began inviting business leaders from organizations to join its students in staff rides of the various battlegrounds.

As the business leaders saw the relevance of the military history to contemporary business problems, they began asking that others in their companies receive the same experience. The customized battleground retreat as described in this article began in the 1990s and has increased in popularity each year. Along the way, a number of innovations have been introduced to make the experience more intense and impactful.

The Battle as a Business Metaphor

Battles make excellent metaphors for studying business issues and problems. They involve lots of people with both competing and complementary agendas. There are at least two sides in competition with each other. During the course of a battle, there is the opportunity to study and observe the whole chain of command, from the top general to the foot soldier. Battles involve the coordination of people in the front line with others in support roles. Battles are fought by teams of people. The success of the team is often based on how well the members work together and support each other. The political and social environment can determine whether a battle is fought and how it is fought. To be successful in battle often requires that the leaders manage the political and social realities of the situation. There is usually a good mix of both strategic and tactical issues. Execution of strategy and tactics, coordination across multiple functional areas, and resource allocation are all critical to success.

Often success on the battleground will depend in part on the use of technology. In some cases, the battles involve the introduction and first time use of a new technology. Alignment of new technologies with old strategies can become a significant issue. Generally, success or failure on the battleground is very clear. The challenge of using a battle as a business metaphor is to sort through all of the potential issues and identify which are most important to a particular organization. Many of the published leadership and management books work well in conjunction with studying a battle. There are parallels to the concepts in these books and to the experiences on the battleground. Examining the role of an individual or group—whether they were effective or ineffective in the decisions they made, how they executed those decisions, and the consequences of their actions—can become very powerful lessons and reinforce the importance of the concepts.

Finding Good Ground

Why actually visit a battleground? Why not study it from a book or video? It is important to be onsite to learn from a battleground experience for two main reasons. First, you need to understand the scale and the context of the battles to appreciate the complexities and challenges involved. Visits to the battleground can be very vivid experiences. They involve the use of all of the senses. Viewing the battleground gives the student a better understanding of the enormous challenges involved.

Often the ground itself becomes the competitive advantage that one side has over the other. It isn't possible to get a sense of this from reading a book, and even the best videos leave out important details. An example of this is the capture of Burnside's Bridge during the Battle of Antietam. What the books and pictures leave out is that there is a bluff on the other side of the bridge. A small group of defenders on top of the bluff could easily hold that bridge for a very long time, which is exactly what happened. You have to be there to understand why this was a costly battle for the Union forces and then begin to question General Burnside's order, especially since his soldiers could have forded the same stream and avoided the bridge and the barrage of bullets.

A second major reason to be onsite is the scale of some of these activities. You don't get the sense of scale from a book. For example, leading a frontal assault, such as Pickett's charge during the Battle of Gettysburg, involved creating a line of infantry attackers almost a mile long. This is also another good example of the need to understand context. Frontal assault against a heavily reinforced stone wall sounds suicidal. Why wouldn't the soldiers just turn and run? When you stand in the field where the soldiers were preparing for the assault, you see that the field is not flat and that they could not see what they were going up against. Understanding the context and the scale of the actions is important to exploring the concepts you want to highlight in your leadership retreat.

Epiphanies on the Battleground

Epiphany is defined in the dictionary as a "sudden intuitive perception of or insight into the reality or essential meaning of something usually initiated by some simple homely or commonplace occurrence or experience." While the experience may not be "commonplace," in every other aspect this definition fits with the intensity of learning that occurs on the battleground.

The reason is that, although the decisions made by these military leaders are similar to the decisions business leaders make regarding issues such as staffing, resource allocation, tactical judgments, and deployment, the results of military decisions are often immediate, clear-cut, and extreme. Bad decisions lead to catastrophic results, and good decisions lead to victories.

In reliving history, the participant can identify with the types of decisions made and, at the same time, be confronted with the rightness or "wrongness" of the decisions. In this way, the learning experience can penetrate a participant's most stubborn defensives. Learning that appears as mere concepts in the classroom becomes painful reality on the battleground.

Take for example the battle of Antietam. Several days before the battle, a Union soldier planning to take a nap under a tree in the countryside discovered several cigars wrapped in a paper. The paper proved to be General Lee's battle plan. It was turned over to the head of the Union Army, General McClelland. Although McClelland first praised providence for the discovery of the enemy's plan, he soon began to mistrust the information. In an attempt to validate the plan, McClelland shared it with a number of people, including, unknown to him, a Confederate sympathizer.

Unable to validate the plan and fearing that he might act on falsified information, McClelland decided to take no immediate action. By the time McClelland decided to act on the information, it was too late. A Confederate sympathizer close to McClelland had already spread the word that Lee's plan was in Union hands. This story has been particularly impactful with combined groups of marketing and business leaders. Discussions emerged focusing not only on collecting competitor intelligence, but also on what to do with it.

Leadership Retreat Versus Field Trip

A good design will differentiate a leadership retreat from a field trip. The process involved is similar to designing other kinds of retreats. The first step is to work with the sponsor to determine the goals, objectives, and intended outcomes (Bolt, 1989). It is important to know your history. As you have these discussions with the potential sponsor, you can describe the historical events that will reinforce the goals and objectives. Sometimes the sponsor has an interest or is a student of the battle and will want to engage you in discussion. You have to know your history! At this meeting, you can also discuss integrating concepts from a leadership book or using a specific leadership development tool that can be reinforced by the battleground experience. For example, team assessment tools often work well because the team can take their analysis on the battleground and learn very graphically what happens when a team does not function well.

The High-Level Flow

Once you know the goals and objectives and you have picked your battle and the leadership concepts you want to reinforce, the next step is to create a high-level flow of the event. The actual number of days can vary greatly, depending on what you want to achieve. A quick staff ride can be accomplished in as little as half a day on most battlegrounds, or you could have an experience that is stretched out over several days, depending on the other elements you are planning for the retreat. The battleground portion of the experience can be compressed or spread out as well. In my view, spreading out the experience over several days is preferable for several reasons. Visits to battlegrounds can be an intense emotional experience for some people. Creating an emotional response can be good when it is channeled to support the goals and objectives of the retreat. However, the participants may need time to reflect and sort through their feelings. By dividing up the battleground portion of the retreat, you can provide time for reflection. Spacing the experience over several days also gives you the opportunity to introduce leadership concepts.

The basic pattern is to share the concepts with the group. Give them assignments to find examples of these concepts on the battleground. When the participants return to the meeting facility, debrief the experience, and then do more work, either individually or in small groups, to identify the examples and report out to the whole group. To illustrate this point, let's look at the high-level flow discussion that resulted at one of our retreats during the discussion of the taking of Burnside's Bridge. After the Union forces finally took the bridge and chased out the Confederate defenders, they proceeded to sit down and have coffee—during the midst of this ferocious battle. The order was to "take the bridge," and that is exactly what they did! The experience on the battlefield led to a discussion among the leadership group about setting objectives and expectations and how people live up to the expectations that are set for them. As they said, if expectations are set too low, then you may receive marginal or incomplete results. At the time of this retreat, this particular company was implementing a new performance management system, and this was an important discussion that secured the support of the leadership team.

After the high-level flow is developed, meet again with the sponsor and go over the event. Once you have approval, then pass the high-level flow on to the historian.

The Art and Discipline of History

It is very important to work with a professional historian on these types of retreats. While you are designing the flow of the retreat, the historian will take the same goals and objectives identified by the sponsor and find examples to illustrate them on the battleground. The "art" involved is to do this in a way that does not disrupt the chronology of the event. When the participants are on the battleground, they are learning how the battle unfolded and connecting with the specific events that reinforce the leadership concepts.

Once the historian has identified the key historical points, you merge your high-level flow with his or her work. The two of you reach agreement on the timing and produce the participant agenda. Coordination can be a challenge at these retreats, because you are moving physically to a number of different sites. It is very helpful to produce a separate agenda for the facilitators, which would have all of the details you would normally expect for each day of the event, including equipment needs, handouts, instructions for activities, and pick-up and drop-off times for the coach or van, among other things. A special feature of the facilitator's agenda should be a section for each day on the battleground that has questions and observations that the sponsor of the event can use to stimulate conversations. This helps the sponsor take a leadership role in the retreat.

The Power of Reflection

Building in opportunities for participants to reflect on what they have learned is extremely important for any type of experience-based retreat (Kimball, 2005). Much of the value in the retreat is the opportunity for participants to reflect on the historical events and derive relevancy to their own work and issues at their company. A couple of tools are used to promote this function. Participants take along a battleground journal that contains pages with probes to record their observations, insights, and applications. This is intended to help draw out their observations and guide their note-taking. Time is allotted while on the battleground to write in the journal. Since the participants usually have assignments to record observations related to key leadership concepts, much of their note-taking occurs around these concepts. As a facilitator, encourage as much writing and note-taking while on the site as possible. The notes are also used for their after-action reports.

After-Action Reports

The United States Army has used after-action reports since before the Civil War. The report is generally divided into three sections: the actions that were intended, what actions were taken, and what actually occurred. These reports are filed as soon as feasible after the conclusion of the event, and the reports are read and catalogued. In a recent National Public Radio (NPR) interview, it was reported that, in the days following the initial invasion of Bhagdad in the Iraq War, over 30,000 after-action reports were filed by U.S. military commanders. In this way, the lessons are preserved and can be transmitted to a next generation of leaders. The after-action report is a powerful too in translating military actions into future learning opportunities. The findings are summarized and sent to senior leadership for review. Later they are incorporated in revised training curriculum. In conducting a retreat, we often read directly from the after-action reports filed after the Civil War or World War II battles. This greatly increases the authenticity of the experience.

Participants at the retreat also create after-action reports. The report format has been modified for a learning experience and is sent to participants at least two weeks before the retreat. The reports are divided into four sections. The first summarizes the purpose of the retreat and the key objectives. The facilitator works with the business unit leader to capture this information. The second section is to be completed prior to the retreat. The participants record their learning goals and objectives. The facilitator works with the sponsoring business unit leader to form the appropriate questions, but often these address the issue of setting personal learning goals, leadership goals, and goals related to development of the organization. Participants are encouraged to look at their developmental plans and identify areas they want to work on at the retreat. The third section of the report is a record of their observations during the retreat. While this is completed after the retreat, participants are encouraged to take notes during the battleground experience to complete this section. In the fourth section, they record their lessons learned from the retreat.

The after-action reports are turned in to their immediate superior, who summarizes the lessons learned and submits the report to the retreat sponsor. The information from the reports can be used for updating personal development plans and group or team development plans, and is incorporated into talent management discussions. The summary reports can be compared against the objectives of the retreat and serve as an important measurement of its overall success. Action steps identified in the reports are monitored for completion in follow-up sessions that occur once a quarter.

At every retreat we have conducted, participants have come away from the experience with some personal learning that has influenced them in profound ways. Sometimes these insights occur and are voiced while on the battleground, and at other times they are written as part of the after-action reports. These are very positive experiences, but not the type that you can plan in your design. As is often the case, some of these unanticipated learning opportunities have created some of the greatest impact. We would like to share a few of these positive experiences, because they have been so memorable and because they illustrate how rich an experience this type of retreat can be.

When we do a retreat at Antietam, we cover two battles that lead up to this major battle: the Battle of South Mountain and the Battle of Harper's Ferry. It was while covering the battle of Harper's Ferry that an epiphany occurred with one of our leadership groups. Harper's Ferry had been the site of one of the Union Army's armories. The commander in charge of the garrison at Harper's Ferry in 1862 was a Colonel Miles. Earlier in the Civil War, he came close to being court marshaled because of dereliction of duty. Rather then remove him from the Army, they decided to find a spot for him where he could do no harm. Unfortunately, the Army leadership did not anticipate that the Confederacy would attack Harper's Ferry. Colonel Miles' actions were so inept that he was later described by the Army as an imbecile. The loss of Harper's Ferry resulted in the capture of 11,000 Union soldiers, 73 pieces of heavy artillery, and 13,000 small arms (Luvaas & Nelson, 1987). In this instance, after this history had been shared with the leadership group, they began to ask whether they too had found "safe" spots for people in their company, rather than move them out. For many of the participants, the experience led to a greater resolve and commitment to the company's performance and talent management process.

Another important personal learning that occurs almost every time we do the Gettysburg retreat is the story of one of the most promising Union generals, John Reynolds. General Reynolds decided to help position troops in the front line while riding his horse, rather than delegate this task to one of his junior officers. A Confederate sharpshooter shot him and he fell from his horse mortally wounded and died on the spot. This usually prompts a lot of discussion about the dangers of micro-management, but at one of our retreats it led to a discussion about the fact that none of the other Union generals, including his successor, knew his battle strategy. Back at the hotel, discussions were held about the importance of documentation and developing your successors.

Summary

In summary, retreats to battlegrounds can provide valuable opportunities for leaders to learn from the experience of others. The battles provide rich metaphors to explore a wide range of issues facing most organizations and to reinforce leadership and team concepts. Participants can have emotionally powerful experiences that can lead to real organizational and behavioral change. The keys to success are (1) to be clear about the objectives and goals of the retreat, (2) to create a high-level flow, (3) to work with a professional historian to lay out the history and choose the most relevant moments, (4) to develop a detailed agenda, and (5) to use tools such as journals and after-action reports to encourage reflection.

References

Bolt, J.F. (1989). *Executive development: A strategy for corporate competitiveness.* San Francisco: Executive Development Associates.

Kimball, R.O. (2005). Using experiential, action-oriented learning for executive development. In J.F. Bolt (Ed.), *The future of executive development.* San Francisco: Executive Development Associates.

Luvaas, J., & Nelson, H.W. (1986). *Guide to the Battle of Gettysburg: The U.S. Army War College guides to Civil War battles.* Lawrence, KS: University Press of Kansas.

Luvaas, J., & Nelson, H.W. (1987). *Guide to the Battle of Antietam: The U.S. Army War College guides to Civil War battles.* Lawrence, KS: University Press of Kansas.

McPherson, J. (2002). *Crossroads of freedom: Antietam (pivotal moments in American history).* New York: Oxford University Press.

Mark Whitmore, Ph.D., *has worked in the insurance and financial services industry for twenty-one years. He is the human resources operation executive at the Westfield Group in Westfield Center, Ohio. In this position, Dr. Whitmore supports compensation, benefits, and HR systems, as well as leadership development and succession planning. He has led many retreats to Civil War and World War II battlegrounds such as Gettysburg, Antietam, and the D-Day beaches at Normandy. Dr. Whitmore received his Ph.D. in industrial organizational psychology from The Ohio State University. He has made numerous presentations and has published articles in the areas of early identification of emerging leaders, personality correlates of leadership, and the effectiveness of leadership development programs.*

Harold W. Nelson, *Brigadier General, U.S. Army (Retired), is a professional historian with particular expertise in the American Civil War. A veteran with thirty-two years of active service, he was the chief of military history from 1989 to 1994 and has taught history and strategy at the U.S. Military Academy, the U.S. Army Staff College, and the U.S. Army War College. As a practicing historian, General Nelson has been instrumental in developing techniques for interpreting military battlegrounds. He has written several books, including battlefield guides to Gettysburg, Antietam, and Chancellorville. General Nelson received his M.A. and Ph.D. degrees in history from the University of Michigan.*

The Role of Peer-to-Peer Networks in Personal and Professional Development

Michael Dulworth and Joseph A. Forcillo

Summary

The authors present evidence that personal and professional networks are an effective, but underutilized, learning method for leadership development. They recommend conducting a self-assessment of the current strengths of an individual's existing network and include a simple, but effective, assessment tool. An overview of network-based learning and its value is followed by an in-depth description of one type of network that the authors' research suggests can be particularly useful—peer-to-peer networks. They summarize findings from their research on the different types of value provided by this type of network, including several case studies that illustrate the personal and organizational impact of network-based learning.

In order to accelerate your personal and professional effectiveness, "relationships" must become a much bigger part of your development plan. That means you need to leverage your networks more than ever before. In a 2003 *MIT/Sloan Management Review* article, "The Social Side of Performance," Cross found that "What really distinguishes high performers from the rest of the pack is their ability to maintain and leverage personal networks. The most effective create and tap large, diversified networks that are rich in experience and span all organizational boundaries" (p. 23).

In a business environment of unprecedented and rapid change, it's no wonder that executives across industries are finding that strong personal and professional networks are an increasingly essential contributor to their own development and effectiveness.

Strong networks, properly used, can help you navigate rapid change in a number of ways, including broadening the breadth and depth of your exposure and access to expertise across a myriad of issues. Effective investments in and use of your networks make you smarter, more knowledgeable, and better grounded, as well as a more agile learner and collaborator overall. These capabilities are critical to solving problems and leveraging opportunities at the pace necessary for success today.

Before making significant investments in network-based learning, we suggest here an approach for helping you better understand the strengths and weaknesses of your existing network and provide you an overview of the opportunities for more effectively using network-based learning. We focus in particular on one type of network that we have significant expertise with—peer-to-peer networks—and share findings from preliminary research that indicates a range of high-value impacts. Our research suggests a general framework for assessing value of network-based learning and includes several case studies. Armed with this information, you'll be better equipped to make informed decisions on the potential use of network-based learning for your specific situation.

Network-Based Learning

An enormous amount of research exists on the two major types of learning currently utilized by most organizations: structured learning (university courses, executive development, coaching, etc.) and on-the-job learning (day-to-day learning, stretch assignments, etc.). However, there is a third, far less systematically used and less studied learning method, called network-based learning. This type of learning is that which occurs in forums (online, in-person, meetings, etc.), where participants or peers share experiences, knowledge, and best practices and often also provide each other support and guidance.

One type of network—peer-to-peer networks—offers particularly significant learning benefits because we tend to learn better, trust more, and gravitate to the shared experiences of people at our level or in circumstances similar to ours. When you are among people with the same challenges, successes, issues, and problems, you increase the likelihood that you'll more rapidly benefit from exposure to the way they think, the problems they've solved, the mistakes they've made, and the people they know.

Peer-to-peer networks take many forms, including those designed to provide executives with a rich and low-pressure forum for exploring issues, weighing options, and probing potential solutions. Such executive forums are fast becoming a critical component for busy executives who need to connect with their peers more regularly and more deeply. Peer-to-peer networks are also for professionals across a broad spectrum of corporate levels—whether you're relatively early in your career in a junior capacity or further along, with more seniority and experience.

What Is Your NQ?

It's clear that today's highly networked business world provides rich rewards for networking maestros—those among us who are skilled at developing varied and effective networks. Having a single measure of your ability to develop strong networks—what we call your networking quotient (NQ)—is crucial in developing effective personal networks. Which begs an important question: Can we create a way to measure your NQ, just as IQ measures your intelligence quotient? We think so. What's more, we argue that one of your first priorities should be to create such a measure in order to chart an accurate roadmap for developing more effective networks.

Let's break the general topic of networking into two key components. The first is comprised of your networking universe, which consists of three primary types of networks: (1) life network, (2) social network, and (3) work network. Each one of these plays a role in determining your NQ. Your *life network* is made up of your family, extended family, your school friends and contacts, all your lifelong friends, and many others. Your *social network* is made up of your active friends (people you see at least once a month), people from your church, fellow club members, neighbors, contacts in online communities, and so forth. Your *work network* includes contacts from previous jobs, colleagues from other firms, contacts in your current organization, mentors/coaches, and others.

Second, before you begin to calculate your NQ, think about three important factors: (1) the number of people in your various networks, (2) the depth of your relationships with those people, and (3) how often you interact with them. Quantity matters (the more people in your networks the better), but quality is just as important (is the person an *acquaintance*—he knows who you are and will probably return a call; a *personal contact*—she'll do you a favor if asked; or a *close friend*—someone you can always count on when the chips are down).

So how can you quickly assess your NQ? Honestly answer the following questions on a scale of 0 to 4:

1. How many total people are in your life, social, and work networks?

   0 = none, 1 = fewer than 50, 2 = 51 to 100, 3 = 101 to 200, 4 = more than 200

2. What's the overall quality of your network contacts?

   0 = Terrible, 1 = Poor, 2 = Good, 3 = Very Good, 4 = Excellent

3. To what extent do you actively work on building your network relationships?

   0 = not at all, 1 = a little, 2 = some, 3 = great extent, 4 = very great extent

4. What is the strength of your relationships with your network members?

   0 = very weak, 1 = weak, 2 = in between weak and strong, 3 = strong,
   4 = very strong

5. How actively do you recruit new members to your network?

   0 = do nothing, 1 = hardly do anything, 2 = sometimes, 3 = often,
   4 = all the time

6. To what extent is the relationship with your network members reciprocal, that is, you've helped them as much as they've helped you?

   0 = not at all, 1 = hardly at all, 2 = sometimes, 3 = often, 4 = all the time

7. To what extent do you leverage the Internet to build and maintain your networks?

   0 = not at all, 1 = hardly at all, 2 = sometimes, 3 = often, 4 = all the time

Multiply your total score by 10. You'll end up with a score between 0 and 280. If your score is from 0 to 70, your NQ is terrible; from 71 to 140, your NQ needs improvement; from 141 to 210, your NQ is good; and from 211 to 280, your NQ is excellent.

So how did you do? Are you a networking neophyte or a world-class contender? Does this self-assessment point to some areas you might want to work on to improve your NQ? No matter how you scored, you can always get better.

Tim Sanders, chief solutions officer at Yahoo, said it best: "All of your knowledge won't amount to much if you don't have a network of people to share it with and enough compassion for the people in that network to understand that your success is a direct result of their success."

The Role of Peer-to-Peer Networks in Your Learning Strategy

Now that you have assessed your own networking skills, it makes sense to more closely examine the potential of network-based learning to fill any existing gaps in your developmental process. Our goal is to make peer-to-peer networks a more understood and used learning and development method, so as to close that gap and accelerate leadership development.

One of the reasons for the effectiveness of peer-to-peer networks is that they create a more secure, open environment that helps accelerate learning and development. The network becomes a safe harbor for executives to more freely discuss issues and challenges of individual and organizational importance with peers who have very similar positions and responsibilities. In this type of low-risk forum, leaders feel far less pressure to be "the expert" and can more openly ask questions and search for answers without the political and emotional weight often present when discussing these issues within their own organizations.

Objectives of peer-to-peer networks can include:

- Sharing knowledge, experience, and wisdom among the members (their collective intelligence), broadening perspectives, and developing new and leading-edge ideas

- Being able to ask for and quickly obtain advice, ideas, information, and support from trusted peers

- Identifying common areas of interest and developing plans and programs to explore those areas

- Presenting and addressing individual member problems by using other members as "consultants"

- Influencing and advancing state-of-the-art practice in one's field or profession

How Does a Peer–to–Peer Network Work?

Peer-to-peer networks can take a multitude of forms. They often include components such as these:

1. *Meetings*—There are typically several meetings each year. Meetings might include the following elements:

    - An in-depth profile of an individual member company

    - A theme chosen by the members for discussion, including an outside speaker as a catalyst for deep dialogue

    - Pure networking time, during which each person has the opportunity to present things he or she is working on that might be of interest to the group and/or to obtain ideas, support, and recommendations

2. *Websites*—Private websites for communicating and networking among members between face-to-face meetings. Members could send out emails to all network members to inquire about some issue or gather information of particular interest.

3. *Teleconferences*—Members networking, supported by regularly scheduled teleconferences on topics of specific interest.

Interview with Etienne Wenger—Researcher, Author, and Lecturer— Communities of Practice (CoP)

What is the developmental value of peer-to-peer networks?

"I think that there is a shift happening in the world today where people are starting to recognize that, in fact, peer-to-peer interactions are one of the keys to learning, not only for professionals but for people in general. It is certainly the key to learning, not only for institutions but for professionals. Because when you have a peer-to-peer network, you hear the story of someone else who is in a similar situation to yours, so there is almost an immediate validity to what you are hearing because you recognize that this person faces the same problems.

"In terms of learning, actually the concept of community of practice came out of studies of apprenticeship, during which we noticed that most of the learning happened among apprentices at different levels of advancement—and not so much from the master. There is something about hearing the words of someone who is a peer that makes the relevance of the knowledge that you receive very immediate. So for me, that is the fundamental value proposition of a peer-to-peer network."

Can you give an example of how a company has used the concept of peer-to-peer networking as a core learning method or approach?

"Many companies today establish peer-to-peer networks as a way to manage their knowledge assets, and part of that strategy is the development of people. The thing about a community of practice is that it does not really distinguish between developing people and developing knowledge assets, because the community itself acts as a living knowledge asset. For example, Chrysler has various car platforms—small cars, big cars, minivans, etc.—where they have cross-cutting communities of practice among designers who are designing similar parts. In many ways, the design of brakes for the minivan is different from that of a small car, but they are similar enough that CoPs are a good mechanism for joint learning. Chrysler has not gotten rid of the training department; in fact, they have an agreement between the community and the training department that when something that the community discussed is well established they hand it over to the training department."

So, for example, you wouldn't use a community of practice to teach the fundamentals of Word, but if you were trying to become a real expert in Word, is using a CoP to listen and interact with others, to share how the program is used to accomplish some more complex objective, a good way to learn?

"It is. If you think about the people in Executive Development Associate's Executive and Leadership Development Network, they come to that network for advanced discussion, not to answer basic questions on executive education . . . and they want to hear stuff like 'What is your learning edge?' They want to hear from another person with a similar level of experience. There are hundreds of companies today that have taken this approach, but they have come more from the knowledge management side and not so much from the education side. For example, many companies like Procter & Gamble really nurture quite formal communities of practice across their business units to do product development. But for most companies that have a community of practice initiative, the goal is really knowledge management."

What Is the Value of Peer-to-Peer Networks?

In the research recently conducted by the authors, peer network members said that the networks they belong to are an extremely valuable developmental experience, producing tangible benefits from a personal and career perspective, plus producing significant organizational benefits. Examples of this value include:

1. Accelerating innovation

2. Reducing risk

3. Improving the use of resources

4. Improving quality

5. Improving executive effectiveness and job satisfaction

6. Advancing the field

Accelerating Innovation

The speed of global change and the increasing demands of global competition require corporations to accelerate their own pace of innovation and improvement, as both a defensive and an offensive strategy in their markets. Networks provide a way to accelerate innovation in human capital management, which then creates the foundation for accelerating the innovation capability of the corporation as a whole. Dr. Richard O'Leary, director of human resources, science and technology, at Corning, commented, "One of the key impacts of my network is in accelerating the speed with which you can get things done. It has accelerated the speed of our executive development work" (personal communication).

In some cases, network members experience this on a very personal basis, in terms of their ability to save precious hours or even days of their own time accessing information on best practices. As Deborah Swanson, national director of talent and organization development for Sony Electronics, noted "I was recently requested to help find a highly credible consultant to facilitate a national sales strategy session. I was able to send a request to the network for recommendations and personal references and was able to do in a few hours what would have taken a week of my time to research" (personal communication).

Reducing Risk

As several network participants have told us, one of the values of their network is not only the knowledge that they gain about best practices, but the opportunity to avoid "worst practices." As in life in general, corporate failures are often as instructive as successes.

The strong level of trust established between network members provides a high level of openness in their dialogue that allows members to share failures so that the entire group can learn from them and brainstorm ways to avoid them.

Improving the Use of Resources

Efficiency has always been important, but withering global competition makes cost control and reduction increasingly critical for business survival and success. Members often find that networks reduce their costs and improve their use of resources in a variety of ways. First, it decreases their reliance on expensive consulting resources by providing them essentially free consulting from a network of their peers. When members do need to use consultants, they avoid costs due to poor vendor selection by having other network members assist them in pooling their experiences with a wide range of vendors.

In addition to these savings, their companies also reap both cost and revenue improvements from the greater effectiveness of adopted best practices. Chuck Presbury, senior director of leadership development for The McGraw-Hill Companies, recounted one example of how his participation in a network enabled him to save several million dollars on one decision alone: "At my previous firm, we were in the early stages of designing a large-scale executive and leadership development process. The COO of the firm was willing to build a physical facility (similar to GE Crotonville) as a focal point for the initiative. I posed this question to the network and the resounding answer was 'Don't do it!' The experience of companies who had such facilities advised that it was too expensive, time-consuming, and would be a distraction from the core mission. The advice was to focus this money on the programs, processes, and people, not on a building. We took this advice and saved an estimated $2 million or more in capital expenditures alone" (personal communication).

Improving Quality

One of the major benefits of network membership is the impact it has on corporate quality. For example, at a recent network meeting, the head of executive development for a major U.S. bank said that she was recently charged with developing a coaching process for the bank. She described the current coaching process as the "Wild, Wild West of Coaching," saying that there were no coaching standards, metrics, hiring criteria, or pricing guidelines currently in place at the bank. In other words, the bank had an out-of-control process with no quality management.

She said that her firm was spending millions on external coaches and that no one had any idea who these coaches were or what value the bank (which was paying for the coaches) was receiving from the coaching engagements. After she recounted this situation to her network peers, two colleagues spoke up and said that they had very recently been in the exact same situation and had spent the last six months putting together comprehensive coaching processes for their companies . . . and they'd be happy to email their completed plans. In addition to the immediate cost savings of $100,000 to $200,000 that this information would have cost to replicate internally, such sharing undoubtedly improved the quality of the solution.

Improving Executive Effectiveness and Job Satisfaction

Belonging to a network benefits executives personally and professionally in a number of ways. They develop strong professional relationships and friendships with true peers in other leading companies—people with similar problems, opportunities, and challenges. There's significant comfort knowing that you have a group of trusted and objective colleagues you can call on when you need help, advice, and support. Beyond the individual level, members and their companies benefit from tapping into what other leading companies are thinking, planning, and doing. As Ray Vigil, vice president and chief learning officer of Humana, noted, "I have found networks to be invaluable to me on a number of occasions, such as conducting best-practice exercises, sharing new and innovative programs, dialoguing with some of the best thought leaders in the field, and gaining valuable input on program design and effectiveness. . . . I consider participation as one of my 'must do' activities in my annual personal development and planning" (personal communication).

Advancing the Field

Networks provide a way of pooling members and experts' intellectual resources to address longer-range challenges of the profession and contribute to the development of their field as a whole. We call these "next practices."

What Is the ROI of Participation in a Peer-to-Peer Network?

As these numerous examples demonstrate, the ROI of a high-quality network can be significant, often as high as 10 to 100 times their investment. Not surprisingly, some of the network members we interviewed stated that a small increase in their time investment into the network often significantly increased their ROI. One way of calculating ROI can be expressed with the following formula:

Learning (best practices) + Problem Solving + Benchmarking
+ Career Support/Membership Fee + Meeting Attendance +
Time Associated with Other Network Interaction = ROI

A critical component of ROI for time-pressed leaders is the speed of the payback that benefits their day-to-day work.

High-quality peer networks provide an extremely powerful developmental experience from a personal and career perspective that is best articulated by participants themselves. To highlight these personal and business outcomes in more detail, we include two interviews with peer network members. We asked these members to recount their experiences and the benefits of participation in a peer-to-peer network.

Interview with Chuck Presbury, Senior Director, Leadership Development, The McGraw-Hill Companies, Inc.

"The peer network that I belong to means a lot to me. I get a renewed sense of 'why we do this work' from every meeting. The network also stimulates my thinking—how people are utilizing different applications, applying different thought processes, etc. I always learn a lot; it's so very different than reading about an idea.

"A great way to learn is via stories, and the network is all about storytelling. People describe experiences in such a way that I gain a fuller understanding of how the firm's culture, strategy, internal dynamics, and behind-the-scene politics affect an outcome. These are the 'real-life' stories, not something that has been filtered for public consumption.

"I use the email-based capability within the network to help solve immediate problems. I also watch the traffic between members to pick up on trends and emerging issues that I need to be aware of to perform my job effectively.

"In terms of the benefits my company gets from my membership in the peer network, the list is long and varied. First of all, my company has access to best practices and 'next practices' from other leading companies. They also receive what I call 'on-the-fly' benchmarking. Once, I put together a benchmarking study via the network in six days with fifteen companies. That is really a time-to-value accelerator.

"In addition, I believe my network membership did a lot to help position my previous company as an innovator and employer of choice. Through the network, positive word got out describing what the firm was doing in the areas of executive and leadership development, and I think this helped our recruitment of talented executives.

"Finally, I believe the elements of a successful peer-to-peer network are

- Focus of the network (same job function, area of interest, etc.)
- Matching of members (job level, organization size, people who are open to sharing and learning)
- Variety of venues and channels for information exchange
- Ability to create close, personal relationships with other network members
- Responsiveness of network members to requests for information or guidance"

Interview with Val Markos, Executive Director, Leadership Development, BellSouth Corporation

"I have learned a lot from my peers in the peer network of which I'm a member. I started in the network when I was new to this job, and the more senior people in the network really helped me out a great deal. They broadened my horizon intellectually, while at the same time providing very practical advice and guidance, such as how large classroom sizes should be, who were the best faculty and consultants, etc. I have been in this network for over twelve years, which really attests to how valuable it is for me. It was a critical component to my success early on in this job, and it continues to be a very dynamic place to learn and to share experiences that are very relevant to my job today.

"I really value the face-to-face meetings, which include in-depth discussions on critical topics of importance to executive development professionals. This is one of the primary ways I keep up on trends and innovations, especially since I cannot attend as many conferences as in the past because of budget restrictions. And the electronic capability (email discussion groups) provides for very quick turnaround on questions I need answers for. For example, recently I was asked to gauge where other companies were on an issue of importance to our board of directors, and they needed this information in a matter of days. I was able to tap into the network electronically, and within forty-eight hours I had six responses, when normally it might take up to six weeks to gather this type of information. These are career defining moments, and the network really helped make me look like a star.

"The benefits that my company has derived, in addition to what I've already covered, include:

- Who's the best faculty to use in executive and leadership development programs
- Guidance on how to structure action learning processes or other learning methods
- Advice on the best learning management systems
- How to evaluate and assess individuals

"Essentially, my membership in the network has led to *enlightened decisions.* I've been able to learn from the experiences of others, and this has helped us not make the same mistakes. We've also learned from the success of others. In addition, my staff has benefited from listening to the teleconferences that are periodically held on topics of interest to the network members and from accessing the archive of documents from the members and the meetings.

"I believe the success criteria for a peer-to-peer network include:

- A broad participation base, that is, diversity. It needs to be large enough, with good industry and geographic participation.
- Someone needs to actively manage and monitor the network.
- You need face-to-face exposure to other members. The electronic stuff is great, but it is much more successful if it is built on strong personal bonds and the type of trust that can only be established with direct contact with the other network members.

"Basically, the network is only as valuable as you make it . . . you get out of it what you put into it."

Conclusion: The Future of Peer-to-Peer Networks

The challenges facing today's organizations are great. New ways of organizing and leveraging knowledge, learning "on-the-fly," and fostering continuous innovation will be at the forefront of business success. Peer-to-peer networks, in both external and internal forms, hold a great deal of promise for helping organizations adapt to and take advantage of the rapid changes taking place internally within their businesses and externally within their business environments.

An increasing number of forward-thinking senior executives tell us that the ability to network will be an increasingly important skill for leaders in their organizations in the future and that developing powerful external networks will be critical to both the success of individual leaders and to their enterprises. These trends suggest that smart investments in improving your networking quotient and improving the size and quality of your networks are not only necessary, but will be rewarding both personally and professionally.

Reference

Cross, M. (2003). The social side of performance. *Sloan Management Review*, p. 23.

Michael Dulworth *is the managing director of Executive Development Associates, Inc. Before joining EDA, Mr. Dulworth was a vice president at The Concours Group, responsible for the firm's learning services practice. Prior to that, he was chairman and CEO of Learning Technologies Group, Inc. (LTG). Mr. Dulworth has also held* *senior positions at Insync Corporation, The Conference Board, Sirota & Alper Associates, and the U.S. General Accounting Office. LTG won the gold medal for online training from the NewMedia Invision Awards in 1999, and Mr. Dulworth was named one of the top 100 multimedia producers by AV/Multimedia Producer in 1998. Insync was awarded the HR Product of the Year Award by HR Executive in 1991. Mr. Dulworth has a bachelor's degree and a master's degree, with a concentration in organizational behavior, from the University of Southern California . He is the author of* Corporate Learning: Proven and Practical Guidelines for Building a Sustainable Learning Strategy *(Pfeiffer, 2005).*

Joseph A. Forcillo *is president of Forcillo Associates (www.forcillo.com), a research, education, and consulting firm based in Grosse Pointe, Michigan. His firm provides solutions to Fortune 500 companies and other organizations in the areas of strategic innovation, competitive value management, network-based learning, and leadership development. Mr. Forcillo holds a B.A. from St. Louis University and a master's from the University of Michigan. He has previously contributed to* Human Capital *magazine and was a contributing author to* Corporate Learning *(Pfeiffer, 2005).*

Introduction
to the Special Challenges
and Opportunities Section

In this section, we present a series of formidable challenges and opportunities that we practitioners face, such as gaining top management buy-in, developing global leaders, assessing and developing high-potentials, on-boarding, ROI, and making sure that what is learned is actually applied back on the job and has a business impact.

Getting Management Buy-In

Engaging the Board and Executive Team in Talent Development, by Annmarie Neal and Eve Dreher

Gaining Management Buy-In: Responding to Unspoken Needs, by Charles Presbury

Developing Global Leaders

Preparing Leaders for the New Competitive Landscape: New Mindsets for New Games, by Gordon Hewitt

Developing Global Leaders: The Critical Role of Dilemma Reconciliation, by Fons Trompenaars and Peter Woolliams

Identifying and Developing High-Potentials

Evaluating Leadership Potential: A Practitioner's Guide, by Val Markos

Identifying and Developing High-Potentials: An Executive Perspective, by Nicole Drake

On-Boarding, ROI, Learning from Experience, and Putting Learning to Work

Successful On-Boarding, by William J. Morin

ROI Comes in Many Forms: Leadership Development
at Baker Hughes Incorporated, by Barbara Reyna

Learning from Experience: Easier Said Than Done,
by Vijay Govindarajan and Chris Trimble

Put Learning to Work, by Andrew McK. Jefferson

Getting Management Buy-In

Engaging the Board and Executive Team in Talent Development

Annmarie Neal and Eve Dreher

Summary

In many companies, analysts, shareholders, and board members are paying close attention to how companies are managing and developing executive talent. We've consulted with several CEOs and senior executives on this issue and are continually surprised and pleased to see that the issues regarding the dearth of good leaders are both understood and felt. CEOs are staying awake at night worrying about how they are going to develop and deploy leaders who can grow and manage their businesses.

Effectively managing this interest, and turning it into true engagement, is key to the success of a well-integrated talent development strategy. In this article, we've provided an overview of some of the most pressing talent development challenges, as well as some ideas and contemporary practices to help engage executives and boards of directors in this important strategic priority.

Strong leadership talent is one of a short list of factors that can truly differentiate good business performance from great. And while acquiring and developing this talent has never been more consequential, it has also never been more complicated. The need to manage talent on a global scale, often at sites in offshore locations, has created increasingly perplexing challenges such as disperse team management and the need to manage effectively around diverse cultures and customs. Every leader, whether or not he or she personally manages global operations, is operating in a global corporate environment.

Why This Matters Now

Successfully navigating in this fast-paced, increasingly global corporate climate requires "horizon leaders," individuals able to see around the corner, understand where the business should go, and with the skill and experience to build and lead an organization. And while finding leaders with these qualities is already inherently difficult, it is further complicated by demographic trends that continue to demonstrate a growing shortage of available leaders. Competition and demand for a shrinking pool of these "horizon leaders" is increasingly intense.

It's no wonder that the way companies are developing and cultivating the next generation of leaders is a top concern for CEOs, senior executives, and company boards of directors. Strong, capable leaders are the basis of a company's ability to create value and compete in the marketplace. In 2004, the Conference Board published a study on CEO challenges that confirmed that "talent-related issues are on the minds of today's CEOs. Leadership, succession, talent identification, and growth all appear important to CEOs with long-range views" (p. 7).

Phase I: Setting the Stage

Aligning talent development to the company's strategic, operational, and financial planning process is absolutely essential to engaging members of the executive team or board. It is the crux of a true engagement strategy.

The significance of this alignment cannot be underestimated. Corporate strategy must be the starting point of all talent discussions. Any forecast of human capital needs must be made in the direct support of strategy. In essence, the question to ask is, "What organizational capability and capacity do I need in order to successfully execute on company strategy?"

Make sure you fully assess and appreciate the attributes and demands of the lifecycle that your organization is working within in order to accurately determine what talent capabilities you have and need. An accurate assessment of what cycle you are in—growth, emerging, mature, or turnaround—will determine how quickly you can move and what your most effective tactics will be. For example, in one of our consulting projects, we were working with a client who found his business in a turnaround situation due to competitive pressures. In this instance, to support the needs of that lifecycle, he needed talent with proven turnaround experience that could build operational and management efficiency quickly.

Regardless of the lifecycle, your main emphasis must always be on solving for business problems and on aligning closely with operational strategy. Create a strong partnership with strategy teams within the organization, making each of your agendas the agenda of the other. Common intent, common purpose, and common alignment

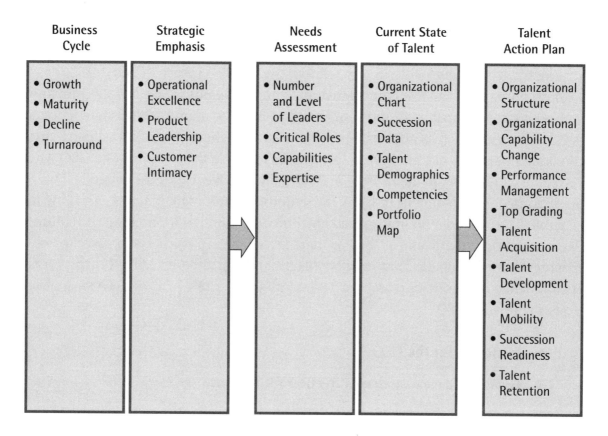

Figure 1. Strategic Talent Management

are integral. Successfully engaging your executive team and board is much more effective when everything you do starts with and is anchored around strategy, as shown in Figure 1.

Know Your CEO

To effectively engage your CEO, you must know your CEO—psychologically, emotionally, and operationally. Consider carefully what your CEO is really capable of and ready for. Be realistic. Sometimes that means your short-term goal can't be hitting best-in-class benchmarks. Your focus needs to be on taking the CEO with you to the next level, at a pace that he or she is capable of and comfortable with.

Clearly understanding where you are starting from and what you want to accomplish is primary to forming an effective phased-in plan. Slow and steady progress is still progress, and it can lead to real change. We worked with a senior executive who stated that he considered all talent development programs "a lot of overhead." While it took him over a year to really get where we needed him to be, when he did get there, he became the driving force propelling talent development forward. Over the course of that year, we took every opportunity to educate and provoke his thinking on the issue. Today, this executive considers the talent agenda critical to strategy execution and a key part of his CEO's agenda. The turning point was when the executive realized that he couldn't achieve his aggressive growth strategy without the people in place to help him.

Any competent CEO is intent on creating competitive advantage for the company. Link your efforts to that goal, and your CEO will begin to appreciate that talent development is as essential as any strategic move made on the business chessboard. And you don't necessarily need to have a strong talent legacy in the company or a CEO who just naturally drives the talent agenda. It is okay to have a "good enough" CEO in place, someone who understands the importance of building talent and is willing to be guided and coached on how to lead and embed talent development in the culture. Passive support is sufficient, as long as there is a continuous process in place for improving the leadership capabilities of people over time at all levels of the organization. The following questions, as presented by Jim Bolt (Bolt, 1989, p. 215), are a great place to start with your CEO.

Critical Questions for the CEO

- Have I set a clear strategic direction for my company?

- Am I committed to seriously using executive development as one way to strengthen my corporation?

- Am I willing to listen to the recommendations generated by my senior management team, take them seriously, and act on them, as appropriate?

- Am I willing to invest my time and energy in participating in the design and implementation of the program?

- Am I willing to participate in the entire program?

Find Your CFO

Another key partner in this work is the CFO. Rather than creating the talent agenda in isolation, engage the CFO to help identify what the most pressing issue for the business is. In the case of one CFO we worked with, the identified issue was adding shareholder value. As a result, we focused all action learning activities on business levers that directly affected shareholder value. In this example, the activities were focused on designing a competitive international strategy that used brand extension and pricing to aggressively compete with a global giant. As a result of this work, the company was better positioned in the global market and experienced increased revenues.

Make the CFO team part of the process and the solution. Be prepared to present integrated talent management as a long-term, financially mandatory investment. Defend your case like a businessperson. Use a financial planning model, and all of the related language, to communicate and forecast your talent strategy. One effective practice we've used is to adopt the language usually associated with financial investment portfolios and present the talent agenda using a portfolio management approach. Keep in mind, when you're seeking funding, that it takes time to sell such a costly initiative and that it's a long-term deal. Be flexible enough to execute in stages that immediately add value and can be de-coupled in times of financial constraints.

Another extremely effective tactic we've used is to have the CFO serve as the executive sponsor of the leadership development initiative. In one case, we selected the CFO because our global development strategy was tightly aligned to her CFO agenda, which was about building stronger leaders. She opened her organization to pilot early versions of development programs and then served as a sounding board on how to take the programs beyond her organization. We met her where her greatest needs and pain were, and we partnered with her to find solutions that helped her *and* the entire organization. A secondary benefit of her sponsorship was that she controlled the company checkbook. Time after time, she proved her commitment by finding ways to fund development when other programs were at risk.

Across the Board

Corporate boards are increasingly demanding more rigorous succession and development plans—and not just for the CEO. The new focus is not on replacement planning, that is, planning for who will fill specific key jobs that come open. Instead, it is on ensuring that companies have the bench strength to execute on the company's long-term business strategy and on developing leaders with the values and culture of the company.

Wall Street, fueled by a new regulatory and legal environment, has put increased pressure on boards to oversee the true financial health of publicly held companies. This pressure has resulted in increased scrutiny, by both Wall Street and the boards themselves, on leadership and talent issues. Analysts are increasingly critical (and their assessments have real influence on stock price) of organizations that lack deep leadership and management capability. The quarterly push to meet Wall Street expectations, or the "quarterly trap," can be an obstacle. Short-term thinking relative to leadership talent must be overcome by presenting talent development as an investment and as a process of building long-term competitive advantage.

Many boards are demanding a non-traditional approach. They recognize that it's passé to approach talent in terms of filling a position or increasing training. Acceleration pools, or pools of many potential successors for a variety of senior-level jobs, are needed to build greater organizational depth. The landscape is far different from that of two or three decades ago, and it requires more creative, more aggressive, and more flexible approaches. Sophisticated boards are wise to this; they are more educated than before, and more demanding of real results. In short—boards are on this issue.

Engage the board by using them as a partner and a lever. Create informal interaction between the board and senior leaders so that board members can make their own assessments. Encourage them to provide constructive challenges and input. Boards can bring their CEO experiences to your CEO and can be a good sounding board and resource on talent and succession issues. They should hold the CEO ultimately accountable to shareholders for leadership development. And most importantly, involve the board, while they're developing annual CEO objectives, to make sure succession and talent development actions are a part of business performance goals.

Phase II: Making Real Engagement Happen

Culture Impact

Once you have closely aligned to strategy, and your executives are on board, embedding your talent strategy into the culture can have a lasting impact on your success moving forward. Leadership development should be front and center to any culture change work. Don't think about leadership development as training, but as a culture-change lever that can be an appropriate and effective tool for the CEO and executive team to use to enroll and empower the organization. Manage the culture and values in a way that emphasizes the right messages around leadership, unity, direction, ethics, operational discipline, and fiscal responsibility. By using culture work to emphasize the strategic, integral nature of talent development, you will be building the support necessary to truly make talent management part of your company's operational fiber.

Human Resources as Business Partner

Human resources (HR) can play a crucial role in engaging the company's executive team. To accomplish this, the HR leader needs to move away from thinking and behaving like a transactional HR generalist. All HR work, and especially talent development work, needs to be done within a business framework and executed on with a complementary HR skill set. In day-to-day development consultation, HR should use the language of the business, link solutions to organizational strategy, and present in terms of operational and financial benefits. In short, company and shareholder value must drive every HR decision and tactic.

It is easy for executives to see talent development as an HR responsibility, because HR professionals are uniquely positioned to have a rich perspective on the skills and potential of the talent in their organizations. The responsibility for talent development, however, is really shared among executives, leadership, the board of directors, and HR. How do you build in natural accountability after the succession planning process and keep executives engaged moving forward? This is where the HR business manager in the field can play a role; he or she can help bring expectations alive in the business with work that is clearly aligned with and supportive of executive goals. Human resources is at greatest risk of failure when they don't have strong linkage and partnership and a concrete, complementary, and fully integrated talent plan. It is the true strategic HR business partner who understands this.

The senior talent officer of the company is not only a developer of people, but also a salesperson of the talent agenda. The priority for the person in this role must be to ensure that talent is at the forefront of the board's, executive team's, and CEO's agendas. Nothing is more vital to its ultimate success! And when the talent agenda has achieved primary importance to this group, it can greatly benefit the company's competitive advantage.

And what's your answer to the question, Who owns talent? The entire organization does, including the board of directors. Thought leaders in talent management are recognizing that being a good talent developer will be a critical competency for all leaders in the years to come.

Phase III: Results

Measure What Matters

One of the biggest mistakes people make is to use training measures to prove the success of talent initiatives. It is a rare CEO who engages readily around training measurement and doesn't ask, "How will it benefit the business?" Our advice is to use operational training measures sparingly. Instead, adopt business measures to illustrate success. In this way, you analyze your work in terms of ROE, or return on expectations. Ask, "What impact did we expect to have?" and "How did we do?" This is the measurement code to crack.

Qualify and quantify—and do this against what's necessary for the business. We had a senior marketing professional as a client who participated in an executive development offering on pricing strategy. After attending this session, he overhauled his pricing strategy, resulting in a $20 million revenue increase. Traditionally, a company would never have measured that revenue increase in a development context, but in a business context, this revenue increase would clearly be counted.

Measurement should monitor strategic impact, not just operational effectiveness. By directly linking pay and performance management to strategic impact, all leaders will have a built-in financial incentive to actively support development. This incentive will help support the shift in accountability from HR to the business.

Tell the Story

By this point, you've built your key relationships and the business case for the talent agenda, all aligned around execution of the strategy. Now how do you tell your story?

One contemporary practice we've implemented is the "talent annual report." By using the language of the business in a familiar, professional format similar to the company's annual report, you create instant credibility around your message. By creating the report year after year, you set deeply ingrained expectations. You also get the board's attention and make sure you stay on the board's agenda. By presenting the best possible report card—as an annual report is—you also have an opportunity to document and demonstrate progress. And with the annual report, you truly engage the "shareholder," which in this case extends to include all of the leadership and potential leadership talent. Begin with your letter to shareholders, as all annual reports do, to engage and invite the entire company to solve for the company's talent and development challenges.

Another effective tactic we've used is making talent a standing item on one CEO's quarterly satellite broadcast to all employees. He uses this forum to send a company-wide message that talent is a real priority of his. Even better, this CEO mentions talent every time he mentions strategy, no matter what the forum.

Beyond using specialized communication vehicles like this, use any communication channel available to drive the importance of leadership development home. Use interviews and case studies, share success stories, and talk up individual efforts whenever possible. Take every opportunity to communicate throughout the company what the executive teams, collectively and individually, are doing around talent. Be both local and global with your messages and your means. Put the issue on your line managers' agendas. Communicate formally and informally. Be creative. But even more importantly, be consistent.

Conclusion

Truly engaging your executive team and your board is crucial to talent development. Look for these signs of success:

- The CEO, executive team, board of directors, and human resources embrace and *share* responsibility (financial, strategic, and operational) for talent development.

- The board of directors is actively involved in the talent and leadership development agenda.

- Talent development is an actionable component of strategy and is embedded in the culture.

- The executive team and senior leaders are accountable for and have financial incentives based on talent development results.

If you build all of your efforts, partnerships, and measurements around corporate strategy, building and developing talent will take its rightful place at the core of your company's strategic imperatives.

References

Bolt, J.F. (1989). *Executive development: A strategy for corporate competitiveness.* San Francisco, CA. Executive Development Associates.

The Conference Board. (2004). *CEO challenge 2004: Top ten challenges.* New York: Author.

Annmarie Neal, Psy.D., *has been applying her unique perspective to leadership and organization development for over fifteen years. An accomplished strategist and architect of best-in-class talent management programs, Dr. Neal takes a decidedly business-centric approach to solving talent issues. Recent highlights of her work include the design and execution of a highly integrated executive talent management strategy that links the acquisition, assessment, performance, development, succession, and recognition of top leaders. Most recently, Dr. Neal has created her own consulting business, focusing on executive coaching and leadership development. Prior to that, she served as senior vice president, talent office, for First Data Corporation and was a corporate psychologist and senior management consultant for RHR International. She received her B.A. in psychology from Boston College, a graduate certificate from Harvard University, a master's in counseling psychology from Santa Clara University, and a master's and doctorate in clinical psychology from the California School of Professional Psychology-Berkeley/Alameda.*

Eve Dreher *has been working in organization development, executive leadership, and employee communications for over twenty years. She has built a reputation as an excellent problem solver, intuitively extracting core issues to deliver both conceptual and practical solutions. Recent highlights of her communications work include building and directing an integrated employee communications function as a vice president for First Data Corporation. Currently, Ms. Dreher is owner of FORETHOUGHT, LLC, a consulting firm specializing in business communications and executive coaching. Previously, she served as a director at Schenkein Public Relations, where she created a new service offering for the company by creating a division dedicated to employee communications. Prior to that, her work focused on helping leaders manage organizational change. She received her B.S. degree in journalism/public relations from the University of Kansas and is a certified professional coach and Emergenetics associate.*

Gaining Management Buy-In
Responding to Unspoken Needs
Charles Presbury

Summary

In seeking buy-in from management for leadership in HRD initiatives, we often rely too much on the factual needs analysis and not on the broader picture of a value proposition, that is, the entire experience clients will receive if they commit to the actions we recommend. The elements of the unspoken experience that a leader seeks can involve things that are not expressed directly, such as concern for one's image as a successful leader, more job security for people, and fear that the resources required may derail another critical priority. The better one identifies these often unspoken needs/issues, as defined by the client, the more likely they will give you a surprising level of commitment.

Listen to a discussion among human resource development (HRD) professionals, and you will inevitably hear the topic of gaining management's buy-in. Our attempts to seek solutions to management buy-in usually result in a quest to find a "Holy Grail"— a rational formula that demonstrates a quantitative or financial ROI that even hard-bitten skeptics would buy into.

But why is it so easy to "sell" some managers, and yet some never seem to be convinced? Why do some managers become highly engaged in development initiatives, while others have only a cursory involvement or none at all? Why do some managers choose not to implement HRD projects, even though it is obvious to an HRD professional that the projects would help solve the organizational performance problems at hand? Why do some managers demand an ROI that no one could ever adequately prove? As a practitioner, I have found that clients often have other unarticulated issues, concerns, and needs that are not always apparent and that, if addressed, make it more likely that I can gain their buy-in. I believe that thinking of a manager's decision in terms of a value proposition will help enhance our ability to gain his or her buy-in. Think of the manager as a customer and consider the wider experience he or she may be seeking to "buy"—beyond the obvious.

A Management Client from Hell

Consider a real situation (the details have been disguised to protect the innocent—mainly me). A new vice president of operations (VPO) joins the senior staff of a business unit. She is probably the shrewdest business person you will ever meet. She can look at any set of business financials and inside of thirty minutes ask highly insightful questions, as if she's run the business for years.

The president brought her into the organization because he needed to inject stronger business savvy in order to help dramatically revitalize the business model. The VPO had fifteen years of senior management experience, including many as a highly successful general manager. She understood how to manage net profit. She rescued several businesses from extinction through insightful analysis and reshaping of the business models.

Her management philosophy and style were relentless. She would not spend a penny unless convinced that she would reap at least an immediate 10 percent return. Her mode of managing and developing people was described by some as the "survival of the fittest." She gathered a small circle of trusted executives around her and gave them enormous responsibility. If they succeeded, they were highly rewarded and given even more bone-crushing responsibility. Human resources (HR) to her was a necessary evil, required to help keep benefit costs in control and keep the business out of trouble with the regulatory authorities. Training was only relevant if it boosted revenue immediately.

After turning the business inside out in her first eighteen months on the job, attaining record performance by challenging the senior managers' business savvy, and personally rooting out inefficiencies, she turned her attention to "training." She requested that HR provide sales training to all employees as a means of refocusing everyone on the fundamentals of the business and thereby improving performance.

Dead HR Team Walking . . .

As the HRD team saw it, there were several issues related to instilling a business mindset throughout the organization. Among the issues were the need to increase the business acumen of every manager regarding attaining profitability; educating managers about setting performance standards and coaching people for performance; and implementing performance management practices that held people accountable for their performance. HR believed that management training and implementing new performance management practices in these areas were the best solutions, rather than company-wide sales training.

HR gathered all the data it could muster. It benchmarked programs at other companies and studied industry norms regarding costs and days of training. HR modeled the costs of building versus outsourcing a curriculum. It outlined the key management practices of high-performing companies and how this type of training was used to support these practices. But it could not find a rock-solid answer to a key question the VPO would surely ask—Precisely what improvement to the business' revenue could it guarantee?

HR passed its thoughts by someone it trusted in the VPO's inner circle. His advice from working with the her was that, unless HR could demonstrate that its solution could guarantee her an immediate ROI, HR should simply provide her with the sales training she requested. Anything else would incur her wrath (and, of course, be career limiting). How was HR going to satisfy her requested improvement on the organization's performance when she was focused on only one part of the problem? Still, HR was determined to do the "right thing" and readied its presentation on the other training and practices she needed to put in place.

The Decision

HR presented a masterful but simple curriculum of training/action learning for nearly 1,500 managers and supervisors around the world, to be spaced out over twenty-four months. It presented learning goals, the number of programs, and participants per program to maximize the return on the expenditures. It also identified the skills managers would develop and how it would measure the results. It then outlined changes to the goal-setting and performance-management process that these resources were intended to support. And finally it described other benefits of this initiative.

Then it braced for the killer questions, expecting to have the proposals ripped to shreds. After a short pensive pause, the VPO calmly said, "That's reasonable. I thought you would ask for more. Go ahead." She asked one more question: "Should we consider investing in space somewhere to run all this training?" Needless to say, the HR team was floored.

The VPO's Value Proposition

Why did this VPO commit hundreds of thousands of dollars and countless hours of her time and her direct reports' time to teach in the programs and implement new training and management practices? Obviously, her decision calculus resulted in a conclusion that the HR proposal was the right investment, even though HR could not possibly have convinced her of the outright financial ROI. Ironically, the concept of the customer value proposition from one of the proposed business training programs helped them to better understand the VP's buy-in decision.

The concept of value proposition was pioneered by Lynn Phillips at Stanford Business School. The basic concept is that customers make decisions to buy a product or service with a sense of the entire experience. They weigh the effect the product or service will have on them, the entire cost (not just monetary but time, effort, aggravation, self-image, etc.), and compare it to alternatives, including doing nothing. By choice or accident, every business presents some sort of value proposition to a customer. However, the more you understand the customer and are able to provide a solution that addresses their spoken and *unspoken* needs as a whole experience, the more value they derive and, therefore, the more they will be willing to invest in your solution over the alternatives.

For example, can you think of two stores with the same product, but one you would never frequent? Why? Perhaps it is because of limited parking, the store inside feels darker or dirtier, you do not like a salesperson, or a good friend shops at the other one and you want to impress him or her. Other factors beside the obvious (the product) often are involved in our decisions.

Take as another example a building supplies firm that sells doors to contractors, a firm that defines its customers as building contractors who want high-quality, durable doors. What if the doors were of excellent quality, yet the customers were not happy. They resisted price increases vigorously, and profits were eroding quickly.

If the supplier started shadowing its contractor/customers, it might discover that architects routinely asked contractors to replace dozens of doors they had just installed, because they were not the shade or texture the architect wanted or because there was too much variation in the shade/texture between all the doors. That might be initially obvious. What would not be as obvious is the fact that contractors typically ordered doors well in advance of when they were needed to assure they were on site when the installation date came, and that this is when the problems would begin for all parties involved. Why? First, doors that are on an active work site for several days are more likely to be damaged by moisture that changes their color and texture, stains, warping, nicks, and dents. Next, the need to reorder and rehang more doors leads to delays in construction schedules, delayed occupancy, increased overtime, and, ultimately, cost overruns. This, in turn, aggravates the architect, which means it tarnishes working relationships with the contractors.

What the building supplier would learn is more important to the contractor/customer than the quality of the door is that he or she can obtain the doors *just in time* so there are no costly delays and frustrated architects. "No hassles. Don't cause me to aggravate the people who I count on to give me business. Help me do the job once." It is easy to hear that they want a door. It takes listening to hear these other things they want you to deliver—and when! And if you delivered their real value proposition, they would flock to your door.

Back to the VPO

HR first assumed that the value proposition for the VPO was purely a rational cost versus revenue decision. It turned out that HR had done a relatively admirable job in her eyes of outlining the costs and minimizing frills. She calculated that she could generate enough savings to cover the cost of training without materially diluting earnings per share. That was the threshold HR had to make to be heard. However, what persuaded her, ultimately, was the benefits discussion that was added to the presentation after talking to the member of her inner circle.

As the HRD team talked to her long-time lieutenant, it assembled a different picture of the day in her life. Although she asked for a training program, she really wanted to remake the organization and her image. She was able to wring 25 to 30 percent of the costs out of the business in the first eighteen months by personally spotting inefficiencies. She realized that she could not continue this for much longer. For her to have a lasting legacy as a great leader, she needed to develop dozens upon dozens of people throughout the organization who could continue rooting out business problems just like she did.

Also, she wanted to demonstrate another side of her leadership capability. Her reputation and image were that of a cost-cutter, not a builder of the business and the talent. She wanted to be seen as a positive top executive who invested in best practices of consistently high-performing companies. HR talked about the systematic development of talent; leading the company by establishing a clear vision and goals; and managing the performance management processes to gain alignment throughout the organization as not only a means to improve the business capability of managers, but to be seen as a best practice of senior management in growing the enterprise over time.

The skills HR targeted made sense to her. She also realized the logic that one training program could not remake a culture or her image. People needed to be educated over time and have many opportunities to apply the skills and practices if she were to remake the business.

She also realized that this gave her a platform to remake her image with the employees, the board, and the industry. She would be seen as investing in the company's future by implementing best practices for developing an organization with long-term performance, viability, and the talent to sustain it. This gave her the opportunity to have very different conversations with the circle of top, highly respected CEOs with whom she frequently met during various conferences and industry forums. She would now be viewed as a CEO-type leader who was capable of growing an enterprise—and not a "slasher."

In essence, she decided to invest in the business and in herself in a different way than she had in the past. We all know leaders who look for and implement best HRD practices on their own because they feel it is the right thing to do. Their decisions are influenced by criteria that have little to do with strict dollars and cents. We just do not have to work as hard to understand their motives because they are already "sold." We need to use a larger viewpoint to help more resistant managers get past the excuses for not giving their buy-in or their involvement in the solution.

Do You Understand Your Client's Value Proposition?

We are usually pretty good at uncovering spoken needs. So continue to do a thorough analysis of the skill gaps, design the right intervention, and craft clear measurable learning goals. Assure the basics are in place. Then look for the unspoken needs that, if addressed, would make the investment of time and money compelling to the client manager.

Uncovering the unspoken needs is more difficult. The manager may not be able to articulate them. You will have to figuratively create what Lynn Phillips describes as "the videotape of a day in the life of the customer" in order to uncover how their operations work, as well as what their desires and challenges are.

Try to look imaginatively at their spoken and unspoken needs to determine what they value, how your solutions can add value to their operations or "lives" as managers, and what hassles or risks they face, and therefore identify things that make the investment in your solutions worthwhile in their minds. Managers who are easier to "sell" on HRD initiatives may not tell you, but they may do it because in their minds it is the right thing to do. Or this may be how their mentors treated them and so they believe they should play the same role for others they now mentor. Or they think it will help their chances for advancement if their people feel positive about them. They are self-motivated. When we hit resistance, it may be because issues like these are lurking in the minds of our clients.

I try to uncover unspoken needs/issue by spending time with clients to understand their operations and by asking some of the following questions of them and of others who know them:

- How would they describe what the perfect experience would feel like for them in their jobs if we delivered the project successfully? What would the experience feel like for *them*?

- What pressures does the client feel beyond the obvious gap posed by the problem as presented?

- If we did provide the obvious solution, is there something that could make it still feel like a "hollow victory"? What is it, and why?

- What are the consequences to them, the team, and the business of this problem?

- What is most worrisome about the problem?

- They may well have to make enormous expenditures, financially or in their personal time, championing the initiative, spending valuable political capital to make room for this extra effort among the already challenging performance objectives and scarce resources. In the end, in their own words, what would they have to see to feel it was worth the risk and effort it will take?

- What is the potential "price" the manager will have to pay for this solution? Does it create added work for him or her? Will he or she lose additional performance during the learning curve of the proposed solution?

- What is the risk of failing to deliver on business results while the group goes through a learning curve, etc.? How much riskier is it to make a major commitment of time to this effort (also leaving other pressing items on the back burner) in order to gain a longer-term solution? Or is it easier to engage enough "window dressing" to take the immediate heat off in the short term and hope it does not come back?

- How will this make their lives as leaders better if we succeed? What could make it even better?

Conclusion

When your client is on the fence, or does not seem to have fully bought in, consider that there may be other concerns and needs that are important to him or her that may not be quantifiable and not directly related to the solution itself. Try to see the value proposition through his or her eyes. Take the time to get to know the unspoken needs of your client. The benefit is that, when those needs are satisfied, you may gain the all-important buy-in you want.

Charles Presbury *is senior director, leadership development, responsible for the assessment and development of the senior-level leadership population at The McGraw-Hill Companies. Mr. Presbury has twenty years of experience in training, human resource development, and human resource management in a wide range of industries, having worked for SCM Corporation, the National Broadcasting Company, Preferred Health Care, and Pitney Bowes prior to McGraw-Hill. He received his bachelor's degree from Holy Cross College and his master's degree from Columbia University.*

Developing Global Leaders

Preparing Leaders for the New Competitive Landscape
New Mindsets for New Games
Gordon Hewitt

Summary

The landscape for leaders has changed dramatically. There is a call for leaders to go beyond execution to what I define as a process of discovery and an imperative for organizations to create new forms of collaboration across organizational sectors. There is a need for leaders to create new business models in organizations and to create new forms of value, involving the consumer, now more than ever, in the development of products and value. This article addresses the new skills and mindsets of the leader of today's global environment and suggests that the time may have come for new governing rules that will support—and not impede—innovation throughout the organization. It also presents key questions that organizations must address if they are to ensure the development of future leaders.

What is the value-added scorecard for leadership development in the modern corporation? What should it be? Is it relevant to the changing nature of the competitiveness challenge facing corporations in the emerging global business system? Is the performance of the leadership development system increasing or deteriorating over time? Are corporations creating enough leaders who can handle new strategic dilemmas? How would we know?

Beyond Execution

As a lifelong student of business strategy, I pose these questions to the leadership development community from a sympathetic point of view. The strategic competence of a business will reflect not the efficacy of the strategic planning system—whose track record has historically been mostly incremental in nature, both operationally and intellectually—but the cognition and capacity of executives who actually run the business. They are the key agents in sensing the nature of the competitive challenge, in defining new opportunities and risks, in setting and communicating a compelling competitive agenda, and in ensuring the organization has the capabilities to deliver results.

By all outward signs, the leadership development industry seems in good health. Certainly the participants in, and expenditure on, the educational and training part of the industry have increased significantly over the last ten years or so. For consultants and educators alike, barriers to entry and barriers to imitation appear low.

Corporations have certainly put more emphasis on relevance, as judged by the marked shift toward action-based learning and customized education. The clinical assessment of executive competencies has become standard within the human resource profession and has provided the foundation for developing "best practice" processes for leadership appraisal, development, and reward systems. Paradoxically, rather than being a tool for competitive differentiation, most competency lists have become as common and undifferentiated as corporate mission statements.

Yet the nagging doubts and echoes of old conversations persist. Are corporations really producing a cadre of executives who are equipped to enable their businesses to become more competitive, especially in the context of the emerging global business system? While the experience of such firms as Enron, WorldCom, and Tyco have put the issue of *ethical credibility* at the center of the governance agenda, today's competitive landscape is posing more widespread and enduring questions about *strategic credibility*—the capacity of business leaders to migrate their enterprises in a new direction and to compete and create value in fundamentally new ways.

In the first few months of 2005, the CEOs of Hewlett Packard, Sony, and Merck resigned. They were only the most notable and publicized examples of a worldwide trend toward volatility in CEO reputation and tenure. As one CEO, still in office, remarked to me recently, "It may take some time to go from good to great, but the journey from great to mediocre can be considerably shorter. And in today's rapidly changing world, you can arrive at the top just when most of what you know is irrelevant to the future."

The changing nature of the competitive and value-creating dilemma for leaders goes well beyond the current obsession with "execution." Clearly, great ideas that lack implementation capability remain great ideas. It is critical, however, to understand the changing nature of the executional challenge. Moving from two sigma to six sigma in operational performance is a sequential and linear journey between two known positions. It demands a certain type of executional discipline around known processes and measurements. It is a journey from A to B. In Sony's case, however, changing the very nature of the corporate concept from a consumer electronics company to a digital entertainment company requires a fundamentally different type and scale of executional capacity, as will be explained later.

One of the key features of leadership positions is the responsibility for creating a strategic agenda. This involves both a robust *framework of direction* and a robust *architecture for implementation*. How these are conceptualised, articulated, and addressed will depend on the competitive context and the previous experience of executives.

A Shift to a Process of Discovery

Legacy factors matter. On the one hand, what many businesses describe as their "strategy" may often be a highly generic mission statement, containing bold promises to all stakeholders, coupled with a detailed operating plan. The legacy of "strategy"—both as a set of analytical constructs and as organizational processes—has traditionally been an exercise in positioning *for cost efficiency or product differentiation* within defined industries with given competitive rules. Not surprisingly, the "strategic agenda" typically contains detailed plans around cost reduction, quality enhancement, productivity improvement, time compression, and so forth.

The nature of the strategic challenge facing more and more businesses today, however, is fundamentally shifting from an exercise in positioning to a process *of discovery*. The challenge of execution goes far beyond implanting disciplines for generating quantitative results. It demands the capacity to create new business and industry models, to discover and access new forms of value and advantage, to pre-emptively build new organizational capabilities, to de-risk the migration path to a foggy and ever-shifting future. This is not simple A to B management. The question is whether we are still developing new leaders with old competitive mindsets.

Strategy in the New Competitive Landscape: New Game and New Rules

Traditional strategy analysis has centered around the question, "Given our industry, how do we outperform the competition?" The key focus for creating advantage has been how to play *better*, rather than how to rethink the nature of *the game and the rules*. The key assumption has been that the secret behind superior value creation lies primarily in extracting inefficiency from an existing value chain.

Executives today, however, are facing a new set of competitive realities. Their landscape is shifting in highly unfamiliar ways as traditional industry structures and boundaries are becoming more fluid spaces, perpetually morphing and reconfiguring. Healthcare, telecommunications, electronics, entertainment, financial services, and energy are all examples of competitive arenas whose definition is becoming highly elusive and whose behavior no longer conforms to established economic norms.

This phenomenon is largely driven by convergence of products, technologies, competencies, functionalities, and formerly distinct consumer segments. The current competitive battle for global standards in hand-held mobile devices illustrates "new game" dynamics. Adverts for cell phones now rarely mention anything about the quality of sound or the consistency of connections. Phones as cameras, VCRs, Internet enablers, and potentially portable digital music players (the potential next evolution of iPod) illustrate new levels of ambiguity for the strategy process.

Consider how aircraft engine manufacturers such as Rolls-Royce and GE are experimenting with new models requiring the integration of engines, service, and inventory logistics systems, plus informatics and finance, in order to provide "solutions" to airlines, which goes well beyond the old game of selling engines on engineering performance alone. Drug companies talk of morphing from "pharmaceuticals" to "pharmacogenomics," as the possibility of combining their existing knowledge base with new genomic insights, as well as advanced technology-based diagnostic systems, opens up new opportunities in the arena of "preventive" rather than "curative" treatment.

The Sony Corporation has declared its intent to move from being a pure consumer electronics company—creating value by making stand-alone "boxes"—to a digital entertainment company. Like so many new game concepts, that under-defined competitive space will evolve like a complex, adaptive system, shaped by the interdependent moves of the participants. This illustrates how strategy is not necessarily about the long term. Next week's actions may vitally affect how the system evolves.

In addition to this, there is the increasing impact of the Internet as a force to change the balance of information and knowledge asymmetry between buyers and sellers. Internet-enabled consumers with previously unattainable levels of insight are altering the traditional dialogue in the marketplace. "Unqualified" medical patients may now carry thousands of globally verified "second opinions" into their appointments with physicians. Auto buyers may have more insight into price spreads and availability than individual car distributors.

With the ongoing digital revolution connecting the above two phenomena, it is easy to see the trend toward *customer centricity* in many markets. This idea goes well beyond the capacity for customer focus and intimacy, although the terminology is often used interchangeably. Customer centric implies having consumers deeply involved inside the firm's value chain, not as a point of delivery outside the chain. It raises the possibility of consumers co-creating value and becoming sources of innovation flows. Further, firms like Skype, which offers its network of users the possibility of free international phone calls via their PCs, and Wikipedia, which, dramatically unlike traditional encyclopaedias, allows users to build the knowledge network, illustrate the growth of user communities as major architects of value creation.

The game and the rules in many industries are also being shaped by developments in "emerging" economies such as India and China. In old game thinking, these countries fit a model of low-cost outsourcing. They are quickly becoming, however, the source of radical business model innovation in industries such as healthcare and recorded music. Several Chinese pop groups now give away their CDs for free to build their reputations and rely on other sources of payment, including more frequent live performances and Internet-based access to earn money. Consumers at the "bottom of the pyramid" may have as much influence in shaping the future of many industries as their more financially endowed cousins in "first-world" countries.

Toward New Collaborative Models: Strategy and Internal Governance

"Structure follows strategy" is a well-established motto and executive behavioral pattern. When executives are put into new leadership positions in a business, how do we develop them to think about how to get the organization to create value? So often, they may reach for the organization chart and realign responsibilities around new strategic imperatives. Additionally, they may devise altered or new measurement and reward systems to encourage and drive behavior that is consistent with their strategy, rather than dysfunctional.

The capacity to operate effectively in the competitive landscape described above, however, often demands resolving deeper tensions in the *internal governance system*— the roles and relationships between different parts of the organizational system. The modern corporation is typically structured as a portfolio of relatively autonomous business units, each with significant strategic and resource independence and responsible for value creation within its defined market scope. Often, the debate goes on within the leadership development community about the desirability of breadth of business unit experience on the way to the top.

Many opportunities, however, to create a new game strategy in a convergent world span multiple businesses. They require the corporation and its leaders to forge new connections across business, functional, and geographical boundaries. Creating horizontal flows of value across the corporation implies the capacity to build shared competitive agendas across different businesses, along with shared views of opportunity and risk. They highlight the need to blend resources in new ways and to create new knowledge, not just transfer best practice across vertically separate silos. Most of all, they require a sophisticated capacity for collaborative, network management, while at the same time preserving efficiency within the business unit system.

This is about creating "next practices," not about benchmarking best practices. For example, Sony's new CEO—British-born Howard Stringer—is examining how a corporation with products and competencies that span consumer electronics, personal computers, and recorded music, with the generic "Walkman" brand in its portfolio, could not develop an "iPod" before the Apple Corporation launched what became the dominant brand in portable digital music. Sony leaders have been highly articulate about the concept of a digital entertainment corporation. Resolving internal governance tensions that would force Sony's notably independent product divisions to collaborate in new ways became the real source of executional inertia.

Developing Leaders for the New Competitive Landscape

Whenever I have the opportunity to discuss these issues in front of executive development specialists, I ask whether new issues and questions on the strategic agenda are receiving a sufficient response from the leadership development agenda. Of course, some of the issues are recognized and are being addressed in some way. But there is still a sense among development specialists that their response is insufficient and partial. The feeling remains that much development activity may still be rooted in old competitive game logic and assumptions. Strategy, I have argued, has been primarily concerned with developing better processes for existing games. The new landscape demands new mindsets for new games.

So here are a few recommendations that frequently arise from my seminars, sessions, and discussions with leadership development professionals. As practitioners, these are the questions to ask your organizational clients as you help them to evolve their leadership development agenda and strategy:

1. How do we ensure that a sufficient number of high-potential executives gain new game experiences early in their careers, and frequently thereafter? How do we coach them to widen the envelope of innovation throughout their careers, going beyond product innovation to the creation of new business models, new platforms and standards, new industry concepts? How do we give them experiences that will force them to think of creating value in fundamentally new ways, rather than trading on legacy factors?

2. How do we develop their strategic competence at an early age? What kind of experiences would encourage future leaders to systematically develop competitive insight and foresight, especially into opportunities that lie at the perimeter of their industry, knowledge, and experience? How do we en-

sure they know that strategy in the new landscape goes well beyond the content of typical business operating plans, and that the two exercises should not be confused? Why do we run educational programs on strategy only for our most senior executives?

3. What kind of experiences would equip future leaders to become comfortable at an early age with ambiguity (not just uncertainty), complexity, and volatility—the drivers of the global business system? How do we ensure they have early opportunities to create value by managing a complex value network—where the roles of customers, suppliers, competitors, and alliance partners are overlapping and simultaneous—rather than a straightforward linear value chain?

4. How do we develop "leadership broadband," the capacity to create and deliver value within tightly organized functions and businesses, as well as through horizontal collaboration across organizational boundaries? Have we developed legitimate metrics of horizontal value creation and reward systems that would encourage this to happen? Do we confuse best practice transfer with high-level convergence management?

5. What is our agenda for being a "next practice" global corporation? How do we inject new forms of "globability" into our leadership development agenda? Are we creating genuinely global executives rather than "multi-domestic" ones who experience country rotation? What assignments are required to develop and master the range of intercultural and competitive skills needed to create value in a genuine global sense—across geographical, functional and product boundaries?

Conclusion

These questions and challenges are just a start. In the same way that business executives are coming to terms with the limits of old ways of thinking about and doing strategy, leadership development professionals may have to experience a similar journey. Yet they hold the key to the most critical ingredient of all. Genuine creativity requires not just learning, but forgetting. I have often argued that building a learning organization may have toxic side-effects if it creates the ability to play the wrong game better. Both the strategy and leadership development professions are going through their own inflection points, which requires confronting the limits of existing knowledge, assumptions, and orthodoxies. As one CEO put it so eloquently, "These are not just interesting times, but humbling times."

Gordon Hewitt *is distinguished professor of international business and corporate strategy at the Stephen Ross School of Business, University of Michigan. He is also a member of the Global Academic Network of Duke Corporate Education and is honorary professor at the Faculty of Social Sciences, Glasgow University, Scotland, where he started his career.*

Professor Hewitt is widely acknowledged as one of the world's leading authorities on how to compete in complex, dynamic markets. He has developed innovative executive education programs for directors of several top global corporations to enable their managers to create credible strategies and corporate value in the context of new competitive realities. His clients have included IBM, Sony, UBS, Merck, Honeywell, Texas Instruments, HSBC, Microsoft, and AstraZeneca. He has worked extensively with Michigan colleagues C.K. Prahalad and Dave Ulrich to develop new frameworks for connecting strategy and HR and has published several articles and book chapters on this issue recently. He has also been a keynote speaker at major CLO and HR conferences.

Developing Global Leaders
The Critical Role of Dilemma Reconciliation
Fons Trompenaars and Peter Woolliams

Summary

Although much has been written and hypothesized about leadership competencies and styles, the advent of global leadership has further complicated the issue. In this article, the authors propose a model of reconciliation based on seven common "dilemmas" that leaders face. The premise is that, by thinking and acting to reconcile these issues, leaders are better able to work globally and cross-culturally.

The Challenge for Global Leaders

The challenge today in leadership models and framework is to include a perspective that transfers to modern global business and international leaders. Attempts to map the personality traits, effective behavioral competencies, contingencies, and transformational styles of outstanding leaders have fascinated a diverse number of practitioners and researchers. But in spite of the extensive proliferation of such models and frameworks, we find that desirable characteristics or effective behaviors of leadership and other frameworks identified in the United States or Anglo-Saxon cultures do not transfer to modern global business. They also fail at home for an increasingly diverse workforce. The question, then, is how leaders can deal effectively within multicultural surroundings.

Take these descriptions of a good leader. Which one would you choose?

1. Good leaders are people who continuously help their subordinates to solve the variety of problems that they face. They are like parents, not teachers.

2. Good leaders occupy a position between that of a private coach and a teacher. Their effectiveness depends on how they balance both roles.

3. Good leaders get things done. They set goals, give information, measure results, and let people do their own work in that context.

4. Good leaders give a lot of attention to work streams, so that goals, tasks, and achievements are aimed at improving those processes.

5. Good leaders get things done. They set goals, give information, and measure results so that everyone is embedded in continuous work streams.

We asked selected top leaders to complete our Intercultural Leadership Assessment (ILA) questionnaire based on this type of question structure. It was consistent with our proposition that leaders such as Richard Branson of Virgin Air, Michael Dell of Dell Inc., Kees Storm of AEGON, and Laurent Beaudoin of Bombardier made significantly different choices from people on our database of more "ordinary" managers. What was the difference?

The leaders described in number 1 look like those of the beginning of the last century: Listen to father and everything will be OK. This style is still very popular in Latin America and Asia, where we have also collected research data, compared to Europe and the United States. There is nothing wrong with this approach, simply that it is limited in its applicability outside these regions.

Number 2 is a typical compromise and will not work very well anywhere—but it is certainly not the optimum approach.

Number 3 is very popular among Anglo-Saxons and Northwest European managers. The ever-popular "Management by Objectives" is again applied recklessly. Add some vision and mission, and you're the modern leader; but the French would quickly argue: "Whose vision and mission is it?"

Numbers 4 and 5 are two alternative ways to integrate seemingly opposing values on a higher level and therefore beckoned our attention. Number 4 suggests that good leaders guide people who make mistakes and learn from them, while Number 5 integrates the dichotomy of task orientation with work streams beginning from the opposite direction. In our research, more-successful leaders selected the last two choices much more frequently.

Using this ILA instrument, we tested some four thousand international managers and leaders and extended our own earlier cross-cultural instruments to account for and assess how leaders reconcile value differences. We have triangulated this with evidence collected from workshops, simulations, and interviews and have found the data supports our core proposition and the topic of this article, namely that high-performing leaders have a higher "propensity to reconcile" than managers or less effective leaders. Furthermore, the business outcome of leaders continually reconciling value dilemmas/value differences manifests directly at the bottom line. Let us share more specifically how this viewpoint has evolved.

A Proposed New Meta-Theory of Leadership

Much attention has been given to the training and development of recognition and respect for cultural differences. However, if we stop at only these first two stages, we run the risk of supporting only stereotypical views on cultures. Our response has been to progress from basic cross-cultural awareness training and consulting to developing the global minds of leaders and beyond and propose that a new meta-theory of leadership was needed to tackle the way in which leaders deal with value dilemmas.

How did we test our proposition? In short, we accumulated a significant body of evidence on how leaders lead by reconciling values across the whole management spectrum. We used customized versions of our profiling tools that collected 360-degree data and found a direct correlation between the measurement "propensity to reconcile," that is, how leaders approach and react to key value dilemmas, and the bottom-line performance of their business units or divisions.

This became our underlying construct in defining cross-cultural competence. Further, from our research findings, we inferred that a successful leader in the current epoch of rapidly changing situations and multicultural surroundings needs to operate with a people-oriented style in order to accomplish his or her task. He or she will have to think logically, fed by an illogical intuition. Finally, a leader must be very sensitive to the situation in order to make consistent decisions, regardless of the situation.

We believe that our work is unique in that our focus has been to extend research on leadership to give much more attention to the competency of reconciliation of differences after the identification of these differences. In other words, the successful leader is able to connect and integrate different points of view over and above compromise through consensus or dictated.

The next thing is therefore to ask what we can do to help leaders make businesses more effective once we cross cultural or diversity boundaries.

Why do leaders need such skills? All organizations need stability and growth, long-term and short-term decisions, tradition and innovation, planning and laissez-faire, order and freedom. The challenge for leaders is to fuse these opposites, not to select one extreme at the expense of the other. As a leader, you have to inspire as well as listen. You have to make decisions yourself, but also delegate, and you need to centralize your organization around local responsibilities. You have to be hands-on and yet hands-off. As a professional, you need to master your materials, and at the same time you need to be passionately at one with the mission of the whole organization. You need to apply your brilliant analytic skills in order to place these contributions in a larger context. You are supposed to have priorities and put them in a meticulous sequence, while parallel processing is in vogue. You have to develop a brilliant strategy, and at the same time have all the answers to questions in case your strategy misses its goals.

We have found that this competence in reconciling differences—or value dilemmas, the term we use in the rest of the article—is the most discriminating feature that differentiates successful from less-successful leaders and thereby the performance of their organizations.

As our own work progressed to be focused on the development of cross-cultural competence, we refocused our interventions for our client organizations to address the need to consider what leadership behaviors were effective in being able not only to recognize cultural differences, but to respect these differences, and moreover to be able to *reconcile* these differences.

Transcultural Competence: The Propensity to Reconcile Dilemmas

Not unexpectedly, the perennial question reappeared! Is this competence innate or acquired? Can it be developed? Or more fundamentally, are leaders made or born? Furthermore, can the leader transform the organization such that it is continually eliciting and reconciling these dilemmas so it becomes the "reconciling organization"?

Readers of our more recent books and other publications will know that we make extensive use of the Internet for collecting primary data from participants from our client organizations. In addition to the main Trompenaars' cross-cultural database, we have also collected and indexed some 6,500 dilemmas faced by leaders in their respective organizations across the world, gathered over the last four years. Coding and subsequent analysis of these dilemmas using clustering and data-mining algorithms reveals a frequently reoccurring series of "Golden Dilemmas" that provide a basis for a structured approach to diagnosing challenges for leaders who owe their origins to cultural differences.

Table 1. A Sample Golden Dilemma

On the One Hand	On the Other Hand
We strive for standard global products and services to benefit from a common universal identity and branding (as well as cost savings through economies of scale).	We try to develop and offer unique products and services adapted to the needs and tastes of local markets.

Table 1 provides a sample "Golden Dilemma" faced by organizations that their leaders must address.

Frequently Reoccuring Dilemmas

At the generic level, the following represent the principal "golden dilemmas" faced by leaders:

Dilemma 1: Standard and Adaptation

It is remarkable how often leaders mentioned this dilemma. Do we have to globalize our approach or do we just have to localize? Is it more beneficial for our organization to choose mass production than to focus on specialized products? Effective leaders found the solution in the "transnational organization," where best local practices are globalized on a continuous basis. "Mass customization" is the keyword for reconciling standardized production and specialized adaptations.

Dilemma 2: Individual Creativity and Team Spirit

A second leadership dilemma is the integration of team spirit with individual creativity and a competitive mindset. The effective leader knows how to make an excellent team out of creative individuals. The team is stimulated to support brilliant individuals, while these individuals deploy themselves for the greater whole. This has been called co-opetition.

Dilemma 3: Passion and Control

Is a good leader an emotional and passionate person, or does the control of emotions make a better leader? Here there are two clear types. Passionate leaders without reason are neurotics, and neutral leaders without emotions are robots. Richard Branson regularly checks his passion with reason, and if we look at the more neutral Jack

Welch, the former CEO of General Electric, we see a leader who gives his controlled reason meaning by showing passion once in a while.

Dilemma 4: Analysis and Synthesis

Is the leader of the 21st century a detached, analytical person who is able to divide the big picture into ready-to-eat pieces, always selecting for shareholder value? Or is he or she someone who puts issues in the big picture and gives priority to the rather vaguely defined stakeholder value? At Shell, Van Lennep's "helicopter view" was introduced as a significant characteristic of a modern leader—the capability to ascend and keep the overview, while being able to zoom in on certain aspects of the matter. Jan Carlzon (SAS) called the integration of specific moments with profundity, as a part of client service, "moments of truth." This is another significant characteristic of the modern leader, namely the ability to know when and where to go in deep. Pure analysis leads to paralysis, and the overuse of synthesis leads to an infinite holism and a lack of action.

Dilemma 5: Doing and Being

"Getting things done" is an important characteristic of a manager. However, shouldn't we keep the rather vulgar "doing" in balance with "being," as in our private lives? As a leader, you have to be yourself as well. From our research, it appeared that successful leaders act the way they really are. They seem to be one with the business they are undertaking. One of the important causes of stress is that "doing" and "being" are not integrated. Excessive compulsion to perform, when not matching an individual's true personality, leads to ineffective behavior.

Dilemma 6: Sequential and Parallel

Notably, effective leaders are able to plan in a rigorous, sequential way, but at the same time have the ability to stimulate parallel processes. This reconciliation, which we know as "synchronize processes to increase the sequential speed" or "just-in-time" management, seems also to be very effective in integrating the long and short term.

Dilemma 7: Push and Pull

This final core competence for today's leaders is the ability to connect the voice of the market with the technology the company has developed, and vice versa. This is not about technology push or market pull. The modern leader knows that the push of technology finally leads to the ultimate niche market, that part without any clients.

If you only choose for the market, your clients will be unsatisfied. We believe that leaders are not simply "adding value," but synergizing through the integration (combining) of values. Thus, a car that is both fast and safe or high-quality food that is also easy to prepare are the integration not the result of either-or choices.

From Values to Performance

We have recently responded to these challenges by moving to a third phase in our approach, in which we now focus on helping leaders by prioritizing and realizing the business benefits of reconciling cultural differences for competitive advantage. Yes, effective leaders can identify and reconcile dilemmas, but which of the dilemmas they face will impact most on the bottom line? Can we develop an objective/analytical approach that gives the best return on reconciliation?

The really exciting part of this third wave, based on our new dilemma database, is that we have been able more recently to converge on a number of key diagnostic measures that reveal how these meta-level dilemmas manifest for the leader and how these link to bottom-line business performance. We first help leaders make such "Golden Dilemmas" explicit and therefore tangible through our structured "Dilemma Reconciliation Process." We then assess the current status of the dilemma against an ideal state that would result when the business benefits had been realized. A typical result, as shown in Figure 1, is that there appears to be a wide variation in the assessment of the current state from an international leadership team, but much more consensus about what is needed in the ideal state. However, closer examination reveals that such assessments are culturally determined. In the example shown, U.S. leaders tend to adhere to the top left, Europeans toward the center, and leaders from Asia/China in the bottom right in terms of current practices. And thus, although our Golden Dilemmas may be universal, how they are interpreted and the starting points for their reconciliation need to account for culture.

Leaders are now in a position to evaluate the business benefits against the costs, time scales to realize benefits, and the degree to which the dilemma solution is located in one profit center or involves cooperation across a number of business units. The example shown in Figure 2 summarizes the top-level descriptions of the Golden Dilemmas faced by the top leadership of a major U.S. organization and how they were subsequently placed on the dilemma relationship matrix using our new measurement techniques.

This type of analysis provides the leader with an objective evaluation of where the highest return on investment can be achieved, and thus secures the best benefits for the business. In this particular case, the most important dilemma that cried to be addressed was the need for technology push (what the company can make from its own

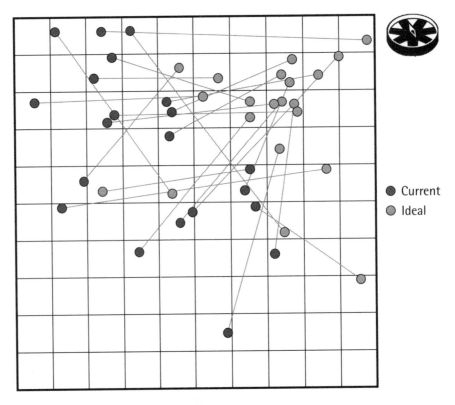

We strive for standard global products and services to benefit from a common universal identity and branding (as well as cost savings through economies of scale)

● Current
◐ Ideal

We try to develop and offer unique products and services adapted to the needs and tastes of local markets

Figure 1.   Measuring Current Versus Ideal Status of Golden Dilemmas

intellectual capital) versus what the different markets want (what the organization could sell).

When leaders are faced with major decisions involving high levels of funding and human capital, such analytical approaches help them to validate their tacit insights by making them explicit and open to debate.

As the world marketplace becomes ever more oligopolistic and more competitive, leaders need such frameworks and their associated tools to provide a decision-making framework that prioritizes actions. How does the new meta-theory (Integration Theory of Leadership) deal with this aspect? Leaders are increasingly confronted with questions from clients of how their knowledge can be embedded into the company's long-term learning processes, or of how they can help the organization build and sustain "cultures of learning," "cultures of continuous development," and "cultures that embrace change and diversity."

We believe that the existing dominant theories of leadership, categorized in three main paradigms known as trait, behavioral, and situational theories, do not resolve the main dilemmas leaders are facing today. Furthermore, they do not give sufficient

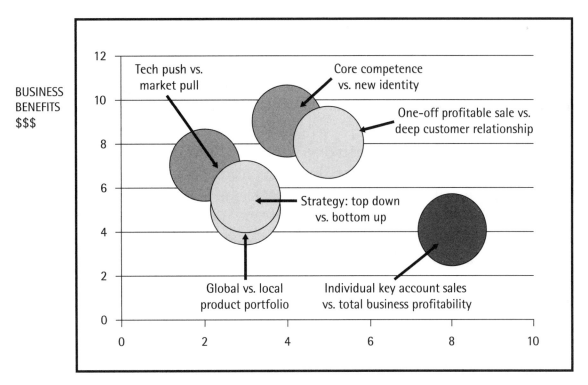

Figure 2. Sample Dilemma Portfolio Analysis

attention to the different perspectives with which different cultures approach frequently occurring leadership challenges. Trait theory claims a "one best" set of traits for the leader and ignores the culture in which these traits need to be brought to fruition. Behavioral theory claims that there are different styles of leaders vis-a-vis task and followers. The weakness of this approach is that one hardly enters the complexity of the world of the relationship between both styles. Again, the cultural context is not taken into consideration. Finally, the situational theory of leadership introduces the (cultural) context as an important aspect in the effectiveness of leadership. One aspect, however, has not been resolved. How can a leader be effective in a multi-cultural environment? We believe our proposed meta-theory resolves most black spots in existing leadership models.

Moving Forward

No one claims that combining values is easy; nevertheless, it is possible. The ever-expanding system of satisfaction of values will form the ultimate test for the leaders of this century. All organizations need stability and change, tradition and innovation, public and private interest, planning and laissez-faire, order and freedom, growth and decay. The consequence is that the systems and processes and challenges for leaders are changing in the world of dilemmas created by the evolving workplace, and even more by globalization. But however complex this world is in all these dilemmas, one discovers an organizational principle that is based on the idea of integration.

To meet the challenges of today's ever-globalizing world, leaders need to develop a new mindset of inquiry and support centered around the reconciliation of dilemmas, and thereby finally reveal their true worth. One approach to help leaders develop this capability we are currently exploring is a competency framework that specifies effective behavioral criteria based on our conceptual framework. Thus, a conventional competency model that prescribes criteria for demonstrating "integrity" might include statements such as "to be direct, open, frank, and honest." Such statements are often (unintentionally) culturally biased and do not embrace reconciliation. Thus, "to be direct, frank, and honest" may work in the United States but be less effective in China (or dealing with Chinese members of your team located in the United States) for whom matters of "face" are different when facing criticism (even if the criticism is constructive). The equivalent behavior description that engenders a reconciliation approach would be "to develop your relationship with your team so that you can be open, direct, frank, and honest." Extending this idea to the complete portfolio of competence descriptors can thereby induce a change of mindset through prescribing behaviors that are reconciling. Living and practicing these develops the aspiring leader to this new level.

Moving forward, we are now researching a fourth phase in which we can quantify the dilemmas between the organization and its societal responsibilities. These will become increasingly important to organizations in the future as G8 world leaders wrestle with their own needs with those of an unhealthy and hungry third world, declining (finite) raw materials, global warming, and poverty, and, of course, the threat from terrorism.

Conclusion

The tensions we have mentioned can all serve as challenges to a leader today, and to practitioners like ourselves, as we work with these leaders to develop the global competency of reconciling these dilemmas and to create a diversity mindset. In all these dilemmas, one discovers an organizational principle, and that principle is based on the idea of integration.

Our hope is that this perspective broadens your viewpoint of leadership theory and helps you increase your value to your global executive clients. Our own satisfaction derives from having reconciled our own intrinsic interest in researching the subject of culture with providing real operational support to our clients that we now know makes their organizations more sustainable.

Fons Trompenaars, Ph.D., *is director of Trompenaars Hampden-Turner Consulting, an innovative centre of excellence on intercultural management. He is the world's foremost authority on cross-cultural management and is author of many books and related articles, including the best-seller,* Riding the Waves of Culture: Understanding Cultural Diversity in Business, *published by McGraw-Hill (1993). This book sold over 120,000 copies and was translated into French, German, Dutch, Korean, Danish, Turkish, Chinese, Hungarian, and Portuguese. He is the co-author of* Seven Cultures of Capitalism *(Doubleday, 1993) and* Mastering the Infinite Game *with Charles Hampden-Turner. He was mentioned as one of the top five management consultants, next to Michael Porter, Tom Peters, and Edward de Bono, in a leading business magazine in August 1999.*

Peter Woolliams, Ph.D., *is emeritus professor of international management at Anglia Ruskin University (UK) and is an owner/partner in Trompenaars Hampden-Turner Consulting. He has collaborated and published jointly with Fons over some fifteen years. He is co-author of* Business Across Cultures *(available in several languages) and* Marketing Across Cultures *published by Capstone-Wiley in 2004.*

Identifying and Developing High-Potentials

Evaluating Leadership Potential
A Practitioner's Guide
Val Markos

Summary

For the past fifteen years, I have worked in a role with responsibilities for developing leaders. This article comes from my experience in evaluating those leaders and the processes I have established to do so. It is written as a guide for practitioners—not so much from a theoretical base, but from a foundation of lessons learned on the ground and the principles drawn from those hard-learned lessons.

In the article, I describe what I have found to be the principles critical to the success of any approach to talent evaluation. I describe various approaches to talent evaluation and what I have found to be the pros and cons of each. I discuss the development and use of leadership models (the desired state) and provide an example of an evaluation system I implemented in one company. Finally, I discuss the use and communication of evaluation results and some of the issues one must consider in any talent evaluation process.

First, let's define the term "talent evaluation." In this article, talent evaluation includes the identification of managers with potential for future positions or roles (as in succession planning). It includes the identification of managers for high-potential or accelerated-development programs. It also includes the identification of specific strengths and weaknesses of individual managers to assist in their growth and development. The aggregation of results of such evaluations serve as an organization diagnostic as well, in order to identify organizational interventions such as education or recruitment.

Criteria for an Effective Leadership Potential Evaluation Process

What makes an evaluation process successful and effective? If I am developing such a process, what do I need to keep in mind to assure it will have an impact in the organization or with the individual? What makes a talent evaluation process effective and provides long-lasting impact in the organization? There are basically four criteria or characteristics that the developmental professional should address in the establishment of any evaluation process. Not all may be equally important, and there will likely be tradeoffs in addressing them together. These four criteria (see Figure 1) are

- *Is it valid?* Does it do what is says it will do?

- *Is it credible?* Does the organization believe in it and accept it as valid?

- *Is it usable?* Can it be implemented and sustained over time?

- *Is it fair?* Will the results be free from unintended and unfair impact on individuals and groups?

Validity

Validity is one of the most important aspects of an evaluation process. If the process does not yield accurate and reliable results, it simply is not a valid process. If you cannot demonstrate in a rationale argument that the process results in reasonable and accurate findings, it should not be used. Further, if the evaluation is repeated, it should obtain the same results. In other words, it should be valid—and reliably so.

Psychologists and psychometricians have various methods for demonstrating validity and assuring that the development of instruments and processes yields valid re-

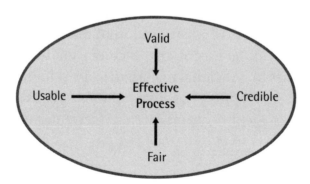

Figure 1.   Characteristics of Effective Leadership Potential Evaluation Processes

sults. These steps include tightly linking results of the measures to performance or demonstration of what is to be measured or predicted by the tests. While the steps followed in developing an evaluation process may not be as rigorous as what psychologists would require, they should assure a rational argument of connection between the results of any evaluation or assessment and the dimension or characteristic the process is intended to measure.

Helpful to this effort is the connection of any framework with the purpose of the evaluation. Training all those involved to assure they understand the framework and the measurement aspects of the process is another dimension of assuring validity. Finally, careful review and monitoring of the process and continued ongoing feedback from those using and involved in the process can aid in demonstrating validity or in diagnosing issues that undermine that validity.

Credibility

Not only does the evaluation need to be valid, but it has to be credible with the organization. These are two very different issues. A process may be very accurate in its prediction of potential or the evaluation of a person's strength and needs, but if the prediction or information is not accepted by the person or the organization, it will not be an effective process. If the organization, the leadership, or the manager does not accept the results of the process, it is virtually worthless to the organization. I once managed a process that our research told us was a valid and fairly accurate process to identify or confirm identification of high-potential managers. Nonetheless, several leaders in the organization had little confidence in the process and therefore paid little attention to the results. Showing our research and defending the process did little to convince them of its value. I finally chose to change the process, *not because it wasn't valid*, but because it wasn't credible. Credibility is critical for the process to be used and to make a difference.

Credibility of an evaluation process may have less to do with the outcome of the process than with how the process was established, how it is managed, and how it is used. Credibility translates into acceptance of the recommendations, use of the findings in decisions and actions, and reliance on them as being valid and valuable.

Credibility of a process is established in several ways. First, it is important to understand the purpose of the evaluation and to make sure all involved understand it. I have found that involving those who will use a process in the creation of that process is an important step in establishing credibility. Sponsorship by those who will use the process is extremely helpful. Involving those who will touch and use the process in the development of its framework helps tremendously in assuring credibility. Finally, managing the process consistent with its purpose will maintain the integrity and the credibility of the process.

Usability

A related concept is usability, which refers to the ease with which those making decisions based on the process can use it and the findings. Do those involved (participants, those doing succession planning, etc.) understand the process? If it is used for development, does it actually provide recommendations that are actionable, realistic, and helpful? Does it require special expertise and experience to understand, or can a participant or user easily understand and use it? Are the results presented in a fashion that one doesn't have to be a trained psychologist to understand?

To assure usability, it is helpful to view the process from the eyes of those involved: those conducting the process, those receiving the recommendations, and those participating in the process. If any of these parties find it difficult to use, the process may die of its own weight. Here again, involvement of participants and recipients in the design is critical. Further, it is best to solicit ongoing feedback from participants and recipients, and then, acting on that feedback, to assure and improve the usability of the process.

Fairness

It is also important that an evaluation process be fair. Fairness includes those issues of race, sex, religion, and so on, that are legal issues and obviously critical, but it also refers to issues of calibration or advantage given to one individual over another. "Fair" basically signifies that participants are distinguished by the factors or dimensions being evaluated and *not* distinguished by extraneous and irrelevant factors. It means that all participants have an equal chance of success, except as they are distinguished by the relevant and valid factors being evaluated. Here again, careful review and monitoring of the process and continued ongoing feedback from those using the process can aid in assuring fairness. Designing the process to accurately identify the factors that distinguish leaders and measuring only those factors assures fairness. Training for all on how the process was developed and what it does is a key to assure that all understand what is being evaluated, as well as what factors (race, sex, etc.) might make a difference.

Framework for Evaluation—The Leadership Model

It seems only natural that, in order to create an evaluation process for leadership potential, a definition or model of leadership is needed. Such models can include abilities, aptitudes, attitudes, skills, aspirations, and other aspects that could be considered predictive of leadership success.

While the approach to how these aspects are measured may differ dramatically, leadership models used across industry today have many dimensions in common. If we analyze all the general leadership models or competency models of the Fortune 1000 companies, we would find that 80 percent of the dimensions are common across most of the models. They may not be worded exactly the same, but you know there is going to be something about leading people or building teams, something about obtaining results or achieving goals, probably one on customers, another on teamwork or relationships. Therefore, I don't suggest spending time and effort in rigorous and time-consuming research to determine which leadership model to use. To assure that the leadership model is effective, (1) spend time gaining agreement and understanding of senior leaders that it represents the model of leadership needed and desired and (2) incorporate the model in all aspects of the talent evaluation process and in key systems (performance management, management development, feedback systems) in the organization. The real work of a leadership model is in implementing the model—not in researching it.

It is important that the model of leadership you choose provide a language and a common framework for evaluation, development, and discussion of talent in your organization. The model should be "owned" by the *senior leadership* of the company, not modified by or owned by human resources or learning and development. This means discussions should be held among the senior team as to what the model and components mean; they should reach a formal agreement on and endorse the model; they should clearly communicate the model to the organization; use the model or components of the model in presentations; and use the model in discussions of talent among themselves. Ideally, the leadership team will want to be involved in the process, further solidifying the model in the organization.

It is tempting to describe dozens of dimensions of behavior to capture all the aspects of leadership and to provide a thorough and accurate evaluation and an opportunity for feedback. Fight the temptation to enlarge the process. Keep the dimensions being measured to a very manageable number (five to eight). Your model should be easy to use, without a manual of definitions. Some models include as many as twenty-five or thirty dimensions—describing almost every aspect of behavior—but that doesn't add to the credibility or usefulness of that model.

The steps in developing a model are fairly straightforward. Usually, interviews are conducted with several leaders of the organization, stimulating their thinking with questions such as:

- To succeed in the next five years, what competencies do we need in our leaders?

- What is the biggest change we have seen in the talents, abilities, or behaviors required to succeed today, versus ten years ago?

- How would you compare those present talents, abilities, and behaviors with what will be needed five years in the future?

- In selecting and developing our leaders of tomorrow, what are the critical dimensions we must measure and consider?

The results of the interviews can be summarized and discussed with the CEO or executive team to finalize the model. This process will usually help to lower the number of dimensions considered. It is important that the leadership team believe in the dimensions that are developed and take ownership for the model itself. Remember that this is not an academic or vigorously researched process, but a way to assure ownership as much as to determine dimensions.

I have formalized such a model by using an exercise with an executive team. I asked them to consider what would happen if they lost (or had to move) ten of their top leaders. I asked, "What would you want in the leaders who would replace them?" The team prepared ahead of time for the ninety-minute discussion, and the outcome formed the basis for their leadership model. While there was a little tweaking after the discussion, it was basically developed in the brief discussion *and* was owned by that team. (I tried to make a change in it once and was reminded that it wasn't mine!)

To be effective, the model has to be communicated to the organization in many ways. It should lead all development, selection, and management of talent. The dimensions of the model should be fully incorporated into the performance management system and into the selection of management recruits. It should be the basis of management development and education of all leaders in the company. It also should be part of the evaluation of both potential and current leaders. While creating the model itself is pretty straightforward, making the model effective in guiding development and selection of leaders often requires great effort.

Approaches to Evaluation of Leadership Potential

Once the definition of what leadership is has been established, you must determine how to measure the components. The measure may be the potential for accelerated development among the managers in the organization or the strength of potential succession candidates—both individual and in the aggregate. The benefit of effective evaluation is that all managers receive feedback on their strengths and flat sides and have a basis and foundation for their own development, knowing not only what leadership really means in the organization but how they compare to the model.

Approaches to measuring leadership talent or potential can range from very basic (self-evaluation or evaluation by supervisor) to very sophisticated (observation in simulated exercises). There may not be one approach that will serve for measuring all aspects of the model. Further, as with the assessment center research from decades ago, it is best to measure each aspect with more than one approach, if possible.

Let's review several different approaches to measuring potential and consider some of the positives and challenges faced with each approach.

Supervisor Evaluation

The simplest approach to potential evaluation is to have the supervisor do it. This is usually done using a leadership model with multiple dimensions and asking the supervisor to rate the candidate on the dimensions during a performance review or talent review process. Often, behavioral anchors describing levels of performance on the dimension are provided to assist the supervisor and to assure calibration across supervisors. This is very often the initial evaluation of talent and potential in a company. In some companies, it is the only evaluation.

Notwithstanding substantial research and clearly described anchors, it is difficult to achieve calibration across supervisors by simply using this technique. Adding a level of review, by either the supervisor's peers or supervisor, can address the calibration issue if they are familiar with the person being evaluated. It usually takes many cycles for calibration and discipline in rating to improve to a healthy level. Progress in such a process can be accelerated by the multi-level review process—rolling up the process several supervisory levels and including multiple leaders familiar with the talent being reviewed.

The supervisor review can be a fairly effective method of initial potential evaluation, but often lacks in-depth feedback and solid development recommendations for the individual. Supervisors often are not skilled in providing feedback or identifying effective developmental recommendations. Substantial support and aids must be coupled with supervisor training to provide quality developmental feedback by using this approach. The aids are readily available from major publishers, and most can be provided electronically from the web for a reasonable investment. Such possibilities include Lominger's FYI (For Your Improvement) and Harvard Business Online's ManageMentor®, both excellent online alternatives. Personnel Decisions Inc. publishes the *Successful Manager's Handbook*, which is also very helpful in providing developmental recommendations.

While the supervisor evaluation is often the initial step in any leadership potential assessment process, it is generally not sufficient as a total process.

Psychological and Cognitive Testing

Cognitive ability and psychological assessment instruments are fairly common in potential evaluations. Most of these instruments require a psychologist to interpret and can be very confusing and easily misinterpreted, if used without proper training and understanding. While such an evaluation does not cover all aspects or dimensions of leadership, this approach can be very helpful in evaluating some dimensions of leadership. The approach can be particularly helpful in determining problem-solving skills, strategic thinking, interpersonal skills, and personality traits that are indicative of influence and social activity.

It is typical to have at least one or more cognitive skills tests and one or more personality tests as part of an overall assessment or evaluation. A number of such tests are on the market. While I have not conducted a formal survey of the most widely used cognitive tests, the Watson-Glaser Test of Critical Thinking and the Thurstone Test of Mental Alertness seem to be very widely used. Many others are available. For personality measures, the Hogan Personality Inventory, the 16PF, and the California Personality Inventory are widely used by psychologists. The Berkman Method, DISC Personal Profile System, and Myers-Briggs Type Indicator™ are also widely used and don't require the credentials of a psychologist to administer. More recently, "emotional intelligence" has received great press and the EQi, while requiring certification, does not require a psychologist.

It is not apparent that any single test or set of tests has demonstrated superiority in measuring potential. Rather, it seems that every psychologist involved in assessing managerial talent has his or her own favorite test and/or combination of tests to provide a good picture of the person being tested. The specific test or combination of tests may not be the critical factor in the validity and usefulness of the assessment. However, the understanding of what is being measured by these instruments and the experience of using them are the more likely factors to consider when determining the quality or validity of the assessment. I do not recommend that psychological instruments be used as the sole or primary methods of evaluating potential, because they rarely provide a total picture of a person's experience and capability. However, they can be very helpful when combined with other methods.

360-Degree Feedback

A very common and helpful method of measuring leadership behavior is the use of a 360-degree feedback instrument, which, when used properly, can contribute to the evaluation of potential. The benefits of using a 360-degree instrument are several, and include the aggregation of views from a number of different raters; the rich feedback, which can be quite helpful in assisting the candidate understand where strengths and development opportunities exist; and the power of the feedback from those who know the candidate well.

The challenges in using a 360-degree instrument in measuring potential include (1) the assurance that raters understand the dimensions evaluated, (2) the calibration of the raters, and (3) the identification of raters to assure fairness in ratings across candidates.

If a 360-degree instrument is used in a leadership potential assessment, one must consider several things. Since 360-degree raters are usually lenient in their ratings, it is helpful to have norms against which to compare the ratings. Ideally, norms are from the population being considered or the population against which the potential is being compared. National publishers of 360-degree instruments can also provide national norms.

Verbatim comments from raters on open-ended questions are helpful in 360-degree assessments and are powerful in providing feedback. They do raise the complexity and cost of the administration, but most users would say that it is an investment that is well worth it. Extra care should be taken to assure confidentiality with verbatim statements.

The 360-degree instrument can be conducted in several ways. Most can now be conducted online and, using the web, are fairly convenient and easy to set up and administer. There is always the paper-and-pencil option, which, these days, actually increases the administration costs. Another approach is to conduct brief interviews with the raters. Although very labor-intensive, it can be very helpful, especially in the assessment of potential. Trained interviewers can gain keen insight and can tailor and direct the questions based on the responses by the raters. This approach is obviously more expensive than the online or paper-and-pencil version, but can provide rich and helpful information regarding the candidate.

Simulations

One of the most sophisticated approaches to potential evaluation is to place the candidate in a simulated environment, observe his or her behavior, and measure the results. This approach takes substantial investment in development of the simulation(s), training of observers (if behavioral observation will be used), establishing the facilities that are conducive to the simulation, and determining the scoring or rating of the results.

The assessment center approach to talent evaluation typically involves one or more simulations. These range from in-basket exercises or other roles plays (e.g., leaderless group discussions, supervisor/direct report conversations, irate customer conversations, etc.) to sophisticated electronic simulations or business games in which the candidate is required to make several business decisions.

Simulations are investment-intensive, but provide helpful feedback regarding the candidate's behavior and style. Consistent with the definition of potential, simulations measure what a candidate can do in a given situation. Therefore, it is important that the situation mirror very closely the type of situations facing managers of the target population. Often, leaders in the target population are used as the observers or assessors to assure an appropriate evaluation.

Although the simulation approach yields very rich feedback, it is not often used because of cost (development and administration), as well as the complex logistics.

How One Organization Evaluates Leadership Potential

I have described several different approaches to evaluating leadership potential. An organization will often use two or more of these approaches in combination to identify and develop their talent. I have designed and worked with a process that combines several of these approaches at different points in the process and for different purposes. The process starts with the supervisors evaluating their talent during the annual organization and talent review—a review that "rolls up" from middle management to the CEO. The review includes, among other things, the evaluation of every middle manager and above on current performance, leadership behavior and potential for growth and promotion, plans for development of individuals and organization, and succession or replacement plans of all critical positions. The review "rolls up" in the sense that each manager presents his or her review to his or her leader with discussion and action planning. The leader then evaluates direct reports and reviews the findings with his or her leader. The process culminates with the chairman's organization review, during which the direct reports of the CEO review their organizations and leadership teams with the chairman. The process results in the initial evaluation of leadership potential from middle managers to officers of the corporation. It is important to note that this process is not a one-time affair, but is repeated annually, forming the basis of all development efforts.

From the organization and talent review, high-potential managers are identified and nominated for leadership development programs. One component of the high-potential programs is an assessment of the participant using a 360-degree feedback instrument and psychological testing. Results are fed back to the participant, and development recommendations are added to the development plan of each participant. This assessment is primarily for development of the manager.

The talent review each year also identifies individuals who may be considered as potential succession candidates for officer roles. As these names surface, a further assessment process is added to their development. This process combines the psychological test results (both cognitive and personality), thorough 360-degree feedback from a dozen or more peers, direct reports, and leaders, and a panel interview with current officers and a senior HR leader. It results in a brief report and profile of the individual that

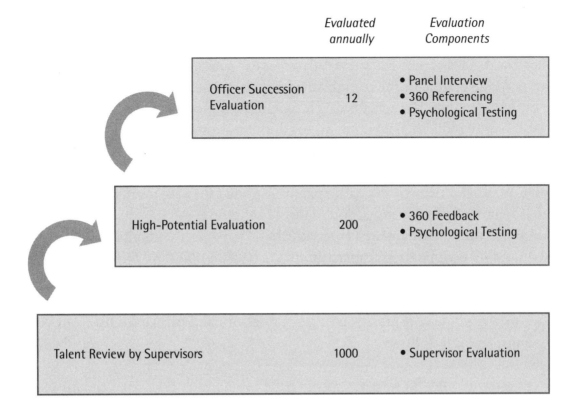

	Evaluated annually	Evaluation Components
Officer Succession Evaluation	12	• Panel Interview • 360 Referencing • Psychological Testing
High-Potential Evaluation	200	• 360 Feedback • Psychological Testing
Talent Review by Supervisors	1000	• Supervisor Evaluation

Figure 2. Leadership Evaluation Process

is fed back to the participant and his or her supervisor, and then reviewed by senior leadership in the organization. The report highlights the developmental recommendations and potential of the participant. Whereas over a thousand managers participate in the organization and talent review annually, about two hundred managers are identified in that review to participate in a high-potential evaluation each year, and at the senior level only a dozen or so go through the evaluation process for officer succession. (See Figure 2.)

Using and Communicating Evaluation Results

An important step in establishing an evaluation process is to determine how the results of the evaluation will be used. Who will "own" the results, that is, who will have access to the results and what are the rules around who can see them? It may seem like a minor point, but it is extremely important to the acceptability of the process to those participating. The anxiety level of anyone being evaluated will be high in the best or "safest" of conditions, but if there is not trust and acceptance of how the results will be used, the process may be viewed in a very negative light.

The answer to who "owns" the results and who can see them is not a simple one. There is not one correct answer for all situations and all processes. For the process to be effective, the answer must address the purpose of the assessment, as well as be consistent with the culture of the organization. In some cases, especially where the purpose of the evaluation is solely for development, the participant may own the results and be the only individual who has access to them. In some processes, not even the supervisor should have access to the results. Often the participant is required to share only an action plan based on the results and share the actual results only if he or she chooses. In other processes, the participant is expected to share results with his or her supervisor and jointly develop action plans for development. In still other processes, not only will the participant and supervisor have access to the results, but the results will be used by organization leadership for succession planning purposes, used for placement, or provided to new supervisors of the participant.

With so many opportunities for use of the results, and so many options, it is important to give some consideration to the guidelines and principles up-front. Here are two principles to follow:

- Ground rules for who has access to the results and under what circumstances should be established up-front, and everyone should understand and be told what the rules are.

- Regardless of who has access to the results, the individual being evaluated should have access to any and all information that can be helpful to his or her development.

Conclusion

Evaluating leadership potential is a critical component to managing leadership talent. The design and approach used in the evaluation are dependent on the needs, practices, and culture of the organization. When planned and conducted correctly, the process and its results can add greatly to the development of individual managers, the future capabilities of the organization, and the current performance of the organization.

Val Markos *is executive director—leadership development at BellSouth. He has over twenty-five years' experience in the areas of human resource selection, executive development, education, and succession planning. He has a Ph.D. and an M.S. in industrial/organizational psychology from the University of Georgia and a B.A. degree in psychology from Weber State University in Ogden, Utah.*

Identifying and Developing High-Potentials
An Executive Perspective
Nicole Drake

Summary

Identifying and developing high-potential employees has become a hot-button issue when addressing sustainable growth and success. Stocking a talent pipeline is a critical factor for all businesses, but not necessarily intuitive to all managers responsible for providing the optimum development of high-potentials, ensuring that they live up to their full potential. We set out to identify criteria, best predictors, and development methods executives currently use to set the standard for maximizing high-potential individuals. I conducted a series of interviews and then performed an analysis, distilling the findings down to usable and practical processes that should be implemented by all managers to address their increasingly important bench-strength shortages.

As Baby Boomers begin exiting the workforce at higher rates and competition for talent has become increasingly fierce, organizations have begun to acknowledge the critical nature of identifying their best and brightest as early as possible. These high-potentials are being tapped earlier in their careers to move quickly through the ranks in order to fill the vacuum at the top.

The topic of talent development was coming up frequently in one of my peer-to-peer networks, the Executive Leadership Development Network. During one conversation, one of the network members mused, "Wouldn't it be interesting if we knew what our best line executives do?" Of course, we all know that in every organization there is someone who has a reputation for being excellent at spotting and nurturing talent—everyone wants to work for him or her! Wouldn't it be great if we could find out the person's secrets! To learn from the best of the best? This led to the idea of surveying executives to find out what the best actually do, rather than listening to theories that consultants, academics, or even the HR community espouse.

High-Potential Executives and Emerging Leaders

Before beginning the interview series, we identified two distinct populations of high-potentials:

- *High-Potential Executives:* Current executives who seem to have the potential to fill positions on the top management team, reporting to the CEO in the future.

- *Emerging Leaders:* Younger leaders lower in the organization who seem to have the potential to fill executive-level positions in the future.

We differentiated between the two groups along the lines of age and level in the organization. We believed, and were proven correct, that there would be distinct ways to identify them and to develop them. In consulting with various organizations and looking over the list of what were called "high-potentials," we were struck by the fact that the lists overwhelmingly consisted of people who were already highly advanced in their careers; often, they were in executive-level positions and, frequently, in their fifties. While it is easier to label someone as high-potential when he or she has a twenty-five-year track record, it can be more difficult but ultimately more rewarding to have criteria to identify high-potentials when they are younger (and emerging) in order to give them more time to be developed. Many organizations we've talked to are currently making a special effort to do so.

The Participants

The twenty-one participants were "role model" executives, with titles ranging from vice president to "C-level," and represented nineteen corporations in varying industries, including the following:

- Abbott

- Aetna

- Battelle

- BP America

- Federated Department Stores

- First Data Corp

- Ford

- Honeywell

- McDonald's

- Navy Federal Credit Union

- Nuvell

- Pimco

- Sonic Automotive

- Texas Instruments

- Visteon

- Westfield Group

The wealth of perspectives from different industries, geographic areas, functions, and levels of responsibility was incredible. Among the participants, we had one chief financial officer (CFO), who gave us a high-level financial view on talent. We interviewed a chief information officer (CIO), who gave us identification and development processes for technology groups. We also gained a global perspective by interviewing a vice president of global business services, along with two senior executives from an emerging talent hot spot, Shanghai. The diverse group of front-line executives and leading organizations made the information from the study rich, practical, and extremely insightful.

Survey Questions

Throughout the interview series, we asked the following questions. The first four differentiated between high-potential executives and emerging leaders; the last four combined the two populations.

Identifying High-Potentials

- How do you determine or decide that a person has "potential"?

- What are the best predictors of future success?

Developing High-Potentials

- What actions do you take to accelerate developments that have the most impact?

- How do you grow leaders fast?

Derailment Factors

- What derailment factors do you look for?

- What actions do you take when you see a high-potential getting derailed?

Quantification Questions

- What percent of your organization is considered high-potential?

- What percent of your time do you spend identifying and developing high-potentials?

The Results

How Do You Determine or Decide Whether a Person Has Potential?

High-Potential Executives

- Track record

- Sees the big picture

- Caring

- Ability to execute

- Active listener

For high-potential executives, "track record," "the ability to see the big picture," and being "caring" were tied as most-cited criteria at 37 percent. The value of looking at an individual's track record as a determining factor of high potential is based on the belief that past performance begets future performance. Simply put, "They have to have a track record of delivering or exceeding my expectations."

"Seeing the big picture" was described as the ability to look beyond quarterly results to the next three to five years down the road. It is also being able to see how all the functions of the organization fit together and what that means for the future. One executive said, "To be a leader, you have to consider multiple dimensions to a problem, not just the technical, but the financial, the political, the social. All of those dimensions become important and when I see a leader, he or she is considering the broadest range of points of view in making a decision." Another executive said, "It is a higher-level thinking. The vision, the strategy, the global perspective. They either have the ability to see that or not. Are they showing that they are thinking that way? Are they interested in knowing that? Are they asking, 'What is the direction of our company?'"

Among the top three criteria, being "caring" is the hardest to quantify. There is no metric that determines whether someone has genuine concern for the people around him or her. While it is, at best, an intuitive measure, one executive described it as the ability to manage up and down and maintain relationships with others. The same executive also said quite bluntly, "I've done a lot of leadership development over the years, and I can't teach someone to be a good leader if he doesn't care for people."

The "ability to execute" was tied with "active listening" as the fourth most-cited criteria. Execution can sometimes be at odds with being caring; however, at the executive level, those who are truly high-potential are able to balance the ability to complete tasks while at the same time caring for the people they work with. It was said that executives who are not high-potential might suffer from the "trail of dead bodies syndrome." They have the results and track records, but they have sacrificed others in the name of those results. This phenomenon was described by one executive when she said, "There are a lot of very bright people, and there are a lot of very good people, but the balance between getting results and at the same time building those relationships is rarer than people are willing to admit."

Other criteria that were cited less frequently were "passion and ambition," "intelligent," and "a team player."

Emerging Leaders

- Track record
- "Shines"
- Passion and ambition
- Sees the big picture
- Team player

At the emerging leader level, "track record" was again cited most often, along with "stands out from peers," both at 37 percent. Responses show that emerging leaders not only stand out from their peers, but their peers also tend to gravitate toward them for their natural leadership and skills. One executive described this as "their ability to act as an influence within a group of their peers. Not to impose their leadership in that position, but clearly, rationally, to start moving the others within that group to that position."

"Passion and ambition" followed at 31 percent and was described as passion for the role and the desire to constantly learn more, work on bigger projects, and involve themselves in all aspects of the organization. One executive put it best, saying, "They want to be a part of something that is high-risk or very important. They just can't stand the thought that they wouldn't work on it. It's kind of a recklessness, but an openness to educate and learn from every experience."

"Seeing the big picture" appeared again for emerging leaders, also cited at 31 percent. Additional criteria for emerging leaders were being a "team player," "passion for learning," "courageous and a risk taker," and "a positive attitude."

After identifying criteria for high-potentials based on what is happening today or has happened in the past, the next question we asked was about what predictors executives use to gauge how high-potentials will do in the future.

What Are the Best Predictors of Future Success?

High-Potential Executives

- Track record

- Sees the big picture

- Team player

- Non-defensive

For high-potential executives, "track record" came in far above the other predictors, at 42 percent. Examining a track record means "looking at goal achievement, what kind of results they are getting. For those individuals who have been assigned a task, did they go from start to finish with everything covered? Did they go beyond what was initially laid out, and did they complete the project with all of the i's dotted and t's crossed and then go on for more?"

Another description of looking at track records was, "I look for people who are successful in what they're doing today, people who are hungry for knowledge, people who work across the organization as well as within their functional environments."

Next, "seeing the big picture" and being a "team player" were cited by 26 percent of the role model executives. A "team player" was described as someone who was skilled at getting the best out of a team. It is also the ability to identify one's own strengths and weaknesses and strategically build a team to support or complement them. One executive asked, "Do they look for key people who supplement their weaknesses as part of team building? We all have strengths and weakness, but high-potentials minimize their weaknesses and build their strengths."

Being "non-defensive" was a characteristic identified in 21 percent of the interviews. This is linked to one's ability to learn and to be continually striving for improvement. Being non-defensive means that high-potentials can accept constructive criticism and coaching from all levels of the organization and then learn from their mistakes. Being defensive is also correlated to having too much ego, which is a derailment factor as well.

The less frequently mentioned predictors of future success were the "ability to manage change," "accomplishments in stretch assignments," and "unanimous support from those around them."

Emerging Leaders

- Track record

- Accomplishments in stretch assignments

- Ability to build and maintain relationships

- Passion for learning

When looking at emerging leaders, three new predictors were introduced into the top ranks. "Track record" was once again the most cited, at 31 percent, but it was closely followed by "accomplishments in stretch assignments," at 26 percent. This is unique to the emerging leaders, and a specific type of track record measures their performance when they were outside of their normal functional area or level of responsibility. One description of what to look for was, "I look for varied accomplishments in areas where they haven't worked before or where there's a significant stretch involved in that accomplishment."

On the other hand, someone may not actually be high-potential, even if he or she is a high performer, if he or she is a "fix-it person." A fix-it person was described as "Someone who keeps accomplishing the same task over and over. He or she can fix one thing after another, but that's the thing, just doing fix-ups. That to me is less of an indicator of potential than someone who takes different things that he hasn't done before and is able to get accomplishments."

The "ability to build and maintain relationships" was also cited by 26 percent of the executives. These are relationships up, down, and across the organization. This seems to be more important at the emerging leader level because the relationships that they develop now that stay strong throughout their careers can be leveraged in the future.

Those who are consistently high performers but fail to create a network to bolster their strengths and supplement their weakness should not be considered high-potential.

"Passion for learning" ranked fourth overall, but those who cited it as a predictor of future success consistently mentioned it as their primary response. One executive said, "They are the ones who are looking to be learning. Quite often, they are the ones who are saying, 'Well, what if we try this? I read about it in a trade magazine. Or I heard that our competitor is doing this, how about if we try something similar?'"

"Being a team player," "seeing the big picture," and being "non-defensive" were also noted at the emerging leader level.

Identifying is only half of the battle. Now you know you have a high-potential, what do you do with him to develop him, and as quickly as possible?

What Actions Do You Take to Accelerate Their Development That Has the Most Impact?

High-Potential Executives

- Stretch assignments

- Rotational assignments

- Increase responsibility

- Conversations around development plans and goals

"Stretch assignments" emerged as the action with the most impact for both high-potential executives, at 57 percent, and emerging leaders, at 68 percent. Stretch assignments can be assignments that are outside of the individual's educational background, functional area, usual level of responsibility, or comfort zone. It would also be considered a stretch if she were being asked to meet nearly unattainable goals with limited resources, limited time, and limited personnel. This is the sink-or-swim test when it comes to high-potentials. One executive said that his preferred method was "giving them a piece of work, giving them the space to show what they can do, but then supporting them in that." He also said, "Invariably I have discovered that has caused people to knock the ball out of the park."

An interesting comment about stretch assignments was, "In 2003, the number of sales in my organization that were in emerging markets of India, China, Mexico was about 6 percent of my operation. My boss gave me a goal to be at 30 percent in one year. Then this year, I have to be at 50 percent. So when I get those kinds of goals, people who are in my organization and around me are going to get stretch assignments."

"Rotational assignments," "increased responsibility," and "conversations around development plans and goals" were equally cited after stretch assignments, at 42 percent each. Rotational assignments were defined as moving an individual through different functional areas, product areas, or businesses for a six-month to two-year period. The goals of rotational assignments are to teach the high-potentials how different pieces of the business work together, to build relationships across the organization, and to round out their skill sets to reflect the core competencies of the organization as a whole. Describing the process used by their organization, an executive said, "I rotate them a lot. I don't let them stay in any one assignment too long. They are rotated from six to eighteen months, but never longer than eighteen months. For senior level, the minimum is two years. I am not trying to build subject-matter experts; I am trying to build leaders."

"Increased responsibility" was related to stretch assignments in this case, but was specific to increasing the number of people or the amount of resources that the individual is placed in charge of. It is also having the person work on initiatives that are more high-profile, more high-risk, and more critical to the success of the company. One executive said, "It really is about giving people increased opportunity, bigger roles, empowering them more, and watching closely to see whether they step up to each increased level of responsibility and how they handle it."

Last, we were surprised that conversations around development plans and goals were more often cited at the executive level (42 percent) than at the emerging leader level (26 percent). An example of the type of conversation that was recommended at the executive level was to "have ongoing developmental conversations that measure the progress versus some pre-established benchmarks and measures [and to] focus on the learning of skills and behavioral development." This is somewhat counterintuitive, but understandable when you consider that part of high-potential development is increasing the time horizon at which the individual looks at the future of the company. People must be highly supported, and a safe space must be created for them to look further down the road and make decisions that will pay off big in the long run, but may lessen short-term profitability. Meeting learning objectives is more important at this stage of development than meeting numbers.

Other developmental actions that were mentioned included "formal training programs," "coaching," and "mentoring."

Emerging Leaders

- Stretch assignments
- Rotational assignments
- Formal training and development programs
- Creating visibility

Preferences for developmental actions had a much more concrete ranking at the emerging leader level. Overwhelmingly, "stretch assignments" (68 percent) and "rotational assignments" (47 percent) were the most often cited. "Formal training and development programs" around leadership skills were the third most highly cited (36 percent), suggesting that they are more valued at this level than at the high-potential executive level. The training programs mentioned ranged from internal teaching to teaming with a learning institution to create a custom curriculum.

"Creating visibility" was cited 31 percent of the time and played a role in influencing what projects the high-potential would be selected to work on. In the interest of getting their work seen by more upper management, suggestions ranged from including the individual on high-profile taskforces, in work on strategic initiatives, and even on drafting the next five-year strategic plan. Exposure to top management can also be achieved through formal and informal mentoring programs.

Other developmental activities that were noted were "conversations around development plans and goals," "increased responsibility," "external coaching," and "mentoring."

How Do You Grow Leaders Fast?

High-Potential Executives

- Stretch assignments with support

- Coaching

- Not a good idea

How to grow leaders fast turned out to be a somewhat contentious question because executives told us that issues of burnout and loss of depth begin to come into play when you do not allow the individual to get the full benefit of developmental activities. "Stretch assignments with support" came in first for both the high-potential executives and the emerging leaders, at 52 percent. Concerning high-potential executives, one respondent said, "When you're giving somebody a fast-track assignment, it means you're giving her an assignment where the risk of failure is substantially higher than her normal duties. And you need to provide a safety net, so you want someone senior enough and seasoned enough not to let this fast-tracker get into serious trouble."

For emerging leaders, another said, "If you want to grow somebody fast, you're taking a risk. You're not fully comfortable that this person has the experience, the development, the expertise. Therefore, when you're taking a fast track, whom you pair that person with is extremely important."

"Coaching," be it internal or external, was ranked as a somewhat distant second-most-cited developmental action at 21 percent. The third-most-cited response was that it was "not a good idea" to try to grow leaders fast, for all of the reasons noted above. "Rotational assignments" and "formal learning programs" were also cited as fast-tracking methods.

Emerging Leaders

- Stretch assignments with support

- Exposure to top management

- Rotational assignments

- Not a good idea

The results for emerging leaders were very similar, with the addition of quicker "rotational assignments." The process used was to "accelerate the job rotations. Although you usually want someone to be there for twelve to eighteen months, you may have to narrow it to eight months."

Again, a concern was that this may lead to lack of depth and derailment further down the road.

What Derailment Factors Do You Look For?

Part of developing high-potentials is making sure that they stay on track. Derailment factors can stop an individual from reaching his or her full potential. There are characteristics, personality traits, or events that must be mitigated or resolved as quickly as possible. Responses for this question were the same for both high-potential executives and emerging leaders, so the responses are combined here.

- Ego

- Developed too quickly

- Self-serving

- Repeated failures

"Ego" was far and away the most cited response to this question. Excessive ego can lead to problems with working in teams, accepting constructive criticism and learning from it, and managing both up and down. One executive said, "They see themselves as too important and it minimizes their positive impact on the team around them. They fail to develop relationships, they demonstrate a defensive form of communication, and they demonstrate a lack of curiosity."

The second-most-mentioned derailment factor, at 36 percent, was that they were "developed too quickly." The effects of this factor were felt by one executive, who said, "If you want to develop them fast, I think that you lose some quality. You can move people too fast; we have suffered from some of that."

"Self-serving" was the third factor (36 percent) and it was also related to ego. It was differentiated from ego in that ego can manifest internally, but being self-serving was characterized as harming those the high-potential works with—and even the organization as a whole. "If they have strong results, but they sacrifice team members or the bigger picture or are too self-serving, they would no longer be considered high-potential."

The last universal derailment factor was "repeated failure," at 29 percent. We were somewhat surprised at this response, because mistakes are supposed to be healthy and allowable, to a point, as an important way for people to learn. However, "high-potential" is such a meaningful designation that there is less tolerance and more is expected. An executive explained, "We work in an environment in which there is a lot of competition. On the one hand, mistakes are healthy because you have a chance to learn from them. However, with high-potentials, it is different because they can't afford to make mistakes very often. Sometimes, they are in a position for a year if you want to move them fast. Everyone is human, but when you make a mistake, sometimes it can kill your career."

One factor that was unique to the emerging leader population was "impatience with the speed of development." This is an increasing concern with Generations X and Y, the so-called entitlement generations. Often, and especially when an emerging leader is identified as high-potential, he may not understand why he is given certain assignments—surely he can be CEO in a week! This is where developmental conversations come into play. If you openly communicate the reasons for the time spent in different roles, you can increase retention and satisfaction for this younger population. One executive said, "They can have expectations of the rate that they are going to move up. They think that they should be moving up very quickly, and when they don't move up, they lose patience. They can become disillusioned."

What Actions Do You Take When You See a High-Potential Getting Derailed?

The actions to be taken are straightforward and, when executed with care, can very quickly put a derailed high-potential back on track.

- Confront with the facts of the issue

- Involve a coach or mentor to correct behavior

- Consider reassignment

The first step is to sit the high-potential down and confront the behavior. Says one executive, "I take a very directive but guiding leadership style that quickly addresses the issue as soon as it develops. I identify and detail the problem behavior and present fact-based, first-hand, specific examples and suggestions of behavior that would be more appropriate."

If confidentiality issues are not a limitation, it is also helpful to involve a coach to help the individual talk about the underlying issues with an impartial party. Coaches may also be able to point out alternative behaviors.

As a last resort, you may consider reassignment. It is possible the individual is performing poorly because he or she is not in an area in which he or she can excel, or perhaps the proper support is not in place. In the most extreme cases, where behavior cannot be corrected, it would be appropriate to remove the high-potential designation.

Unfortunately, although these seem like simple steps to take, they may require a potentially uncomfortable confrontation. An executive noted, "We are not very good at this. We are so polite, and we are so nice to one another, that we let things go without pointing them out." With the huge investment that is made in high-potentials, one cannot afford not to be direct and honest.

What Percent of Your Organization Is Considered High-Potential?

The organizations that were represented in this study are very diverse, and so we expected some variation in what percent of each organization was considered "high-potential." We were not disappointed. However, the average of 5 percent was about what we expected.

- High: 20 percent

- Low: .01 percent

- Average: 5.07 percent

When asked to identify his high-potential population, one executive said, "Ten percent who have officially been identified as high-potential and another 10 percent who could be high-potential." The relatively high numbers in this quote suggest that the currently used process and criteria in this organization were not sufficiently selective in identifying high-potentials.

What Percent of Your Time Do You Spend
Identifying and Developing High-Potentials?

The last question we asked was to get an idea of the amount of time executives actually take out of their day to identify and develop high-potentials. While time spent does not guarantee quality, it is a measure of their commitment to this activity.

- High: 75 percent

- Low: 5 percent

- Average: 24 percent

The common lament that we heard echoed in nearly every interview, "I wish that I could say 80 percent, but it is closer to 15 or 20 percent."

Words of Advice

The last thing we asked the executives was what advice they had for other leaders about identifying and developing high-potentials. Here's what they said.

High-Potential Executives

- "Find ways to have multiple perspectives. If you're making an assessment of people, have two or three other people you have confidence in also making assessments."

- "It is the most important thing I do. I have a friend who says if people were truly our most important asset we'd paint them every year."

- "I think it comes down to risk. What I have found in a lot of cases is that people have never been pushed, but they have always had that ability—it has just never been tapped."

- "If you give them feedback on where they need to improve, most high-potentials really embrace that feedback, and when they get it, they get it forever, so it's a lesson learned."

Emerging Leaders

- "You just can't watch and expect people to grow. You've got to get involved in it very personally for the person, as well as just to build your skill sets around what's going on as the market changes, as graduates change, as talent changes. You have to be out in the middle of it."

- "Lots of people have the potential to do well at higher levels in the company, and only a few are chosen to do that. If senior leaders and colleagues believe people will be successful, it is very frequently a self-fulfilling prophecy, because other people's beliefs engenders a commitment to that person's success."

How to Act Differently

I believe that all members of an organization can benefit from our interview results. Corporate executives can better understand the key emerging competencies of future leaders and expand their knowledge of ways to develop them. Coaches can share parts of this data with their executives and coaching clients. For example, in coaching a client, I might share some of the derailment factors so that he or she does not fall into the derailment camp.

All parties can realize that there is an imperative to start acting *now* to develop talent and that the tendency to put it off will have major consequences.

Last, it gives employees of all levels a clear vision of what characteristics they should develop and emphasize within themselves in order to be the best that they can be. For me, it is a playbook for success, pinpointing the programs that highly motivated people should pursue to get noticed and to meet their long-term career goals. Aligning all members of the high-potential process is a powerful way to ensure the future success of the organization.

Nicole Drake *recently joined Executive Development Associates as a consultant. She is currently a project manager for EDA's High-Potential Interview Series. Prior to joining EDA, Ms. Drake was an associate with Dr. John Sullivan & Associates, a strategic advisory services firm focused on the development of world-class human resource practices in HR planning, employment branding, HR metrics, and talent management. In her role as an associate, she was responsible for identifying, researching, and documenting best practices in both the public and private sectors. Ms. Drake has also served as a co-teacher for a capstone course on business strategy at San Francisco State University, where she has earned a bachelor of science degree in business administration, with an emphasis in finance.*

On-Boarding, ROI, Learning from Experience, and Putting Learning to Work

Sucessful On-Boarding

William J. Morin

Summary

It's estimated that 35 percent of C-level executives get new jobs each year in Fortune 500 corporations. Of course, starting a new job has always been challenging. For the presidency of the United States, we call the first phase of the President's performance "the first 100 days." Executives experience very similar challenges when being promoted or recruited into a new position.

This article is about this up-front critical time period, which we are calling the *on-boarding* process. I will discuss the pitfalls, opportunities, and the correct way of conducting this process during the first six to twelve months of an executive's time in a new position. I will also examine the roles of HR, the supervisor, and all other interested parties.

Every day of my professional life, I advise executives on performing more effectively. I have been doing so for thirty years. Over those years, I have observed that the most critical time period for any executive is the first several months of performing in a new position.

Even if an executive has been promoted into a position with the same company, the new position requires new thinking and new approaches. If he or she comes in from the outside, he or she will face an even greater challenge in doing the right thing at the right time because of the need to learn the culture.

David Fowler, ex-CEO of Chubb Life Institute, states in an article about advising CEOs that 55 percent of CEOs don't last eighteen months in their jobs (*Harvard Business Review*). In addition, according to *The Wall Street Journal*, C-level executives' tenures are becoming increasingly "nasty, brutish, and short." Some 60 percent of today's Fortune 500 C-level executives have held their jobs for just six years or fewer.

These startling revelations continue to hit American corporations and organizations where they can be hurt most—in the pocketbook. Considering that 35 percent of CEOs and other C-level leaders in the Fortune 500 change jobs every year, the money spent on recruiting top talent adds up.

The responsibility of controlling and reducing the cost and potential harm to the organization falls squarely on the organizations' leading HR professionals.

In addition, it may sound silly, but bosses need to be trained (or at least advised) on assimilating new hires. They need to be checked on at the highest levels to determine how they feel their new hire(s) are doing. Many C-level recruits feel waltzed into the job and then abandoned to dance solo. Articles and surveys routinely speak of the "abandoned stage," when an executive is hired and then dropped into a position without proper orientation and support.

Misstatements and Poor Guidance

Most of the time, new executives are told they have been brought into the company to bring about change and to meet specific expectations of the board of directors, shareholders, stakeholders, and, of course, other top management members. They are most often directed to be a change agent as soon as possible. Unfortunately, nothing could be further from the truth. This is especially the case if an organization has any history at all (companies like General Electric, DuPont, General Motors, or Avon). Even if the company must be turned around quickly, even a new CEO, or any other executive, would be foolhardy to act quickly without knowing the true challenges facing the company and having the time to attain subordinates' support. In fact, the deadliest action a new hire can take within the first several months is attempting to change anything. Interestingly, a major pharmaceutical company requests that new executive hires do nothing and say little for six months or more. In essence, peers, subordinates, and management expect new hires to learn what's going on first before making any real suggestions.

The Truth

Now let's go for a real-life story (of course, names and titles are changed to protect the innocent—or the not so innocent).

Joe came on-board as the new chief financial officer. On his first day, a gentleman showed up at his door. This man introduced himself as Mike and said he was in charge of corporate purchasing. "Because of your level in the company," said Mike, "you have the privilege of selecting new furniture for your office." So the new CFO picked out new furniture from Mike's catalog, and the furniture was to be delivered within a week's time.

When the CEO found out that his new chief financial officer had ordered new furniture on his first day, there was hell to pay. Fortunately, an on-boarding coach was involved. As the coach explored how this event happened, it came to light that the new furniture purchase was part of a normal policy instituted several years ago by the CEO. Frankly, the CEO, not having brought in new C-level executives, had forgotten about establishing this perk.

Had the on-boarding coach and appropriate HR executive not been involved, the CEO probably would have removed the chief financial officer because of lost confidence in his new hire's sense of judgment. In this case, the search fee was $380,000, and the severance, due to a contract, would have been $1,000,000. In addition, other stock offerings totaled $3,000,000 for the new hire. All of these factors brought the potential cost of termination close to $5,000,000. Unfortunately, this story is not unusual. Protecting the investment of the organization is usually an afterthought.

Another unfortunate factor is that people are likely to make quick, personal, judgmental decisions when first meeting someone. For example, can the person be trusted? Is he worthy of respect? Can she do her job? If a new colleague, peer, or subordinate doesn't measure up to our expectations in any of these areas, we tend to hold him or her accountable forever. We might not even give him a second chance to rectify any poor decisions made when coming on-board. This makes the following question extremely important.

What Is an Appropriate On-Boarding Process?

We strongly recommend the following eight steps:

1. The most important first step is to *establish clear expectations for the position.* This seems logical, but often, job descriptions and mandates are outdated and various constituencies' expectations are unclear. Since the boss is usually the most important member of these constituencies (versus subordinates or peers), it's imperative to clearly understand his or her expectations. However, peers can also sabotage an individual's potential and growth opportunities within the first six months.

2. *Develop a system of peer checks.* Peers are critical to a new hire's success. Peers perceive a new hire as a competitor for the boss's attention and speculate what the new person will be like as a team member. Peers wonder what authority they

may have to give up or how much cooperation they must offer to a new person. In many cases, peers have limited interaction with a new executive and may withhold vital support, information, and cooperation. A system of "peer" checks conducted by HR and the new hire can go a long way toward winning the peers' support. Simply asking peers for feedback on the new hire's performance is a good move for the new hire and for the HR professional to take.

3. *Prepare an announcement that sets the tone.* Often, written and verbal announcements of new hires are no more than several sentences or statements about the individual coming on-board and his or her job description. It is much better to describe the individual's background and outline some of his or her major responsibilities.

4. *Conduct a real orientation* that is not limited to one or two visits to the stakeholders' offices. In fact, the orientation should be a well-planned, well-calendared event that has the executive visiting and speaking with individuals for at least several hours each over a six-month period.

5. *Review the results of the orientation process.* The boss, the HR professional, and the new recruit should discuss the recruit's experience during the orientation period. An agenda may be set for each individual who meets with the new recruit during the orientation. This is an important business venture and should be conducted accordingly.

6. *Establish an inside-the-organization mentor* to look after the individual during, as well as after, the orientation. This internal mentor (a seasoned executive outside of the new hire's chain of command) should be trained on how to mentor and how to reach out to the new executive on a regular basis. An HR professional could certainly play this role if trained to do so.

7. *Conduct a 360-degree review with peers and subordinates* after two or three months so that the on-boarding coach can evaluate the new hire's progress and give the new hire some helpful, constructive feedback. Obviously, everything—from dress code, manners, and style of communication—can be critical to the new hire's success. This 360-degree feedback can be provided on a group basis, with subordinates in one group and peers in another.

8. The boss should *frequently ask subordinates and other interested executives* how the new executive is doing—and should be prepared to intercede if issues, questions, and/or perceived challenges related to the assimilation process are uncovered. All too often, it seems the boss is the last to know there is an issue.

Do C-Level Executives Need On-Boarding?

The answer, of course, is "yes." The higher up you go in an organization, the more critical a new hire's success is for both the organization and the individual.

Recruiting fees, sign-on bonuses, severance payments, and organizational impact of a poor hire all add up to very high cost and risk factors when hiring or promoting a C-level executive. When on-boarding C-level executives, several other factors must be considered:

- Dealing with the board of directors. Is the new hire prepared to interact with the board? Analyst? Investors?

- What was the reputation of the executive before joining the company or being promoted? What is good about it or what is not so good? How should his or her reputation be managed?

- What is the potential for greater negative impact if the person makes wrong business decisions?

- Should an advisor be identified to coach him or her into the position?

Should You Have an External On-Boarding Coach?

Clearly, if you have a strong internal mentoring program with individuals well trained to look after new recruits, perhaps you can avoid the cost of having an external on-boarding coach.

Although most on-boarding coaching costs in the $30,000-plus range for a six-month program, it seems a small price to pay for the assurance of on-boarding a high-potential executive in a proper way. Using an outside coach is a good idea because objectivity and confidentiality can be maintained.

The Achilles' heel of using on-boarding coaches is the fact that they often lack solid understanding of the organization's culture and the established expectations for a new executive. As with everything else, on-boarding coaches have to be well trained in coaching and oriented to the organization. They also have to know where to go if a problem arises during the on-boarding process. Confidentiality is not enough; all on-boarding coaches need to be reminded that they work for the company, as well as for the individual being coached. We all know that expectations for the coaching relationship are sometimes too loose and not defined well.

Coaching for on-boarding generally requires a great deal more sharing of information with human resources professionals and with the individual's supervisor than does coaching used for development, and it is important that all parties, including the new hire, be aware of the communication and feedback processes.

It could be argued that everyone needs to be coached or mentored into an organization or position. As a process, on-boarding should be well-thought-through by human resources professionals as well as by the rest of the management teams. It should never be taken lightly.

What Role Does the Executive Search Organization Play in On-Boarding?

When it comes to on-boarding, most executive search organizations claim to follow and support a recently placed candidate as he or she becomes active within a new company. However, although well-intentioned, search firms tend to move quickly to the next assignment and wash their hands of the executive once he or she has been placed.

It's appropriate that a corporation, having spent a tremendous amount of money on executive search fees, should hold an executive search firm accountable for supporting the new recruit for at least several months. A search firm may not be as objective or as confidential as an executive coach, yet they can add value to the on-boarding process. At a minimum, the search organization should assign someone to check on the new recruit's well-being and ask about challenges he or she may be having in the new assignment.

Usually, the search organization has a meaningful relationship with human resources, as well as with the hiring executive. These relationships could both support and provide helpful direction to the new hire in his or her efforts to succeed. In addition, the executive search organization usually has a good understanding of how the company functions and any expectations for the new recruit. After all, they searched for the new recruit following company specifications and competencies for the position.

Danger Signs of an Unsuccessful On-Boarding

If all constituencies are paying attention to the new recruit, it should quickly become obvious if the individual isn't working out. Some signs of poor on-boarding are

- The recruit communicates very little because of obvious insecurity. This speaks volumes about his or her feelings toward the position and the on-boarding process. A questioning attitude is a good sign the recruit is in the right place.

- The recruit appears out-of-sorts, in over his or her head, or indicates that he or she may have made a bad decision by accepting the position (by acting confused or negative, for example).

- Obviously, being absent or tardy are signs that the new hire is not into his or her new position.

Discussing any of these signs with the new hire is appropriate. Putting the issue on the table is better than assuming the person's feelings can be ignored, which can prove to be a disaster for the company and for the executive.

HR's Job—The Four Takeaways

Four activities should always occur to make successful on-boarding a way of life, rather than a rare event. They are

1. Management has to be trained on bringing people on board successfully. For example, a proper orientation to the on-boarding process would include (1) what should be discussed with the new recruit and (2) how to obtain (and give) feedback on how the new recruit is doing.

2. The new executive must feel supported and know that he or she can ask questions without fear of reprisal. Often, the individual feels left out, not communicated with, isolated, and under-appreciated. We all need feedback, as long as it is positive or instructive.

3. Internal on-boarding mentors should be trained on advising and supporting new hires. This process won't happen without training.

4. Human resources professionals must ensure that on-boarding is a way of life and not just a rare event. HR needs to lead this process to make sure it is being carried out properly.

If a company undertakes these four activities, it can anticipate a successful on-boarding process.

Conclusion

Organizations must be aware that human development is not an event, but a way of life. Certain clichés are popular today, such as, "We are on a continuous learning curve" or "We want to be a learning organization." These terms are replacing the old statement, "Our number-one asset is our people." We now recognize that executives must be nurtured from their first days on the job, not six months into their positions when problems arise.

William Morin, *founder and chairman of WJM Associates, Inc., has advised numerous CEOs, presidents, and other C-level executives of leading corporations in a variety of industries. A recognized leader in the human resources consulting industry, Mr. Morin has developed many effective HR management strategies for top corporations for the past thirty-one years and has personally worked with over two hundred of the Fortune 500 corporations. He established WJM, a leading executive and organization development consulting firm, in 1996, following a twenty-two-year career as chairman and chief executive officer of Drake Beam Morin, Inc., the international career continuation and organizational consulting firm. During his tenure as CEO, Mr. Morin directed the growth of DBM from a U.S. company with sales under $1 million to a worldwide organization operating in nineteen countries with over $210 million in revenues. Mr. Morin has authored or co-authored seventeen books and numerous articles about conducting successful staff reductions, corporate trust, coping with job loss, and corporate revitalization. Mr. Morin received his master's degree from Southern Illinois University.*

ROI Comes in Many Forms
Leadership Development
at Baker Hughes Incorporated
Barbara Reyna

Summary

An enterprise-led leadership development strategy launched in 2001 at Baker Hughes Incorporated included an executive development program called the Business Leadership Institute (BLI). After collecting three years' worth of evaluations, performance measurements, and organizational impact outcomes, Baker Hughes Incorporated looked at various quantitative and qualitative forms of measuring return on investment (ROI). The question as to whether development programs can always be quantified in terms of hard business results led to tracking various forms of ROI measurement.

Baker Hughes traces its roots back to the early 1900s, when R.C. Baker and Howard Hughes, Sr., began oilfield service companies based on innovative technology. For the next eight decades, their respective companies grew and acquired a number of other oilfield companies with diverse histories and cultures. Ultimately, Baker International and Hughes Tool Company merged in 1987 to form Baker Hughes Incorporated (BHI), headquartered in Houston, Texas. Today, we have more than 27,000 employees in seventy-two countries, with a diverse mix of skills, nationalities, and backgrounds.

Through all the years of growth, Baker Hughes achieved success because each of its operating divisions focused on being the best at providing products and services in a specific technical area, such as drill bits or well completion systems. This "best in class" strategy helps drive our quality and customer service models. In addition, strong pride and a unique culture are alive and well in each business unit.

Why Invest in Enterprise-Wide Leadership Development?

In 2001, a new CEO, Michael E. Wiley, came to Baker Hughes with a plan to drive company performance by creating an enterprise spirit and common alignment around core values, keys to success, and a BHI high-performance culture. To deliver on this plan, he established a leadership development strategy and sponsored the launch of the Baker Hughes Business Leadership Institute (BLI) for selected executives and managers with high potential throughout the global organization. The two-week BLI course was designed to provide advanced management training tailored to the needs of a decentralized, worldwide corporation. During the program, participants were encouraged to think strategically while studying issues specific to the international energy business.

Program curriculum, case studies, and discussions had elements relating to our core values (*integrity, teamwork, performance, learning*) and keys to success and decision making (*engage people, deliver value, be cost-efficient, resource effectively*). BLI also emphasized common models of Baker Hughes' business processes, culture, and leadership style.

Business Leadership Institute and ROI

As many practitioners know, linking ROI to a development program can be a bit like the search for the Holy Grail. Once you think you've found it, you find yourself again on the journey for a more explicit "hard" measurement.

Our Baker Hughes Business Leadership Institute represents a substantial investment. Since BLI was launched in 2003, 225 top managers have attended the course. Program costs, travel, accommodations, and time away from critical jobs add up to a significant expense.

In the development arena, most ROI efforts demonstrate a clear link between "soft" development processes and "hard" business results. As we all know, learning is not something that can be easily quantified in the way that profits and losses can be. Although at Baker Hughes we have chosen to focus our efforts on the *quality* of the leadership development process rather than the "hard" measurement validity, we have potentially identified five forms of ROI that we can use to measure effectiveness and to justify investment.

Five Forms of ROI

The five ways that BLI can be linked to ROI are (1) business results, (2) applied learning, (3) high-performance culture index, (4) succession planning outcomes, and (5) feeling valued (perhaps immeasurable, but quite worthy of inclusion).

1. Business Results

Many of our BLI alumni claim that the experience had an impact on their businesses. Whether a case study discussion relayed a valuable idea about a business application or a new working relationship revealed a collaborative business deal, many believe that the ten days spent together at BLI improved their overall business skills and business results.

BHI Business Results

An August 2005 report in the *Houston Chronicle*, "Baker Hughes' Profit Hits $218.8 Million," stated that BHI booked almost $2 billion in sales for our second quarter of 2005, which drew 64 cents per share profit, 87 percent over the same period of 2004 and 22 percent over the last quarter.

Our company saw an increased demand for drill bit rentals and wire line logging services. Revenue per employee was up 14 percent, and operating profit per employee was up 67 percent over the same period last year.

This report may sound like "easy earnings," in a high-demand environment, yet it's tough to find people and materials in this "up" business cycle. BHI had to pay more for these resources—not to mention deliver performance under increasing competitive forces.

Here's a recent quote from our president and chief operating officer, Rod Clark: "I can't say enough about the conscious efforts people are making. I'd really hate to compete against us. Our business results speak volumes about unified leadership, common enterprise spirit, and a high-performance culture that fortunately was planted and nurtured before the up-tick in the market. I believe that our BLI program has had a profound impact."

Another business result: BLI brought together the general manager from a Baker Hughes cable operations plant and one of our company's financial executives, who otherwise would never have had the opportunity to meet. At lunch one day, the plant manager complained about the rising cost of copper and, as a result, his division's challenges to meet its financial goals. Working together, they developed a plan to hedge the division's cost of copper by entering into copper swaps on the London Metals Exchange.

---

2. Applied Learning

Most programs emphasize evaluation. The classic Kirkpatrick model (1975) shown below gives the progressive levels of initial reaction, actual applied learning, demonstrable behavior change, and last, over time, actual "hard" results. The four levels are

- Level 1: Reaction—Measures satisfaction with aspects of program (topic, speaker, schedule, etc.)

- Level 2: Learning—Measures knowledge acquired during program (improved skills, attitudes changed, etc.)

- Level 3: Behavior—Measures extent to which participants change behavior on the job as a result of the knowledge obtained in a program

- Level 4: Results—Measures results of a program (higher productivity, quality, sales, profits, turnover, costs, etc.)

Level 1, program evaluations, have been called "smile sheets." However, evaluations are designed to align closely to program objectives and overarching company goals. In our case at Baker Hughes, the major considerations of the evaluation process are the relevance and value of the courses, the probability that our leaders will use the insights from the classes, and the overall satisfaction with BLI. Shown in Table 1 is evaluation data that indicates subtle and increasing value to individuals.

The data from Table 1 shows that BLI met the expectations of participants, but does not necessarily measure ROI. The Level 4 data validates that BLI had an impact on business results.

Level 4: Results

One executive member of our company, a vice president of technology for our largest division, has a compelling story of moving through the Kirkpatrick model to Level 4.

"After discussions during and after BLI, a seed was planted in my mind and others' regarding our supplier strategy. In my previous position at one of the BHI drilling divisions, we recognized the importance of aligning our strategy with key suppliers. We shared elements of our long-range plan, giving them 'line of sight' to the end product application and performance requirements. Working with their main supplier, this process enabled them to develop the technology and products that contributed to increased performance of the final product. This resulted in a *win-win* situation, as both companies increased market share and profitability in a very competitive environment."

Table 1. Level 1: Reaction

BHI Business Leadership Program Evaluation: 12-Month Comparison, May 2004 to May 2005
Distribution of Scores: 1 (low) through 6 (high)

Please evaluate how effectively the following program objectives have been met	May 2004	May 2005	Change
To help you develop global leadership and management skills	5.25	5.29	+.04
To advance your understanding of global strategic issues, both analysis and implementation	5.19	5.29	+.10
To gain a better understanding of key business issues facing your company	4.81	5.29	+.48
To share best practices and develop better working relationships across business units	4.81	4.82	+.01
To develop personal action plans that, when implemented, will add value to your company	4.43	5.18	+.75

3. High-Performance Culture Index

When designing BLI, we wanted to create a program to drive our enterprise culture from one that was strong on divisional focus to one of alignment across the corporation. We also wanted to provide a common ground of networks and relationships to build a high-performing organization. We had to decide how to measure that.

We conducted our first global, all-employee high-performance culture survey in 2004 with an impressive 68 percent response rate. A benchmark comparison will be conducted in 2006.

It may be unrealistic to consider that BLI can have an impact on employee-wide high-performance culture survey results. Yet, aspects from the survey, such as leadership behavior and better understanding our strategy and company goals, may serve as indicators. After we complete our benchmark analysis in 2006, we will assess a high-performance culture index and potential ROI indicators, as laid out in Table 2.

4. Succession Planning Impact

We wanted to create a leadership development program that supported our succession planning process. As participants got to know other management team members better, the relationship building naturally created alliances across divisions.

Cross-divisional career development experiences were not previously an embraced practice. As the numbers in Figure 1 show, our organization has leveraged BLI as a talent

Table 2.   2004 High-Performance Culture Exhibits

Overall, Baker Hughes as a Place to Work (By Job Category)			
	Favorable	Neutral	Unfavorable	Different from Norm
Total Baker Hughes	67%	28%	5%	+9
Senior Management (n = 72)	78	18	4	+5
Management (n = 1,775)	71	26	3	+5
Supervisors (n = 2,298)	69	27	4	+3
Professionals (n = 4,856)	68	28	4	+13
Field Services/Support Technicians (n = 2,590)	63	31	6	+11
Administrative (n = 1,615)	72	24	4	+20
Hourly Production and Ops/Prod Support	66	28	6	+4

Strategic Framework			
	Have a Good Understanding		Understand What I Must Do to Support Goals	
	Agree	Disagree	Agree	Disagree
Total Baker Hughes	60%	14%	65%	12%
Senior Management	86	3	86	5
Management	69	11	69	11
Supervisors	63	13	67	12
Professionals	57	16	62	14
Field Service/Support Technicians	56	16	63	13
Administrative	64	9	69	7
Hourly Production and Ops/Prod Support	58	14	67	11

- 225 attendees through 8/31/05
  - 41 cross-divisional moves involving 34 BLI attendees
  - 168 progressions or promotions involving 119 BLI attendees

Figure 1.   BLI Attendees 2003 to 2005

development resource. Ultimately, a succession planning impact measurement has evolved.

5. Feeling Valued

Last but not least, there is nothing more motivating to encourage and drive performance than the awareness of and appreciation of feeling valued by an organization.

One of our corporate officers stated it quite well in a recent discussion: "Learning, for me, is a motivating force. Knowing that the company was willing to invest a significant sum of money and ten days in my continuing education made me feel truly valued as an employee and a leader in Baker Hughes."

Continued Learning and Global Relationship Building

The primary purposes of BLI were to expose senior managers to strategic ideas, to encourage decision making consistent with the core values, and to develop relationships among senior leaders throughout the company. Because it included senior managers from all over the world, BLI promoted communication across our divisions and advanced the understanding of our global businesses, challenges, issues, and common experiences.

To build on the success of BLI, we will offer in 2006 a "next level" program to address strategy, execution, and growth in our global businesses. Chad Deaton, Baker Hughes Incorporated's chairman and CEO since October 2005, stated recently, "When I first joined Baker Hughes, I attended the BLI programs to meet our participants and to discuss the challenges and opportunities from their points of view. I could see that the program had helped facilitate a strong cultural foundation for engagement of our top team. The 'next chapter' of BLI will be critical in supporting our long-term strategy for achieving continued global growth, world-class service delivery, and optimal customer relationships. In assessing our progress, it's clear that we have achieved a 'return on investment.'"

Conclusion

It is always difficult to directly tie increases to productivity and profits to training and development initiatives. However, at BHI we have gathered data and analyzed correlations that strongly suggest that BHI benefits from the Business Leadership Institute. Not only has the performance of the company been outstanding, but employees are finding BHI a great place to work and in which to build careers.

Over the years, management theorists have known that organizations, business plans, and management theories don't really achieve results. Endeavors succeed or fail because of the *people* involved. Only by attracting and developing the best people, can we accomplish long-term stretch goals. Our goal at Baker Hughes Incorporated is to create an environment in which the best, the brightest, and the most creative are attracted, retained, and, most importantly, contributing to their full potential. Now that's ROI!

Reference

Kirkpatrick, D. (1975). *Evaluating training programs.* San Francisco: Berrett-Koehler.

Barbara Reyna *is the director of leadership and organization development for Baker Hughes Incorporated, a leader in worldwide oilfield services, providing technology to produce and manage petroleum reservoirs. She specializes in designing and delivering programs and processes to support leadership teams, global succession planning, and high-performance cultures. Her career experiences include Tenneco, Chase, Compaq, Conoco, and Harvard Business School's Executive Education Center. In her various capacities, she focused on strategic human resources and management consulting. Her education was at the University of Texas-Austin, University of Houston-Houston, and Simmons College-Boston.*

Learning from Experience
Easier Said Than Done
Vijay Govindarajan and Chris Trimble

Summary

Learning from experience is commonly assumed to be a natural process. It is not. Without a disciplined approach to drawing inferences from experience, learning is much less likely. The core learning step is analysis of disparities between predictions and outcomes—critical for the planning process. Yet most organizations suffer from numerous barriers to insightful analysis. Part of the problem is that the analytical framework embedded in most planning processes is not conducive to learning. The other part of the problem is that the predictions themselves are mistreated, through several prevalent organizational mechanisms.

Companies adopt a wide variety of strategies to train and develop leaders. They send their managers for classroom instruction, assign them action learning projects, engage them in business simulations, mentor them, connect them with outside leadership coaches, and more. Without any doubt, these efforts bolster a company's executive bench strength.

Still, there is no substitute for direct experience. Management is an art, learned over decades. Thus, among the most important elements of a leadership development program are well-constructed rotation programs and career paths that give managers broad exposure to multiple business disciplines.

It is commonly assumed that experience is the best teacher. But how does learning from experience actually happen? It is easy to dismiss the question. Isn't learning from experience a natural accumulation of wisdom and judgment? In fact, learning does not always follow from experience. It is not automatic. *Learning from experience requires effort and discipline.*

This discipline is teachable, but few companies teach it. This leaves a crucial element of leadership development to chance. Managers should be trained in the basics of learning from experience, and they should understand the many reasons that the learning process breaks down.

In this article, composed of three parts, we will first illustrate the mechanics of the process of learning from experience. In the remaining two parts, we will show why managers struggle to learn. First, we will show how six specific planning practices inhibit learning. Then, we will demonstrate how a number of common organizational dynamics interrupt the learning process.

The Science of Learning

Experience is valuable to the extent that it makes managers better decision makers—better predictors of the outcomes of actions. Every time a manager makes a decision, at least implicitly, he or she also makes a prediction of what will result from the decision. Young managers make many decisions for the first time. As a result, they are poor predictors. They make a lot of guesses. How quickly can they get better?

There are certain contexts in which managers can learn quickly. In particular, if they can run a lot of experiments cheaply, and get very rapid feedback, they can learn very quickly. These conditions are like those associated with learning to play a new video game. You can run the game as many times as you want. You try things that work, and things that do not. Soon, you figure out what it takes to win.

Under such ideal conditions, people are very good at learning from experience—without even thinking explicitly about *how* they are learning. Certain business problems approach these ideal conditions. A front-line employee on a manufacturing line may be able to learn from experience fairly quickly and inexpensively that certain processes are more efficient than others.

But with each promotion and increase in responsibility, learning conditions get further and further from the ideal. Decisions become much more expensive, so there is little chance for repetition. Furthermore, feedback is less immediate and less clear. A general manager might have to spend millions and wait several quarters before getting a clear picture of whether a new product is a success or a failure.

The scientific community has perfected a process for learning under any conditions—the scientific method. Managers may not be able to create ideal learning conditions, and they may not be able to afford the repetition that scientists find desirable. But this does not make the scientific method any less relevant. It just makes learning more difficult. In certain disciplines—social sciences, environmental sciences, and more—scientists deal with imperfect conditions too.

Science is a process of developing theories, using them to make predictions, running experiments, measuring results, and analyzing disparities between predictions and outcomes. This last step is the crucial learning step.

Managers can also employ the scientific method to ensure that they learn from experience. It becomes more and more critical that they do so as they advance in responsibility. Managers do not typically think of themselves as scientists, but they are already familiar with a process that, at least in its basic structure, is similar to the scientific method—the planning process. In it, they devise a set of action steps and predict what will happen as a result. Later, they compare outcomes to predictions, and here they have the opportunity to learn. Whether they actually learn is another question entirely.

We proceed to describe two major categories of learning inhibitors. The first is simply poor analysis of predictions and outcomes. The second is organizational interactions that corrupt any analysis of predictions and outcomes before it even begins.

Analysis of Predictions and Outcomes

Drawing lessons from experience—interpreting disparities between predictions and outcomes—is not straightforward. Once removed from ideal learning environments, humans are subject to many pitfalls, including:

1. A bias for simple, linear explanations of cause-and-effect.

2. An overemphasis on recent events to explain current causes (when more distant history may actually be more important).

3. An assumption that cause-effect relationships in familiar contexts also hold in unfamiliar ones.

4. An assumption that big effects have big causes. (Suppose you made two investments to improve performance, and the second cost ten times more than the first. It would be natural to attribute any performance improvement to the second investment.)

5. A bias for ignoring failures.

6. A bias for paying too much attention to major events (entry of a new competitor, unexpected manufacturing crisis), especially those with strong metaphorical power, such as changes in leadership.

7. A bias for attributing success to our own actions.

8. A bias for attributing failure to the actions of others or to luck.

To dodge these pitfalls, managers must be aware of them. They must also apply an appropriate analytical frame when comparing predictions and outcomes. The analytical frame is crucial because it serves as a filter. It highlights certain data points and obscures others. It shapes how experience is viewed—and the lessons drawn from it.

Managers analyze predictions and outcomes as part of the planning and performance review processes. Typical planning processes achieve many things—setting stretch goals for managers, allocating resources among competing alternatives, coordinating actions within a complex organization, and more. Several specific planning practices support these purposes better than they support learning, despite the fact that the overall structure of the planning process is similar to the scientific method.

Thus, managers are more likely to learn from experience if they make some changes to the way they plan. Learning is more likely when the following six attributes of the planning process are altered:

Attribute 1: Level of Detail

Typical plans show predictions in small increments. They may show revenue by product line, by region, and by month, for example. This has a purpose. It makes it easier to troubleshoot problems. For example, if the red widget sales in the northwest sub-region unexpectedly decline, it will be observed right away, and corrective action will be taken more quickly.

Such an approach, however, depends on business operations being stable and predictable—that is, well-known, and well-understood. If this is the case, there is much less of a need to learn from experience. Knowledge of how the business works can simply be passed down from one generation of managers to the next.

But in most industries, business conditions are changing. Learning from experience matters. Learning is more likely when managers identify a handful of critical assumptions that need to be tested. For example, a manager may believe that demographic shifts are making certain product attributes more desirable. Detailed breakdowns will not help determine whether such a conjecture is true or false; it will only distract. Learning-oriented managers always have a small number of critical unknowns that they are trying to resolve.

Attribute 2: Numbers Orientation

Look at almost any business plan, and you will see tables and tables full of numbers. But underlying any such set of predictions is the *theory* used to generate those predictions. In effect, the theory is the set of assumptions that were made in the process of calculating forecasted revenues and expenses. Unfortunately, between the time predictions are made and the time that those predictions are compared to outcomes, those assumptions are often long forgotten. One reason is the inadequacy of spreadsheets to the task of recording assumptions, rendered nearly unrecoverable by arcane codes and complex equations.

Especially when conditions are uncertain (and learning is most important), the theory is every bit as important as the predictions themselves. When uncertainties are high, predictions are usually wrong anyway. Some practicing managers cringe at the word "theory." It sounds like the opposite of "practical." But it is not. Theories are the raw materials of the learning process. Managers who are quick learners go to the effort to record assumptions in a way that they can be easily recovered and reexamined later. Many use simple diagrams to record their theories, clearly showing the hypothesized linkages between actions and outcomes.

Attribute 3: Format for Predicting

Typical plans will highlight outcomes for a period of time—revenue forecast for the coming fiscal year, for example. This does more to motivate and focus a group than it does to accelerate learning, however. Learning is an ongoing process, not something that happens all at once at the end of a reporting period. Furthermore, single numerical comparisons provide thin bases for drawing conclusions.

Learning is much more likely when managers monitor trends over time (performance trajectories), rather than single numbers for a certain time period. Admittedly, trends tell you little when each week looks exactly like the previous one. But most businesses are dynamic. When conditions are changing quickly, trends tell you more.

Thus, rather than forecast numbers, managers should forecast trends. This may at first seem more difficult, since a trend is many predictions at close time intervals. But accuracy is less important than the shape of the curve—whether it is exponential growth, a sudden jump, a worse-before-better pattern, or whatever. For learning purposes, it is adequate to describe the shape of the curve and give rough estimates for the timing and magnitude of the changes. If the assumptions underlying these predictions are flawed, it will be evident more quickly than if a manager tries to decipher what has gone wrong by comparing a single numerical prediction to a single numerical outcome.

Attribute 4: Low Propensity for Retrospective

Most plans are about looking forward, about building a better future. They do not dwell on the past. At most, they include results for the most recent period. But if it is worthwhile to predict trends, it is worthwhile to retain history. Predicted trends can then be compared with outcome trends.

This comparison is most useful if it extends back several periods. Often, lessons overlooked when a narrow focus is taken on what has happened over only the last period become abundantly clear when a wider window on performance is viewed.

Attribute 5: Low Planning Frequency

Typical planning practices call for thorough reviews of strategy only annually. There may be status checks more frequently, but the purpose is to identify and repair any unexpected operational problems. These more frequent reviews can also be an opportunity to test more fundamental assumptions—and accelerate learning—provided that there are only a few assumptions being tested.

A manager who reevaluates assumptions monthly has the potential to learn twelve times faster than one who only does so annually. Such high planning frequency may seem impractical. But if planners reduce detail and focus on only a few critical unknowns, a higher planning frequency is reasonable.

Attribute 6: Focus on Financial Outcomes

Plans tend to focus on financial results. Learning-oriented managers, however, will select measures that are most closely tied to the most critical assumptions that they need to verify. These measures will sometimes be financial. But more often, they will be more directly tied to core processes. For example, to test whether customers are responsive to a new sales channel, salesforce productivity is the most telling indicator.

Organizational Barriers to Learning

Altering the planning process is an important step in improving the odds of learning from experience. But it is insufficient. Even with the best possible analytical frames in place, learning can be blocked by a host of other problems created through the ongoing political jockeying that is present in any organization. Predictions, outcomes, and perceptions of performance are not just the raw materials of the learning process; they are also powerful game pieces in the ongoing struggle for power and influence within an organization.

Learning barriers can arise in the most innocuous ways. One manager asks another, "How's business?" The answer inevitably references a previously existing prediction—as in "as good as we expected." Without caution, ongoing conversations such as these—gossip—can become a substitute for careful analysis of predictions and outcomes.

To learn, predictions must be protected. They should be treated as the cornerstone for ongoing learning. They should be revised carefully—only when there is clear evidence that resolves an unknown.

Instead, predictions are mistreated. They become rigid, they are ignored, or they are manipulated.

Predictions Become Rigid

Whenever a management team learns something new about its business—whenever it resolves an unknown in its business model—the best estimate of future performance changes. Yet, predictions are often not updated when more is learned. Thus, the lessons learned are not validated. They are lost.

The most common reason that predictions become rigid is an excessive desire to hold managers accountable for the numbers in their plans. Comparisons between predictions and outcomes can lead to one of two possible conclusions—either the prediction was wrong, or the execution of the plan was flawed. A disciplined culture of accountability biases all analyses toward the latter—blaming managers for shortfalls. It is not acceptable to say that the prediction was wrong. After all, it is the manager's job to hit the prediction.

Rigid enforcement of accountability to plans can be a good practice. Many senior executives believe that a relentlessly practiced discipline of holding managers accountable is a crucial driver of high performance. But there is a cost. Under strict accountability, it is much harder to learn from experience. Thus, the practice is most sensible in businesses that are proven and stable—that is, where the opportunity to learn from experience is relatively low.

Predictions may also become rigid as competing executives work to sway perceptions of performance. Suppose one executive has lent his support to a new growth business, backing aggressive revenue growth targets. Should the business stumble, other executives who are competing with the first will continually remind him of his earlier prediction. This will likely have the intended effect—reducing his credibility. But it will also damage the learning effort.

Predictions Are Ignored

Predictions might be ignored for any number of reasons. It may simply be a lack of investment in the planning process. Managers of new and uncertain businesses may take the view that planning is pointless—the uncertainties are so high that it is impossible to predict. But these are exactly the times when disciplined learning is most valuable, and the planning process is the setting for the learning effort.

Even if leaders of uncertain businesses do invest in planning initially, perhaps just to win funding for a new product, they may later try to discount the value of the plans.

If outcomes fall short of expectations, they will do everything they can to maintain a positive perception of how their business is performing. They will argue that the predictions were based on minimal data or point out how much has changed in the external environment since the initial plans were made. They will do whatever they can to create as much ambiguity as possible around how their business is performing—so they can create favorable stories about how the business is likely to succeed in the future. But there is a cost. In succeeding in dismissing past plans, they discard the opportunity to learn.

Senior executives who are typically disciplined about holding managers accountable for performance may relax their standards when it comes to risky innovations. They acknowledge the uncertainty and agree to evaluate those leading the innovation in a different way. This is a step in the right direction, but it can easily go too far if it encourages the leaders not to take planning seriously. Predictions in plans are the basis for learning, even when they are not the basis for performance evaluation. Past predictions should never be discarded.

Predictions Are Manipulated

Leaders may try to manipulate the predictions for their own businesses for several reasons. If a manager needs additional resources, she may elevate predictions just to establish credibility. Later, if she is to be judged by performance against the prediction, she may look for ways to revise the predictions downward, just to ensure a more favorable personal performance evaluation. Leaders also sometimes manipulate predictions and performance perceptions to motivate their staffs. By creating a perception that the business is on the threshold of a major success or on the threshold of failure, leaders may push the staff to buckle down and work harder.

Competing executives may also manipulate predictions. For example, they may insist on imposing standards of performance that are accepted as normal in other parts of the organization—even if the same standards may not apply. Doing so can make their own business look better.

Recommendations

Regardless of the motivation, and regardless of whether predictions are becoming rigid, being ignored, or being manipulated, learning is the victim. To accelerate learning, senior executives must fight attitudes that diminish the importance of planning, particularly when uncertainties are high. Emphasizing planning is not the same as strengthening accountability to plan. Plans are important under uncertainty because they provide the basis for learning, not the basis for evaluating managerial performance.

Further, to overcome learning disablers, it is crucial that managers recognize that predictions are the basis for future learning, and that they must be treated with care. Although it is not possible, or even desirable, to put a stop to competition between executives, it is possible that, if a management team collectively values learning and is aware of learning pitfalls, then the likelihood of predictions being treated well rises.

A possible stronger step is to separate planning processes for mature and predictable operations from those that are more innovative and uncertain. In one set of meetings, emphasize accountability to plan. In the other, focus on learning.

Developing Leaders Through Learning

The steps outlined here are not easy. But as driving forces such as globalization, technological advance, demographics, and regulation all change the business playing field, the value of learning from experience goes up. The value of mentoring and coaching drops, because the lessons of the past no longer apply. Lessons learned do not just magically accumulate. Learning from experience requires skill and discipline. And it requires removing the many barriers to learning described here that are prevalent in most every organization.

Bibliography

Edmondson, A. (1999). Psychological safety and learning behavior in work teams. *Administrative Science Quarterly, 44*, 350–383.

Govindarajan, V., & Trimble, C. (2004, Winter). Strategic innovation and the science of learning. *MIT Sloan Management Review, 45*(2), 67–75.

Govindarajan, V., & Trimble, C. (2005). *Ten rules for strategic innovators—From idea to execution* (Chapters 6–8). Boston, MA: Harvard Business School Press.

Hedberg, B. (1981). How organizations learn and unlearn. In N.C. Nystrom & W.H. Starbuck (Eds.), *Handbook of organizational design*. Oxford: Oxford University Press.

Levinthal, D., & March, J. (1993, Winter). The myopia of learning. *Strategic Management Journal* (Special Issue: Organizations, Decision Making, and Strategy), *14*, 95–112.

Levitt, B., & March, J. (1988). Organizational learning. *Annual Review of Sociology, 14*, 319–340.

March, J., Sproull, L., & Tamuz, M. (1991, February). Learning from samples of one or fewer. *Organization Science, 2*(1), 1–13.

Russo, J., & Schoemaker, P. (2002). *Winning decisions* (Chapters 8 and 9). New York: Doubleday.

Vijay Govindarajan and Chris Trimble *are on the faculty at the Tuck School of Business at Dartmouth College. In 2005, they completed a five-year research effort that culminated in* Ten Rules for Strategic Innovators—From Idea to Execution *(Harvard Business School Press, 2005). They have also published in the* Harvard Business Review, MIT Sloan Management Review, California Management Review, Across the Board, *and* The Financial Times, *and publish a monthly column on* Fast Company's *website, www.fastcompany.com.*

Dr. Govindarajan *is the Earl C. Daum 1924 Professor of International Business (www.vg-tuck.com). His area of expertise is strategy, particularly strategic innovation, industry transformation, and global strategy and organization. He has been recognized by* BusinessWeek, Forbes, The Wall Street Journal Online, *and* Across the Board *as a top thought leader in the field of strategy. He received his doctorate and his MBA (with distinction) from the Harvard Business School and his Chartered Accountancy degree in India, where he was awarded the President's Gold Medal for obtaining the first rank nationwide.*

Chris Trimble *(www.chris-trimble.com), in addition to his faculty position at Tuck, is a senior fellow at Katzenbach Partners LLC (www.katzenbach.com), a New York-based consultancy. He holds an MBA degree (with distinction) from the Tuck School and a bachelor of science degree (with highest distinction) from the University of Virginia.*

Put Learning to Work

Andrew McK. Jefferson

Summary

There is an undeniable relationship between leadership excellence and organizational performance. The future performance of an enterprise is predicated, in large part, on the successful development of new leaders. How then does an organization ensure that it has the right people at the right time to drive the successful evolution of the enterprise? The organizations that are most adept at producing great bench strength are those that ensure that executive education is transferred, applied, and put to work.

Leadership excellence and organizational performance are directly linked. A 2003 study, for example, found that organizations with top-tier leadership teams realized a 10 percent higher total shareholder return then their industry peers (Corporate Learning Council, 2003a). Clearly, ensuring an adequate supply of leadership talent is an organizational imperative. Yet fewer than one in four leaders is confident that they will be able to find qualified successors in the coming years—a problem exacerbated by the pending retirement of a large number of "baby boomers" in the next five to ten years (Corporate Learning Council, 2003b).

Turning Learning into Results

Taken together, these trends suggest a strong need to improve both the efficiency and effectiveness of leadership development to prepare the right numbers of leaders with the right skills to meet the leadership demands of tomorrow. But where will these improvements in efficiency and efficacy come from? What needs to change in leadership development in order to meet the demand?

In Fort Hill Company, our consulting experience continues to suggest that the key will be to put more learning to work, that is, to ensure that the results of executive education and leadership development are transferred and applied to the work of the leader and that he or she continues to learn on the job. That, in turn, requires thinking about leadership development systemically and holistically, as an ongoing *process* rather than an isolated *event*. Well-planned, strategically linked, superbly delivered leadership development programs will continue to be essential, but they will no longer be considered *sufficient*.

Professor Herminia Ibarra of the INSEAD International School of Business, writing in the *Harvard Business Review*, put it this way: "In fact, the personal learning catalyzed by a top-notch program can be tremendous. The problem, my research suggests, is what happens when a manager comes back to the day-to-day routine of the office. . . . In a series of studies ranging from the introduction of new technologies, to managers' approaches to taking on new roles, behavioral scientists have found a consistent 'window of opportunity' effect: We have only a short time to make a real change after any break from routine. After that, things slip quickly back to business as usual" (Ibarra, 2004).

Improving the effectiveness and efficiency of executive education requires doing a better job of seizing this window of opportunity and helping executives make real changes for their own benefit and the company's. Not surprisingly, "creation of a strategy and system that integrates all executive/leadership development" emerged as the top-ranked strategy and policy activity for the next two to three years in Executive Development Associates' 2005 Trends Survey (Bolt, 2005, p. 13). There is growing awareness of the need to tie together developmental activities, and, in particular, to link development to on-the-job learning and application.

For the past six years, we have focused our training and consulting efforts on the post-course period—on that short "window of opportunity" that executives have to put their learning to work and change their habits and effectiveness. Time and again, we have seen that, when organizations pay more attention to what happens after formal training and developmental programs, they are able to improve the impact of already effective programs. As a result, an increasing number of organizations and companies— from the Center for Creative Leadership to Agilent, Sony, Honeywell, and others—have put in place formal follow-through systems to enhance the transfer and application of their most important leadership development programs.

Managing the follow-through period provides tremendous leverage to ensure that leadership development yields meaningful impact. But it is no magic bullet. Putting learning to work effectively requires a process that begins with strategic planning and continues through measuring the impact and feeding the results back into the planning for continuous improvement of subsequent cycles.

In our experience, three key elements need to be in place to maximize the effectiveness and return on leadership development:

- Strong and unambiguous links to strategy

- Emphasis on transfer and application

- Support and coaching

Strong Links to Strategy

"It is not only the strategy and the financial resources that makes a company win in the marketplace, but the quality of their talent" (de Herde & Ogg, 2005, p. 112). Given the strong correlation between the quality of executive leadership and overall organizational performance, no strategic plan should be considered complete unless it includes a clear process for developing, extending, and renewing executive leadership. The leadership supply chain needs to be an integral part of the company's strategy, as much as the product supply chain or the new product development pipeline.

Ensuring linkage between strategic business needs and leadership development requires ongoing dialogue between the business leaders and the learning organization. At Honeywell, for example, the chief learning officer and his team review the strategic plans of each of the strategic business units and the challenges they face. They have face-to-face meetings with each of the business presidents to validate that what learning and development is offering continues to meet the strategic needs of the business. Sony Electronics uses a Talent Management Council to firmly link development programs to business needs and to ensure execution of learning transfer objectives. The council includes the president's direct reports, ensuring strategic input from the company's most senior leaders. The council reviews the current business objectives and strategic direction and then identifies the leadership competencies needed to achieve the business goals.

The critical factor is what Bolt and Consolver (2005, p. 150) have defined as "strategic unity" of executive development. It is characterized by:

- Shared vision, values, and strategy (understood and committed to)

- Aligned priorities and processes

- Leaders equipped with the capabilities needed to execute

Just as the executive development process must be an integral part of the business strategy, the business strategy must be a visible and integral part of the program for executive development. In other words, the connection between the business strategy, expected leadership capabilities, and what is being taught in executive development should be abundantly clear and repeatedly emphasized. Doing so acknowledges fundamental characteristics of adult learning (Knowles, Holton, & Swanson, 2005), specifically:

- *Need to know.* Adults need to know why they need to learn something before they will undertake to learn it. This is especially true for busy and experienced leaders. Clearly relating the topics covered in leadership development to the business strategy and imperatives provides legitimacy and relevance and helps create the need to know. Even more potent tools for creating the need to know are 360-degree feedback tailored to the organization's leadership model and competencies and real or simulated exercises in which the participants discover for themselves the gap between their current performance, knowledge, etc., and where they want to be in their careers.

- *Readiness to learn.* A second core principle of adult learning is that adults are ready to learn those things that they recognize as essential to succeed in the real world. Applied to leadership education, this means that the material must be anchored not only in the company's strategy, but also in the leader's priority work. Throughout the program, leaders should be encouraged to stop and reflect on how what they have learned relates to the real-world tasks facing them when they return to the office. There should be the opportunity to discuss real-world application to take advantage of the exceptional breadth of experience and expertise present in any group of learners.

- *Motivation.* Finally, firm links between the business strategy and the educational program and objectives help ensure the motivation that adult learners need to master new materials and, in particular, to adopt new approaches and behaviors. As discussed below, setting the expectation for learning transfer and application is the other key to ensuring and sustaining motivation. (Knowles, Holton, & Swanson, 2005, p. 201)

Emphasis on Transfer and Application

Leadership development only fulfills its promise and provides a meaningful return on investment when it is transferred and applied to the work of the organization. Therefore, improving the transfer and application process improves the overall value of the output.

Too many programs still focus exclusively on the "placemat" (the formal instruction period) and completely neglect what must happen after the course if the new learning is to be assimilated and applied to good effect back on the job. Participants are given the unambiguous impression that on the last day of class they cross the "finish line." Painstakingly prepared course manuals are brought back to work, only to become bookshelf ornamentals.

In fact, the real work begins when the formal program ends—the work of translating the theory, instruction, simulations, and skill sessions into effective on-the-job behaviors and habits. The truly effective courses redefine the "finish line" in terms of results—evidence of successful implementation of course materials in the ensuing weeks and months.

We coined the term "follow-through management" to describe the process of actively managing the post-course implementation/execution phase. For the past six years, we have focused exclusively on optimizing this phase of the learning process and have now helped companies implement follow-through in programs involving more than 40,000 managers. While our own work utilizes a family of web-based Follow-Through Tools®, the principles can be applied to any program with good results. There are three keys to success:

1. *Secure meaningful management endorsement.* Given the many conflicting demands on executives' time, they focus on those tasks that they perceive are most valued by their management. In our experience, the successful development initiatives are those that have had strong support from the leaders the executives respect and/or who are in a position to influence their careers. This support needs to be concrete (actions, not just words) and modeled by the manager himself or herself. Savvy executives (the sort in whom we invest education and development efforts) immediately see through empty endorsements ("Do as I say, not as I do"). If senior leaders want to improve results, they need to improve application by actively participating in the follow-through process.

2. *Provide reminders and reinforcement throughout the follow-through period.* Establishing a new work habit or pattern requires repetition and practice over time. Results are better and longer-lived in programs that provide reminders and reinforcement in the weeks immediately following the course. Without a mechanism to trigger awareness and provide support, the rate of recidivism—falling back into old habits—is unacceptably high. Executives attending leadership development programs are simply adult learners in a corporate setting, and as such should be afforded the time to act and reflect periodically on the goals they have set.

3. *Facilitate collective learning and peer accountability.* Collaborative learning is an important feature of successful leadership development programs and adult education, but usually stops once the course is completed, especially among

geographically dispersed groups. Systems that make individual progress and "lessons learned" available to the group as a whole accelerate organizational as well as individual learning. It provides a platform for a broadly distributed group of player/coaches to provide rapid feedback on progress being made, thus enabling necessary course adjustments during the action/reflection cycle.

Support and Coaching

While some programs provide coaches to ensure follow-through action that causes learning transfer, most leave it up to the participants' individual initiative. In fact, one learning leader said, "Our responsibility ends when the participants walk out the door."

How different this is from other professions where improvement is not just a desired result, but is mandatory. Olympic gold medalists, concert musicians, and extraordinary leaders all have one thing in common: the benefit of coaching. Coaching and support during the critical "window of opportunity" immediately after a program greatly augments the impact. "Coaching is an opportunity to share experiences and best practices, and support someone as he or she tries a new skill" (Duke Corporate Education, 2005, p. 76). It also enhances the probability of retaining talent. According to Beverly Kaye, founder of Career Systems International, "those employees with mentors are twice as likely to stay on the job as those without" (Kaye & Jordan-Evans, 2005, p. 117).

There are four main sources of coaching and support for learning transfer: the learner's manager, facilitators and professional coaches (internal and external), and peers in the program. Numerous studies have demonstrated that a participant's manager is far and away the most important influence on the transfer of training. Broad and Newstrom (1992) found that involvement by the manager before and after the program were ranked as the first and third most-potent learning transfer strategies, respectively. Yet involvement by the manager after the course was the *least frequently used* of the nine role/time combinations they studied. They concluded: "Managers do not consistently and powerfully support the transfer of training in the work environment" (Broad & Newstrom, p. 53).

So a major challenge for companies that want to maximize learning transfer is to make certain that participants' managers are properly informed and actively involved in the post-program coaching effort. One simple, but important step in this direction is to be sure that the more senior managers know what their direct reports' goals are. No company could function effectively if managers did not know their reports' business goals; yet it is common for them not to know their reports' developmental objectives. In our systems, we solve the problem by sending managers their reports' learning application goals electronically, but it could also be done by sending a paper copy.

A second important source of support for learning transfer should be instructors and facilitators who participated in the learning and development program. When we surveyed participants at a leading technology firm about what they valued most about a program and follow-through, they ranked ongoing contact with the instructor very highly. Similarly, participants in Notre Dame's innovative Integral Leadership Program indicated on follow-up interviews that they would like to have ongoing support from the faculty should they need on-the-job advice. Writing in *Best Practices in Leading the Global Workforce*, Teresa Roche, vice president, global learning and leadership development, at Agilent Technologies, said:

> "Facilitators are selected for their superior knowledge and teaching ability. During the program, participants come to value the facilitator's knowledge, opinion, and advice. Yet, historically, teaching ended when the class ended; communication was cut off. As a result, there was no support for learning transfer from the facilitators—the very people with the greatest insight into the material and whose opinion the learners value most." (Roche & Wick, 2005, p. 6)

There is an obvious opportunity to more fully leverage their knowledge and skills in follow-through management.

Facilitator's New Role

To address this issue, Agilent redefined the role of the facilitator so that their responsibilities now extend beyond the last day of class and into the learning transfer period. That is a significant departure from the prevailing paradigm that the purpose of educators is to deliver courses and requires reallocation of resources. The new role suggests a focus on providing "service after the sale." It supports the proposal by Broad and Newstrom (1992) that trainers should redefine their roles from "strictly trainers/presenters to *facilitators of behavioral change on the job*" (p. 113) and the Robinsons' (1996) concept of "performance consultants." Roche and Wick (2005) put it this way: "Facilitators must move from the 'sage on the stage' to the 'guide by the side', from facilitator of learning to facilitator of performance" (p. 13). Agilent achieved this shift in roles by lightening the teaching schedule of their facilitators. If you don't have such flexibility or resources, you can begin the process of change by asking your instructors to simply contact each participant and ask, "How are things going in your effort to transfer your new skills?" Or you can investigate other means of providing more systematic follow-up.

Recognizing that facilitators' time is valuable and limited, the support process must be efficient as well as effective. Agilent uses an electronic follow-through management system to streamline support by facilitators. The system provides a "dashboard" that allows facilitators to efficiently identify and communicate with individuals in need of encouragement, recognition, or help.

The facilitator's comments can be targeted and personally relevant, because they are provided in the context of the participant's goals, progress, and issues. Over time, the process becomes increasingly efficient. Participants tend to encounter the same kinds of challenges and questions. Facilitators can create a personal library of suggestions/responses for the most frequently encountered issues. When one of the issues to which they have already responded recurs, they can quickly personalize a prior response, gaining efficiency with each iteration of the program. An outstanding example of this approach is Richard Jolly at the London Business School, who sent more than six hundred messages to his executive MBA students during their three-month follow-through period. Given that these students represented more than a dozen countries and as many time zones, no other approach would have been practical.

Conclusion and Recommendations

The link between leadership excellence and organizational performance is clear, and the demand for effective leaders will only increase over the next ten years. A company's leadership bench strength is a bellwether of future enterprise success. As Noel Tichy noted: "The most important task for the leader who wants to win in the 21st century is to create more leaders, at more levels of the company, than the competition." The challenge for leadership development, then, is to increase the rate at which it is refilling the leadership pipeline by improving both the effectiveness and efficiency of the process.

To achieve the greatest possible depth of leadership talent, organizations need to ensure that optimal results are obtained from leadership development initiatives. Put simply, the results of executive education and leadership development are only realized when the learning is put to work. Well-designed and executed programs strongly linked to business strategy and supported by follow-through management and coaching are the keys to avoiding a shortage in the leadership pipeline.

References

Bolt, J.F. (2005). Mapping the future of executive development: Forces, trends, and implications. In J.F. Bolt (Ed.), *The future of executive development* (pp. 3–24). San Francisco: Executive Development Associates.

Bolt, J.F., & Consolver, G.A. (2005). Creating strategic unity through executive development. In J.F. Bolt (Ed.), *The future of executive development* (pp. 150–158). San Francisco: Executive Development Associates.

Broad, M.L., & Newstrom, J.W. (1992). *Transfer of training: Action-packed strategies to ensure high payoff from training investments.* Cambridge, MA: Perseus Publishing.

Corporate Learning Council. (2003a). *Hallmarks of leadership success.* Washington, DC: Corporate Executive Board.

Corporate Learning Council. (2003b). *High-impact succession management.* Washington, DC: Corporate Executive Board.

de Herde, G., & Ogg, S. (2005). Building global bench strength and filling the talent pipeline. In J.F. Bolt J.F. (Ed.), *The future of executive development* (pp. 112–130). San Francisco: Executive Development Associates.

Duke Corporate Education. (2005) *Translating strategy into action.* Chicago, IL: Dearborn.

Ibarra, H. (2004, February). Breakthrough ideas for 2004. *Harvard Business Review,* p. 24.

Kaye, B., & Jordan-Evans, S. (2005). *Love 'em or lose 'em* (3rd ed.). San Francisco: Berrett-Koehler.

Knowles, M.S., Holton, E.F., III, & Swanson, R.A. (2005). *The adult learner: The definitive classic in adult education and human resource development* (6th ed.). Burlington, MA: Elsevier.

Robinson, D., & Robinson, J. (1996). *Performance consulting: Moving beyond training.* San Francisco: Berrett-Koehler.

Roche, T., & Wick, C. (2005). Agilent Technologies: Global leadership training with an on-the-job focus. In P. Harkins, D. Giber, M. Sobol, M. Tarquenio, & L. Carter (Eds.), *Leading the global workforce.* San Francisco: Jossey-Bass.

Andrew McK. Jefferson *is president and chief operating officer of the Fort Hill Company in Wilmington, Delaware, the global leader in follow-through management technology and know-how. He is an accomplished executive, with a career spanning both operational and legal roles. He has significant line management expertise and is experienced in strategic planning, sales and marketing, productivity, and technology development in large and small corporate environments. Mr. Jefferson is passionate about his work and research into transfer and application and about helping people change and fulfill their potential. He is a co-author of* The Six Disciplines of Breakthrough Training, *published by Pfeiffer in April 2006. He is a graduate of the University of Delaware and graduated Phi Kappa Phi with honors from the Widener University School of Law, where he currently serves on the school's board of overseers.*

About the Editor

James F. Bolt is chairman and founder of Executive Development Associates, Inc. (EDA), a leading consulting and networking firm specializing in the strategic use of executive development. EDA develops custom-designed executive development strategies, systems, and programs that ensure clients have the executive talent needed to accelerate strategy execution. EDA also supports the success and effectiveness of executives through powerful peer-to-peer networks and conducts research that supports network members. EDA's clients have included half of the Fortune 100 companies and many other leading organizations around the world. Mr. Bolt was recently selected by the *Financial Times* as one of the top experts in executive/leadership development. Linkage, Inc., named him one of the top fifty executive coaches in leadership development in the world. He is an online columnist for *Fast Company* magazine.

Contributors

James F. Bolt
Executive Development Associates, Inc.
225 Bush Street, Suite 770
San Francisco, CA 94104
  jbolt@executivedevelopment.com

Nicole Drake
Consultant, BTS
456 Montgomery Street, Suite 900
San Francisco, CA 94104
  (415) 362-9563
  nicole.drake@bts.com

Eve Dreher
Principal, Forethought LLC
1694 Muirfield Lane
Evergreen, CO 80439

Michael Dulworth
Managing Director
Executive Development Associates, Inc.
225 Bush Street, Suite 770
San Francisco, CA 94104
    (415) 399–9797
    mdulworth@executivedevelopment
      .com
    www.executivedevelopment.com

Joseph A. Forcillo
President
Forcillo Associates, Inc.
18530 Mack Avenue, #450
Grosse Pointe Farms, MI 48236
  (313) 881–4026
  jforcillo@forcillo
  www.forcillo.com

Dr. Barry Frew
Frew & Associates
Monterey, CA
  (831) 372–3932
  barry@frewassociates.com
  bfrew@executivedevelopment.com

Marshall Goldsmith
Founding Partner
Marshall Goldsmith Partners
P.O. Box 9710
16770 Via de los Rosales
Rancho Santa Fe, CA 92067-9710

Vijay Govindarajan, Ph.D.
Tuck School of Business at Dartmouth
100 Tuck Hall
Hanover, NH 03755
  (603) 646-2156
  vg@dartmouth.edu

Alice Heezen
Human Resource Manager
BG Group
Thames Valley Park Drive
Reading, Berkshire RG6 1PT
United Kingdom

Gordon Hewitt
Distinguished Professor of International
  Business and Corporate Strategy
West Grange
12A West Grange Road
Bearsden, Glasgow G8a SPL
United Kingdom
  drghewitt@aol.com

Andrew McK. Jefferson
President, Fort Hill Company
  (302) 651-9223
  www.ifollowthrough.com

Betty Kovalcik
Navy Federal Credit Union
820 Follin Lane SE
Vienna, VA 22180
  (703) 255-7908
  Betty_kovalcik@navyfederal.org

Robert W. Mann, Ph.D.
UBS AG
677 Washington Boulevard
Stamford, CT 06901
  (203) 719-3000

Val Markos, Ph.D.
  vmarkos@bellsouth.net

Jeff McCreary
Senior Vice President, Texas Instruments
  (retired)
2570 Atalaya Hill Road
Santa Fe, NM 87505
  (505) 920-2006
  jeff@jeffreymccreary.com

William J. Morin, CEO
WJM Associates, Inc.
675 Third Avenue
New York, NY 10017
  (212) 972–7400 (office)
  bmorin@wjmassoc.com

Annmarie Neal, Psy.D.
Senior Vice President, The Talent Office
1694 Muirfield Lane
Evergreen, CO 80439
  (720) 332-5291
  fax: (720) 332-0531

Brigadier General Harold W. Nelson
United States Army (ret.)
25 Derbyshire Drive
Carlisle, PA 17013
  (717) 243–3502
  halwnelson@earthlink.net

Dan Parisi
Executive Vice President
BTS, Catalysts for Profitability & Growth
456 Montgomery Street, Suite 900
San Francisco, CA 94104
  (415) 362-9516
  dan.parisi@bts.com
  sww.bts.com

Charles Presbury
Senior Director, Leadership
   Development
The McGraw-Hill Companies
1221 Avenue of the Americas
New York, NY 10020

Barbara Reyna
Baker Hughes
3900 Essex
Houston, TX 77026

Julie Staudenmier
   Julie.M.Staudenmier@aexp.com

Chris Trimble
Tuck School of Business at Dartmouth
100 Tuck Hall
Hanover, NH 03755
   (603) 646-0463
   chris.trimble@dartmouth.edu

Fons Trompenaars, Ph.D.
Trompenaars Hampden-Turner
   Consulting
   info@thtconsulting.com
   www.thtconsulting.com

Dr. Raymond Vigil
Humana Inc.
500 W. Main Street
Louisville, KY 40202

Mark Whitmore, Ph.D.
Director, Career Enhancement Center
The Westfield Group
1 Park Circle
Westfield Center, OH 44251

Dr. Warren Wilhelm
   Warren@WilhelmConsulting.com

Peter Woolliams, Ph.D.
Trompenaars Hampden-Turner
   Consulting
   info@thtconsulting.com
   www.thtconsulting.com

Ashley Keith Yount
Senior Manager, Global Talent
   Management
Dell, Inc.
One Dell Way
Round Rock, TX 78682

How to Use the CD-ROM

System Requirements

PC with Microsoft Windows 98SE or later
Mac with Apple OS version 8.6 or later

Using the CD with Windows

To view the items located on the CD, follow these steps:

1. Insert the CD into your computer's CD-ROM drive.

2. A window appears with the following options:

    Contents: Allows you to view the files included on the CD-ROM.

    Software: Allows you to install useful software from the CD-ROM.

    Links: Displays a hyperlinked page of websites.

    Author: Displays a page with information about the Author(s).

    Contact Us: Displays a page with information on contacting the publisher or author.

    Help: Displays a page with information on using the CD.

    Exit: Closes the interface window.

If you do not have autorun enabled, or if the autorun window does not appear, follow these steps to access the CD:

1. Click Start -> Run.

2. In the dialog box that appears, type d:<\\>start.exe, where d is the letter of your CD-ROM drive. This brings up the autorun window described in the preceding set of steps.

3. Choose the desired option from the menu. (See Step 2 in the preceding list for a description of these options.)

In Case of Trouble

If you experience difficulty using the CD-ROM, please follow these steps:

1. Make sure your hardware and systems configurations conform to the systems requirements noted under "System Requirements" above.

2. Review the installation procedure for your type of hardware and operating system.

It is possible to reinstall the software if necessary.

To speak with someone in Product Technical Support, call 800-762-2974 or 317-572-3994, M–F 8:30 a.m.–5:00 p.m. EST. You can also get support and contact Product Technical Support through our website at www.wiley.com/techsupport.

Before calling or writing, please have the following information available:

- Type of computer and operating system

- Any error messages displayed

- Complete description of the problem.

It is best if you are sitting at your computer when making the call.

Pfeiffer Publications Guide

This guide is designed to familiarize you with the various types of Pfeiffer publications. The formats section describes the various types of products that we publish; the methodologies section describes the many different ways that content might be provided within a product. We also provide a list of the topic areas in which we publish.

FORMATS

In addition to its extensive book-publishing program, Pfeiffer offers content in an array of formats, from fieldbooks for the practitioner to complete, ready-to-use training packages that support group learning.

FIELDBOOK Designed to provide information and guidance to practitioners in the midst of action. Most fieldbooks are companions to another, sometimes earlier, work, from which its ideas are derived; the fieldbook makes practical what was theoretical in the original text. Fieldbooks can certainly be read from cover to cover. More likely, though, you'll find yourself bouncing around following a particular theme, or dipping in as the mood, and the situation, dictate.

HANDBOOK A contributed volume of work on a single topic, comprising an eclectic mix of ideas, case studies, and best practices sourced by practitioners and experts in the field.

An editor or team of editors usually is appointed to seek out contributors and to evaluate content for relevance to the topic. Think of a handbook not as a ready-to-eat meal, but as a cookbook of ingredients that enables you to create the most fitting experience for the occasion.

RESOURCE Materials designed to support group learning. They come in many forms: a complete, ready-to-use exercise (such as a game); a comprehensive resource on one topic (such as conflict management) containing a variety of methods and approaches; or a collection of like-minded activities (such as icebreakers) on multiple subjects and situations.

TRAINING PACKAGE An entire, ready-to-use learning program that focuses on a particular topic or skill. All packages comprise a guide for the facilitator/trainer and a workbook for the participants. Some packages are supported with additional media—such as video—or learning aids, instruments, or other devices to help participants understand concepts or practice and develop skills.

- *Facilitator/trainer's guide* Contains an introduction to the program, advice on how to organize and facilitate the learning event, and step-by-step instructor notes. The guide also contains copies of presentation materials—handouts, presentations, and overhead designs, for example—used in the program.

- *Participant's workbook* Contains exercises and reading materials that support the learning goal and serves as a valuable reference and support guide for participants in the weeks and months that follow the learning event. Typically, each participant will require his or her own workbook.

ELECTRONIC CD-ROMs and web-based products transform static Pfeiffer content into dynamic, interactive experiences. Designed to take advantage of the searchability, automation, and ease-of-use that technology provides, our e-products bring convenience and immediate accessibility to your workspace.

METHODOLOGIES

CASE STUDY A presentation, in narrative form, of an actual event that has occurred inside an organization. Case studies are not prescriptive, nor are they used to prove a point; they are designed to develop critical analysis and decision-making skills. A case study has a specific time frame, specifies a sequence of events, is narrative in structure, and contains a plot structure—an issue (what should be/have been done?). Use case studies when the goal is to enable participants to apply previously learned theories to the circumstances in the case, decide what is pertinent, identify the real issues, decide what should have been done, and develop a plan of action.

ENERGIZER A short activity that develops readiness for the next session or learning event. Energizers are most commonly used after a break or lunch to stimulate or refocus the group. Many involve some form of physical activity, so they are a useful way to counter post-lunch lethargy. Other uses include transitioning from one topic to another, where "mental" distancing is important.

EXPERIENTIAL LEARNING ACTIVITY (ELA) A facilitator-led intervention that moves participants through the learning cycle from experience to application (also known as a Structured Experience). ELAs are carefully thought-out designs in which there is a definite learning purpose and intended outcome. Each step—everything that participants do during the activity—facilitates the accomplishment of the stated goal. Each ELA includes complete instructions for facilitating the intervention and a clear statement of goals, suggested group size and timing, materials required, an explanation of the process, and, where appropriate, possible variations to the activity. (For more detail on Experiential Learning Activities, see the Introduction to the *Reference Guide to Handbooks and Annuals*, 1999 edition, Pfeiffer, San Francisco.)

GAME A group activity that has the purpose of fostering team spirit and togetherness in addition to the achievement of a pre-stated goal. Usually contrived—undertaking a desert expedition, for example—this type of learning method offers an engaging means for participants to demonstrate and practice business and interpersonal skills. Games are effective for team building and personal development mainly because the goal is subordinate to the process—the means through which participants reach decisions, collaborate, communicate, and generate trust and understanding. Games often engage teams in "friendly" competition.

ICEBREAKER A (usually) short activity designed to help participants overcome initial anxiety in a training session and/or to acquaint the participants with one another. An icebreaker can be a fun activity or can be tied to specific topics or training goals. While a useful tool in itself, the icebreaker comes into its own in situations where tension or resistance exists within a group.

INSTRUMENT A device used to assess, appraise, evaluate, describe, classify, and summarize various aspects of human behavior. The term used to describe an instrument depends primarily on its format and purpose. These terms include survey, questionnaire, inventory, diagnostic survey, and poll. Some uses of instruments include providing instrumental feedback to group members, studying here-and-now processes or functioning within a group, manipulating group composition, and evaluating outcomes of training and other interventions.

Instruments are popular in the training and HR field because, in general, more growth can occur if an individual is provided with a method for focusing specifically on his or her own behavior. Instruments also are used to obtain information that will serve as a basis for change and to assist in workforce planning efforts.

Paper-and-pencil tests still dominate the instrument landscape with a typical package comprising a facilitator's guide, which offers advice on administering the instrument and interpreting the collected data, and an initial set of instruments. Additional instruments are available separately. Pfeiffer, though, is investing heavily in e-instruments. Electronic instrumentation provides effortless distribution and, for larger groups particularly, offers advantages over paper-and-pencil tests in the time it takes to analyze data and provide feedback.

LECTURETTE A short talk that provides an explanation of a principle, model, or process that is pertinent to the participants' current learning needs. A lecturette is intended to establish a common language bond between the trainer and the participants by providing a mutual frame of reference. Use a lecturette as an introduction to a group activity or event, as an interjection during an event, or as a handout.

MODEL A graphic depiction of a system or process and the relationship among its elements. Models provide a frame of reference and something more tangible, and more easily remembered, than a verbal explanation. They also give participants something to "go on," enabling them to track their own progress as they experience the dynamics, processes, and relationships being depicted in the model.

ROLE PLAY A technique in which people assume a role in a situation/scenario: a customer service rep in an angry-customer exchange, for example. The way in which the role is approached is then discussed and feedback is offered. The role play is often repeated using a different approach and/or incorporating changes made based on feedback received. In other words, role playing is a spontaneous interaction involving realistic behavior under artificial (and safe) conditions.

SIMULATION A methodology for understanding the interrelationships among components of a system or process. Simulations differ from games in that they test or use a model that depicts or mirrors some aspect of reality in form, if not necessarily in content. Learning occurs by studying the effects of change on one or more factors of the model. Simulations are commonly used to test hypotheses about what happens in a system—often referred to as "what if?" analysis—or to examine best-case/worst-case scenarios.

THEORY A presentation of an idea from a conjectural perspective. Theories are useful because they encourage us to examine behavior and phenomena through a different lens.

TOPICS

The twin goals of providing effective and practical solutions for workforce training and organization development and meeting the educational needs of training and human resource professionals shape Pfeiffer's publishing program. Core topics include the following:

Leadership & Management

Communication & Presentation

Coaching & Mentoring

Training & Development

e-Learning

Teams & Collaboration

OD & Strategic Planning

Human Resources

Consulting